GENDERING RADICALISM

Women in the West

SERIES EDITORS

Sarah J. Deutsch
Duke University

Margaret D. Jacobs
University of Nebraska, Lincoln

Charlene L. Porsild
University of New Mexico

Vicki L. Ruiz
University of California, Irvine

Elliott West
University of Arkansas

GENDERING RADICALISM

Women and Communism in Twentieth-Century California

BETH SLUTSKY

University of Nebraska Press | Lincoln and London

Library of Congress
Control Number: 2015941635

Set in Sabon Next LT Pro by
L. Auten.

This book is dedicated to
activist women everywhere—
their contribution, their
identities, and their legacy.

Contents

Illustrations

Acknowledgments

This book has been a community effort. The History Department at the University of California–Davis supported this project in its earliest stages and has since continued to help bring the book to fruition. Joan Cadden, Eric Rauchway, Alan Taylor, Cecilia Tsu, Clarence Walker, Louis Warren, and Michael Parrish of the University of California–San Diego all offered guidance to this project. Lorena Oropeza and Lisa Materson have been ongoing enthusiasts for this project with their incisive questions and comments, which continually pressed me to reconsider these three generations of Communists and how gender truly shaped their identities. Above all, Kathy Olmsted offered more patience and support to me than I could ever have hoped for from a mentor. From the day I walked into her office with a vague idea about writing about Communist women, her enthusiasm for the project, support for my scholarship, and selflessness to the historical discipline have impressed me beyond words.

Beyond the Davis academic community, this project was made

possible by the financial support of the Department of History's Teaching Fellowships, Block Grants, and Summer Research Grants from the Roland Marchand Funds. UC-Davis gave me additional financial support through the Humanities Research Award. The Institute for Governmental Affairs also awarded me the Dissertation Improvement Award, which allowed me to travel and conduct research at various archives throughout Northern California. A research grant from the Historical Society of Southern California and John Randolph Haynes and Dora Haynes Foundation afforded me the opportunity to spend time at various archives and libraries in Southern California.

My research at these institutions was made possible by a community of warm and generous librarians and archivists. Kristie French with the Special Collections at California State University–Long Beach, Daniel Goldstein in Shields Library at UC-Davis, Lucy Barber at the California State Archives, Lisa Rubens at the Regional Oral History Office at UC-Berkeley, Jeffrey Rankin at the Special Collections at UCLA, and the late Edith Laub at the Niebyl-Proctor Center for Marxist Research spent invaluable time with me as I navigated my way around numerous materials and questions. Beyond these people and their institutions, the Tamiment Institute and Wagner Labor Archives at New York University, the Southern California Library for Social Studies and Research, the Labor Archives and Research Center at San Francisco State University, the Bancroft Library at UC-Berkeley, the Special Collections at Mills College, and the University Archives at UC-Davis provided excellent environments in which I spent many days researching.

In the process of crafting this narrative, I had the opportunity to share my research with a broader community of scholars and scholarly organizations. Bill Issel graciously invited me to present my work in progress at the Bay Area Labor History Workshop. The Cross-Cultural Women's History group at UC-Davis also allowed me to share my research. I was also fortunate enough to give conference papers at the annual meetings of many historical associations and especially benefited from the guidance of scholars I met through the

Western Association of Women's Historians and the Pacific Coast Branch of the American Historical Association.

This book was considerably improved when it found a home with the University of Nebraska Press. Two anonymous reviewers, Dr. Kathy Cairns, and the editorial review board sharpened the focus and central arguments while always supporting the overall merit and goals of the project. Sabrina Ehmke Sergeant and several other press authors helped to see it to fruition. And Bridget Barry, who from day one has been a fan of this book and what it proposes to do, has more than anyone helped make this book happen.

Ultimately, this project would not exist without the three women around whose lives the book revolves. Although none of them survived to participate in the creation of the book, I was able to connect with them and their memories through their close friends and relatives. Sally McKee first introduced me to Kendra Alexander. Because of her, Giuliana Milanese spent dozens of hours poignantly reflecting on her years with Kendra. In addition, the generous time given through the interviews of Marian Gordon, Charlene Mitchell, and Patrice Sewell gave me firsthand access to Kendra's world. Richard Healey, Dorothy Healey's son, enthusiastically read and commented on the chapter that highlights his mother's life. Earl Ofari Hutchinson, Maurice Isserman, and Josh Sides also kindly shared their oral histories and related materials with me.

Finally, this book is the product of a community of friends and family. Brian Behnken, Robert Chester, Lori Clune, Kim Davis, the late Chris Doyle, Wendy Jorae, Denise Lynn, Elisabeth Ritacca, and Greg Wigmore have been fantastic friends and colleagues, sharing in the humor, emotions, and scholarly dedication to our discipline. As this project transformed from a dissertation to a book I found a home with the California History–Social Science Project at UC-Davis, where Shelley Brooks, Shennan Hutton, Nancy McTygue, and Tuyen Tran have not only supported the project but have reminded me, through our shared pursuit of quality history education, that a key goal of history scholarship is its accessibility. It is my sincere hope that this book is not only readable but relatable to history students everywhere. My family—Dianne Slutsky, Allison Slutsky, Michael Slutsky, and Kathy Hawkins, Mike and the late Peggy Wilson, along with Lynn Wilson—have encouraged this project and continue to selflessly cheer me on, and they have my unending appreciation. And finally, this book is possible because of Josh Wilson, my best friend, my research assistant, and my middle-of-the-night editor. He has spent nearly half of his life trying to understand why his wife wants to be a historian of radicals, all the while being my biggest fan and loving me unconditionally. And through all this we have created three sons—Benjamin, Aaron, and Noah, who certainly delayed the book, spilled milk and juice on drafts of it, and helped me realize just how remarkable these professional revolutionaries were with their commitment to both motherhood and a demanding and isolating Communist Party.

GENDERING RADICALISM

1   Three Generations of American Communist Women

In October 1919 an educated, wealthy, white woman who loved to wear colorful hats and had grown up with pedigree in a prestigious California family sat quietly in an Oakland meeting hall while votes were being tabulated. Moments earlier she had cast her ballot in favor of her branch of the Socialist Party breaking off and becoming a pioneer branch of the Communist Labor Party. Within days the members of the charter group of the Northern California Communist Labor Party affirmed their commitment to the revolutionary organization's constitution and its article supporting the overthrow of the capitalist American government. On the day her group pledged its devotion to the Communist Party (CP), Charlotte Anita Whitney (1867–1955), the distinguished clubwoman, suffragist, Socialist, and now Communist, proudly and politely received one of the first membership cards given out to Californians.

Less than a decade later, on December 1, 1928, a self-conscious,

1

awkward, but thrilled fourteen-year-old girl with a strong working-class Jewish heritage went to the Berkeley, California, home of one of her brother's friends. She had convinced her older brother to take her along to a Young Communist League meeting, where she thought she might finally find her social and political niche. That evening Dorothy Ray Healey (1914–2006) paid her initial dues and became a card-carrying member of the Young Communist League, pledging her allegiance to an organization committed to a revolution led by the proletariat.

Nearly forty years later, in early 1966, a tall, thin, dark-skinned nineteen-year-old young woman from Los Angeles, who had already established herself as a seasoned civil rights activist, launched her career as a Communist in Southern California. Born to a black man and a white woman who taught their daughters to ignore racial distinctions and actively fight for equality, this mixed-race woman determined that promoting class equality through an older radical organization would be the best way to advance her vision of the world. Kendra Claire Harris Alexander (1946–92), a second-year college student, enlisted wholeheartedly with the Los Angeles branch of the Communist Party of the United States of America (CPUSA).

These three women joined and eventually led the California branches of the Communist Party of the United States of America through a period that stretched from its founding in 1919 to its near dissolution in 1992. Separately, each woman represents a generation of the membership and the activism of the Communist Party. Each woman chaired the state Party, represented the state at national and international Communist events, and led California radicals through pivotal moments in the twentieth century. But collectively, their identities, Party involvement, and leadership tell the story of one of the most infamous and legendary organizations this country has ever known. Just as important, their experiences tell the story of women who devoted their lives and livelihoods to radicalism in America. Over nearly a century these female activists found the Communist Party's organizational structure to be useful for their purposes as they waged their diverse struggles through the Party apparatus.

While these women lived at different times, in somewhat different regions of California, and nearly in different worlds from each other, they made the decision to enlist with a revolutionary, stigmatized, and at times banned organization. Each joined for different reasons, and each expressed her activism in distinct ways. But together, at their core, all three women agreed with the philosophical premise of communism: equality (whether economic, racial, or gender) could only be fully realized by ending the capitalist system. While the Party occasionally changed its strategies, it never wavered in its efforts to achieve its two overarching goals of abolishing capitalism and ending an inherently unequal competition-based way of life. Whitney, Healey, and Alexander are united in retrospect by their willingness to consider communism as a viable way of life in the United States and by their drive to convince others that only communism could bring about true equality.

This study into the lives of three generations of women who lived in and led the Communist Party in the United States seeks to answer five interrelated questions. First, why did Whitney, Healey, and Alexander join the Party? What did the Party offer these women? How did the Party change over time because of and for its female members? To what extent did its members' race and class shape the Party's changing agenda? Finally, how and why was California central in their experiences with radicalism? The historical contexts of their entry into the Party varied enormously over time: Whitney entered in the wake of the Bolshevik Revolution, when America had been struggling to define its positions on radicals; Healey became a member at the height of labor organizing; and Alexander joined during the Cold War but also in the context of a radicalizing civil rights movement. But the devotion of these women to the Communist Party and all that it represented did not waver.

Investigating these women as separate individuals, members, and leaders who lived in different temporal moments and sociopolitical environments not only illuminates their particular historical contexts. Such an analysis also helps to expose both the significant chronological continuities and the key changes over time in Party members' attitudes, actions, rhetoric, and identities. Using Whitney, Healey, and Alexander as windows through which to analyze the Party, women, and California over three generations summons a broader view of the past. Not only do the evolving and shifting contours of the Party, the history of women, and California become more apparent through this generational study, but situating these three women in such a framework provides a much more complex and nuanced understanding of the past. Analyzing the three generations of women as part of a broader movement and an ongoing conversation among women in the twentieth century deepens historians' understanding of the Communist Party in general and of these women in particular. Through the coalitions they built and relationships they sustained, these American Communist women pushed components of their radical agenda into the mainstream.

This book spans the lives of each woman. The first section chronicles the life of Charlotte Anita Whitney. Living all but five years of her life in the Bay Area, Whitney was a socially elite leftist. The Communist Party proudly championed Whitney as its matriarch. And as the public leader of the first generation of the Party, she forged a Communist identity in the radical environment of the 1920s and 1930s. Mainstream progressive organizations and radical movements alike welcomed Whitney's membership and leadership. Most notably, Whitney drew widespread attention during her arrest, trial, and pardon campaign for violating the California Criminal Syndicalism Law. After she was convicted of conspiring to overthrow the government, mainstream organizations actively supported Whitney and even found common ground with the Communist Party over the defense of free speech rights. Capitalizing on her fame and coalition-building ability, Whitney ran for the office of state controller on the Communist Party ticket in 1934 and received well over one hundred thousand votes, more than any other California Communist ever received in an election. In commemoration of her seventy-fifth birthday, the Communist Party published *Native Daughter*, a biography that painstakingly recited the details of Whitney's increasingly radical life. The book also showcased her feminine qualities, which helped the Party disseminate an image of its idealized woman leader. Her life reveals how radical and non-radical female activists in the early twentieth century cooperated across political boundaries on multiple occasions.

By the 1940s and 1950s the Communist Party had a new woman to hold in esteem, Dorothy Ray Healey. Representing a new generation of Communist leaders, Healey was a tireless labor organizer and independent wife and mother. Born into a radical family, Healey spent most of her life organizing labor unions and leading Communists in Southern California. More than either Whitney or Alexander, the Party kept Healey within its insular world; her family life, marriages, and professional life centered on the Party. For a time the raging anticommunism of the Cold War forced her to live in a more isolated political world than her counterparts. During the late 1940s and early 1950s she hid underground, served jail time for violating the Smith Act (the Alien Registration Act of 1940), and argued her case in front of the U.S. Supreme Court, which overturned her convictions in 1956. Healey remained a leading activist in the Party from the turbulent years of the popular front (when the American Communist Party aligned itself with mainstream political parties in a united opposition to fascism and supported some New Deal policies) to the anti-Communist hysteria of the 1950s. But as the domestic Cold War terror eased within the United States, Healey began to criticize the Party's hierarchical political structures and bureaucracies. Although she resigned in 1973 over international and internal struggles, Healey was a key figure in the Party's battles stretching from the depths of the Great Depression to the height of the Cold War and through the civil rights movement.

Characterizing the third generation of American Communist women from the late 1960s through the early 1990s, Kendra Alexander found and sustained the Party at a moment when most had dismissed it and believed it to be outdated. Alexander, a teenage civil rights activist in the 1960s, eventually became one of the most prominent and high-ranking Communist Party officials in the United States throughout the 1970s and the 1980s. Spending her life in both Southern and Northern California, Alexander held an unusual role as an intellectual woman who embraced Black Power movements and simultaneously had an allegiance to the Communist Party and its commitment to class and racial struggles. She served as the head of Angela Davis's defense committee in 1972, when Davis faced charges of murder, conspiracy, and kidnapping. But Alexander was also intimately tied to non-Communist California radicals and labor organizers. Like Whitney and Healey, she succeeded in building coalitions with other radical and non-radical groups on specific issues such as police brutality, poverty, housing segregation, and unemployment. Thus, despite ideological differences, notions of justice and equality often united Party faithfuls such as Alexander and non-radicals.

Although Whitney, Healey, and Alexander led different generations of activists, these women were all part of an ongoing attempt to sustain a radical political movement in the United States. Each headed the second largest Party chapter in the country and served as the California representative (or chair) to the Central Committee of the Communist Party. In other words, each held the same title and had similar responsibilities. While the American Communist Party underwent a number of name changes (switching, for example, from the Communist Labor Party to the Workers (Communist) Party of America to the Communist Party of the United States of America) and organizational shifts in terms of mission, these women all belonged to the Communist Party that grew out of the Comintern that V. I. Lenin created in Russia in 1919 and which was aligned with the Soviet-directed parties around the world. At its core the Party advocated abolishing capitalism and social democracy and replacing it with a proletariat-led state. Whitney, Healey, and Alexander all agreed to support these tenets, which also included overthrowing the existing government to attain this workers' utopia.

Although Whitney and Alexander never met—Whitney died when Alexander was still in grade school—Healey knew both women and served as a bridge between the beginning and ending generations of Communist women. These women's lives and experiences with the Party challenge previous assumptions about the ways in which women integrated their American identities with their radical involvement. Whitney's gender and elite class background, for instance, often enabled liberals to support this revolutionary, while the Communist Party enhanced its legitimacy by proclaiming her to be its domestic matriarch. Indeed, throughout her 1920 criminal syndicalism trial and ensuing pardon campaign, Whitney's liberal and radical supporters alike characterized her as a wealthy social do-gooder incapable of inflicting harm. Thus, they united around a highly constructed image of an American-born revolutionary. Through such episodes the biographies of these three women leaders deepen and broaden historians' understandings of female radicals across the twentieth century.

Whitney, Healey, and Alexander not only became powerful figures within the CPUSA, but they also remained deeply rooted in mainstream society. Their families, friends, and cultural understandings centered on American notions of identity and femininity. They lived their lives deeply connected to their local communities—from community centers to women's clubs to student organizations to local politics. In other words, they blended, and at times purposefully adapted, Communist political culture with American society. What emerged in the lives of these three women was a profoundly American—if not Californian—version of communism, which allowed them to subscribe simultaneously to both mainstream and unconventional ideologies. By analyzing Whitney, Healey, and Alexander's experiences, this study argues that a deeply American version of communism developed and persisted throughout the twentieth century. This approach was characterized by conventional American gender roles, often assuming a separate spheres ideology; American notions of citizenship (relying on guaranteed civil liberties such as free speech and the right to organize); an embrace of consumer culture and American standards of beauty; and most important, a commitment to racial equality.[1]

Central to Whitney, Healey, and Alexander's collective experiences with American communism was gender, specifically the Party's reluctance to challenge gender inequalities. This reluctance stemmed more from conventional American gender roles than from any critical application of theory about gender hierarchies. Indeed, a gap emerged between philosophical arguments about gender inequalities and their lived experience. In its purest theoretical explanation, communism located women's oppression in the structures of capitalism. Resulting from the industrial-era division of labor between work within and outside of the home, communist theory reasoned that women's production became less important than men's production. Writers of a propaganda pamphlet observed in 1972: "Production in the family is unpaid; it is not recognized as valuable. Production outside the family is paid, therefore it is considered valuable."[2] Because of women's integral roles as stabilizers of capitalism, freeing the proletariat required women's participation. Without the private unpaid sphere of women's traditional work, capitalism would not function. Moreover, Karl Marx and V. I. Lenin contended that the abolition of private property, fostered by a proletariat-led revolution, would help emancipate women. Under communism the sexual division of labor would disappear, no assigned roles within a family would act as restraints, and the lines between public and private, male and female, would blur. Thus, historically, communism recognized the numerous economic and social problems caused by separate gender roles.[3]

Despite its theoretical commitment to women's equality, however, the Communist Party in the United States did not practice these principles in its daily activities. While consistently pronouncing that gender equality would only come out of proletariat-led revolution, the Party nevertheless expected its female members to serve as professional revolutionaries but remain subordinate to the Party's primarily male leadership. In much the same way that men in civil rights organizations did not practice gender equality in their daily operations, men in the Communist Party discouraged women from taking leadership positions but also relied on them to organize and facilitate events. But the paradox was made all the more puzzling because readings from Marx and Lenin that Communists regularly discussed addressed female inequality. Thus, the CPUSA eagerly discussed gender inequality, but daily Party activities often perpetuated inequality.[4]

The existing paradox about gender norms became apparent through the Party's operational structure, democratic centralism. Following from the logic that direction should come from one national center that coordinated the activity of the whole Party, democratic centralism meant that the Party functioned hierarchically. At local, regional, and national conventions Party leaders encouraged members to discuss openly, debate freely, and reflect critically on policies and goals (termed "self-criticism" by the Party). But after discussion was exhausted and a policy was determined, no dissent could occur. In order to have the most uniform positions, democratic centralism demanded that all Party members fall in line with whatever policies the Central Committee adopted.

When this structure was applied to recruiting directives, the Party leadership feared alienating its male base by targeting working women with gender-specific appeals. For this and other reasons, working women's concerns did not consistently appear on the national Communist Party's agenda. Throughout virtually all of its existence the Party subordinated concerns about sex and gender to a broader class-based approach to pursuing equality. But its reluctance to consider feminist causes put it in an awkward position: rather than support the potential industrial workplace opportunities and equalities that might come about through passage of the Equal Rights Amendment, for example, the Party did not support the amendment out of fear that it would do away with protective labor legislation. Women in the CPUSA had to accept that class would always be the first interest of the Party. As Kate Weigand, a historian of American Communist women, has observed, "Because of the Communist Party's social and cultural conservatism, individual Communists accepted traditional notions about women's natural submissiveness and subordination."[5]

These generally conservative attitudes toward gender that Weigand describes were reflected in the Communist Party's daily activities as male leaders typically restricted women to serving as organizers rather than as policy makers. Conversely, women who became outspoken proponents and leaders of the Party became the victims of vicious stereotypes. Communists and anti-Communists alike often assumed that women "gravitated to the Party's supposedly promiscuous environment in order to avoid becoming old maids," as historian Robert Schaffer has explained.[6] In theory Communists shunned traditional monogamous marriage (because it rested on capitalist assumptions about the private and public spheres) and embraced sexual openness. And in reality the world found vivid examples of women who fit this mold. Famed Communist spy–turned–FBI informant Elizabeth Bentley, for example, carried on a five-year romantic affair with a Soviet agent, which convinced many Americans of the subversive sexual power and promiscuity of Communist women.[7] Regardless of their roles within the Party, female members faced sexual stereotypes assigned to them by the outside world as well as Party structures. Its conflicting and contradictory positions on gender and sexuality in general, and of its female members in particular, begin to explain the complexities that three women leaders faced in trying to reconcile their individual and group identities.

Furthermore, although the female Communists differed significantly in terms of age, class, and race, the Party's idealized image of them rarely wavered. Throughout the twentieth century the CPUSA needed to have female leaders fulfill a public image of an idealized traditional American Communist woman. This venerated woman did not appear to be a feminist. For the sake of the Party, Whitney, Healey, and Alexander reflected this image, which typically went hand in hand with traditional American gender roles. In fact, rather than championing gender equality within the ranks of the Party, male leaders often attempted to confine professionally ambitious women to a less threatening subordinate sphere. Female Communist Party members rarely held real leadership roles; in this regard Whitney, Healey, and Alexander do not represent the average Party woman's experience. Their experiences, however, highlight the tension over gender issues within the Party; the primarily male leaders occasionally called for gender equality by accepting and ultimately appointing a few women to high-ranking positions. Whitney, Healey, and Alexander became exceptions by eventually holding their privileged posts of California state representative and/or chair of the Party.

In taking these prestigious Communist Party positions, Whitney, Healey, and Alexander did not push the Party to place gender equality higher on its agenda. By tolerating discriminatory treatment from inside the Party and refusing to recognize women as an oppressed category, these three leaders did not prioritize gender inequalities. For nearly a century they repeatedly insisted that social oppression stemmed directly from economic oppression, which made them relegate the importance of gender discrimination to the bottom of their agendas.[8] While there were small groups of female members such as Mary Inman, Betty Gannett, and Claudia Jones who attempted to draw attention to the sex discrimination within the Party, for the most part Whitney, Healey, and Alexander "didn't consider that what was happening was a general problem; it was a private individual thing, and what good was it to dwell upon it," as Healey recalled several years after leaving the Party.[9] Weigand has argued that Communist women who protested sexist treatment within the Party, especially Mary Inman, found themselves ostracized. Even as conversations about women's inequality and struggles as revolutionaries made their way to the pages of Communist publications, those that prioritized gender were not maintained by the Party's leadership circle for long.[10] In this regard Whitney, Healey, and Alexander resembled non-Communist female political activists. Women such as Francis Perkins and even Eleanor Roosevelt while she was first lady, for example, often subordinated concerns about gender inequality in exchange for other campaigns for political or economic rights.[11]

Thus, strikingly, a Party with such progressive and occasionally introspective ideologies and practices—which carefully considered class and racial inequalities—did not look at gender with the same critical eye. Both female and male members could not escape to the confines of popular notions about gender. For more than eight decades Communist leaders succeeded in convincing members of the need to privilege class and race inequalities above gender. Yet in spite of their seemingly complacent positions on gender inequalities, Whitney, Healey, and Alexander confronted, contested, and overcame personal gendered criticism from male comrades. And although they all resisted the label "feminist" (because they believed class rather than gender to be the central contradiction in American society), each woman found professional opportunities in the Party that would not have been available elsewhere. As Weigand has asserted about Communist women in the Cold War, "Communist women were the most radical of the antifeminist 1950s."[12]

Indeed, some historians of the American Communist Party argue that "no matter how much evidence of sex and race discrimination scholars can detect in the Communist Party and its auxiliaries, the culture these radicals constructed was a far cry from the brutally racist and sexist universe that surrounded them."[13] While that was true in the Party's public world, the private lives of these women reveal a more complex and negotiated Communist culture. Gender helped to shape a distinctly American Communist culture among Party members in the mid-twentieth century. From Whitney's lifetime ties to her elite cadre of Wellesley alumnae to Healey's privileging of her mother-son relationship above all else to Alexander's close familial ties, these women rooted their Communist identities within their personal communities. In many of the choices they made and values they held, Whitney, Healey, and Alexander replicated American feminine standards and conventional notions of domesticity. While on the one hand they pushed forward as leading political actors, on the other they became mired in mainstream cultural expectations regarding gender. And in this regard they lived feminism but were not feminists.

This book also explores the lives of three women in order to gain a greater understanding of the American Communist Party as a whole throughout the twentieth century. While the democratic centralist structure of the Communist Party changed little over the course of the century, the Party did shift its revolutionary agendas, tactics, and even name (throughout Whitney, Healey, and Alexander's lives the Soviet-led Comintern directed its member parties to dissolve and re-form a number of times, though for most of its existence the Party was known as the Communist Party of the USA). The story of the Party told from the perspectives of Whitney, Healey, and Alexander presents an alternative and nearly foreign image of the organization. While geographically separate from many of the national decisions, these women nevertheless held positions on the Central Committee in New York City, which meant that at least in a formal capacity they interacted with other national leaders and responded to international policies. And whereas they obviously differed from each other in terms of how they reacted to and were received by other Party officials, their changing experiences with the national Party explain a great deal about the Party's internal dynamics and its relationships with both local and international events. Moreover, telling the story of the Communist Party through Whitney, Healey, and Alexander's eyes not only sheds new light on the experiences of these women and of their Party, but it changes historians' understanding of the Party's relationship to the rest of American society. These women all built coalitions with non-Communists. Most consistently, the Party (and particularly the California Parties under the leadership of these three women) forged relationships with other people and organizations over common issues.

Communists frequently aligned with non-Communists on the legal battlefield. Sympathizers often came to the side of Communists not because they necessarily supported Communist theories or broader agendas but because they believed in the civil liberties implied in the American Constitution and legal system. In building support for Angela Davis's 1972 murder trial, for example, the Communist Party founded the National United Committee to Free Angela Davis (NUCFAD), which solicited and received support from such diverse organizations and individuals as the Black Caucus, the Southern Christian Leadership Conference, labor unions, student activists, and entertainers. Often non-Communists who aligned with Communists simply believed that all American citizens, even radicals, deserved to have their constitutional rights protected (particularly free speech and due process).[14]

Communists also aligned with non-Communists through political coalitions and labor organizations. In much the same way that historian Jacqueline Castledine has explained how women in the Progressive Party saw themselves as members of a broad popular front advocating for the rights of oppressed workers and minorities, Communists positioned themselves within the same political environment.[15] Communists of course have a storied history in the labor movement. Historians have explained their involvement in official and unofficial capacities in certain industries, cities, and specific unions. The Trade Union–Unity League (TUUL); the Congress of Industrial Organizations (CIO); the United Cannery, Agricultural, Packing, and Allied Workers of America (UCAPAWA); the auto industry; and municipal organizations all have connections with the history of communism in America.[16] At certain moments in the twentieth century, especially during the "heyday" of organizing during the Great Depression, Communists worked relatively openly with labor. And much of the Party's successful grassroots organizing occurred in conjunction with its involvement in the labor movement.

Similarly, the California branches of the Communist Party also found common ground with non-Communists in struggles for racial equality. As several historians have documented, American Communists advocated and promoted racial equality long before the rise of the southern civil rights movement of the mid-twentieth century, and hence the Party gained members because of this issue.[17] Minutes before Oakland police arrested Whitney in 1919 for violating the California Criminal Syndicalism Law, for example, she had made a speech to a crowded room of clubwomen denouncing lynching and Jim Crow laws in the South. And once the mainstream civil rights movement came to the fore, Party members (although not the formal Party apparatus) actively participated in its programs and activities. Healey, for example, spoke on college campuses to advertise the Party's long-standing commitment to civil rights, while

Alexander traveled to Louisiana in 1965 to attempt to register disfranchised black voters.

Whitney, Healey, and Alexander led a Party that continually pursued relationships with non-Communist organizations. Free speech and racial equality dominated their attempts to build coalitions, but they certainly sought to find common ground with groups broadly focused on helping workers, the unemployed, and the underrepresented. By extension, rather than envisioning the Party in isolation from other radical and non-radical organizations, the efforts of Whitney, Healey, and Alexander demonstrate that a new understanding of the Party is to be gained from considering it as part of an ongoing dynamic movement that was not always stigmatized by non-Communists. This frame of reference should be central to a broader analysis of communism in America. Indeed, Communist Party members were part of a multidimensional and multigenerational Left and must not be isolated historically and historiographically from other progressive activists.[18]

In addition to using Whitney, Healey, and Alexander's lives as lenses through which to explore women Communists, the Party in general, and its relationships with non-Communist organizations, this book examines how the geographic and social space of the state of California affected their experiences. The fact that each woman spent the vast majority of her activist life inside the state affected her identity, outlook, agenda, and priorities. Throughout the 1930s and 1940s (the years when the national Party membership peaked, with around one hundred thousand members) California proudly held the second highest number of card-carrying Communists, after New York. Still, being geographically separate from the powerhouse of New York, California Communists retained a certain amount of distance and independence. Members in this West Coast state pursued agendas, formed alliances, and took positions that in many regards ran counter to or at least challenged stances determined on the East Coast or in Europe.

California's own geographic, political, and social diversity created the space for radicalism to develop. Within the state three regions—

the Bay Area, Southern California, and the Central Valley—stand out as distinct sections that produced their own local versions of radicalism. Each region possesses a distinct climate, landscape, history, and source of economic opportunity. Whitney, Healey, and Alexander crossed through each space over the course of their Party involvement and recognized the unique economic, political, and social circumstances that fostered interest in communism. In the Bay Area radical ideas made sense to workers on the docks, in the fields, and in factories. These workers listened to explanations of their struggles and the advantages of Communist Party involvement in a way that seemed to be a reasonable extension of their understanding of the freedoms that came along with being American citizens. Whitney, for example, first supported members of the Industrial Workers of the World because she wanted to defend their free speech rights, and in Bay Area courtrooms, as she helped to protect and promote their rights, she became an even stronger advocate of the rights of the most vulnerable Californians. Similarly, in Southern California radical ideas made sense to those who worked in the harbors and in many factories as well as to those who felt that the local government and police force repressed these groups. Healey and Alexander were able to find a broad base of support in Los Angeles by explaining to residents that their rights had been violated by the Los Angeles Police Department's famous Red Squad, by anti-Communist forces in the local government, or by businesses that refused to sell to or buy from minorities. Furthermore, in the Central Valley the diverse pool of migrant labors who toiled in the expansive agricultural fields were willing to work with labor organizers who understood their uniquely weak position. Healey, for example, worked openly as a Communist by encouraging agricultural workers to support strikes and join a union that was violently repressed by landowners.

Moreover, California has a history of nurturing extremist movements. While this book explains how and why over the course of the twentieth century California was home to a significant group of Communists on the Left, the state also fostered equally strong movements on the Right. As Healey persuaded some baby boomers to join the New Old Left, others found a home with Barry Goldwater and a much more conservative Republican Party. Many historians have written about the diverse forces in the agricultural regions and suburbs that encouraged this increasingly radical strand of conservatism in California. This characterization of California—as somehow more extreme than the rest of the country—has long been highlighted by popular writers, politicians, and academics alike. As Wallace Stegner wrote, "California has not only been America only more so, it has sometimes been America in the worst sense of the word. It has plundered itself, it has permitted the wide excesses of wide-open opportunism and uncontrollable growth."[19]

This book engages the California exceptionalism framework by locating its sources rather than merely accepting its fictive power. It assesses whether California may have indeed facilitated a Communist Party that was separate from eastern Parties because of the diverse members, their understandings of California, or the ways in which radicalism operated in this distant space. In analyzing the connections, tensions, and relationships among California branches, other western Parties, and the East Coast headquarters, this study complicates how historians understand the forging of political and social movements. A bottom-up explanation of grassroots radicalism will contribute to a broader understanding of California and its diverse localities, which gave rise to many state and national coalitions.[20]

In addition to participating in the ongoing attempt to characterize California politics and radicalism, this book contributes to a large body of scholarship about the Communist Party in the United States. Historiographical debates about the Party's relationship with the Soviet Union and the Comintern dominate a significant part of the scholarly discussion of American communism. On the one hand, traditionalist historians of American communism have emphasized the foreign roots and hierarchical nature of the Party. By extension they tend to highlight the nonautonomous aspects of the Party, maintaining that Soviet authoritarian power essentially made American Communists tools of the Kremlin.[21] At the opposite end of the spectrum revisionist and some neo-orthodox historians of the American Communist Party underscore the distinctly "American" aspects of Parties to prove their autonomy from the Soviet Union. These studies document the roles that Communists have played in American domestic affairs, specifically in relationship to the Congress of Industrial Organizations, and in politics. They frequently expose common ground shared by Communists and non-Communists about political concerns.[22]

Scholarship of American communism has also dealt comprehensively with the underground and above-ground Party apparatus and leadership. Several historians have studied the extent to which American Communists aided in espionage. Dividing the Party between the underground covert networks and public worlds has become a framework for contextualizing this component of American communism.[23] Likewise, many of these scholars have chronicled the lives and experiences of top-level Party officials. Biographies, including autobiographical works, enable writers to account for changes over time and in perspective. With a few notable exceptions, these accounts focus on leaders from the East Coast.[24]

Recently, several important studies have documented the Party's local activism. In particular historians have constructed a narrative away from the leaders in the East by focusing, for example, on Communists in the South and radicals in labor organizations in Chicago as well as Party members' relationships with African Americans and their connections with women's rights activists.[25] This research recreates an American Communist Party that was distinct from the Soviet Union and, more important, one that was grounded in local communities that pursued issues that appealed directly to residents. What these studies share is not simply an indigenous American communism but also a grassroots Communist movement that elicited support from what might otherwise have been skeptical people and organizations. This recent scholarship tells the story of communism through the lens of grassroots movements that struggled to produce concrete changes in local communities. Participants in these Parties tended to be rooted in their physical neighborhoods and thus were more aware of and responsive to immediate and relevant problems. On some level Whitney, Healey, and Alexander fit into all of these strands of American communism.

But more than situating these leading women in multiple radical traditions, this book describes leftist activism in America generationally.[26] Identifying, characterizing, and analyzing its leaders throughout and across lifetimes draws attention to both continuity and change in revolutionaries and their agendas over the twentieth century. The Progressive Era, Great Depression, Cold War, and social protest movements of the 1960s serve as central backdrops that frame this study and contextualize each woman's life. Weaving the story of American radicalism through these eras reveals the extent to which time and place affected radicals' identities. The following chapters survey radicals' engagement with California mainstream politics and society, enabling this book to extract broader temporal and thematic generalizations. By the same token it scrutinizes how Whitney, Healey, and Alexander led lives that appeared to straddle deviant and mainstream definitions of womanhood.

The resulting study considers how the profoundly American Communist world in which Whitney, Healey, and Alexander lived and participated embodied contradictory attitudes to women. It was also marked by coalition building as a routine tactic of the California members of the Communist Party. Together, these two points demonstrate that radical politics were not disconnected from mainstream politics. Whitney, Healey, and Alexander were rooted in the culture around them. Their local activism illustrates how the Party worked within and not by definition against the formal political structure, and because of this flexibility, members were able to maintain organizational integrity into the early 1990s. Ultimately, analyzing the Communist Party over this expansive period of time demonstrates the Party's continuity across the three generations of its female leaders' lives.

2 Parlor Pink Turned Soapbox Red

*Charlotte Anita Whitney, the American
Communist Matriarch, 1867–1955*

On October 23, 1925, the Women's Christian Temperance Union
(WCTU) unanimously passed a resolution declaring its commitment
to help Charlotte Anita Whitney, a card-carrying Communist, avoid
prison. "We, as members of the WCTU," it proclaimed, "hold it deplor-
able in the extreme that a law the alleged purpose of which is to
protect society against the violence of the evil minded, should have
been so interpreted as to entrap within its coils one whose gentle
life has been devotion to service of the betterment of humanity."[1]
A longtime progressive organization, the WCTU offered important
broad-based support for Whitney's pardon campaign. Nearly six
years earlier Whitney had been convicted of violating the California Criminal Syndicalism Law. After making its way to the U.S.
Supreme Court, Whitney's case had reached a dead end; her one-

to fourteen-year prison sentence seemed imminent, despite years of appeals. Still, the WCTU came out loudly in support of Whitney and her pardon campaign, illustrating that in spite of her Communist Party affiliations, progressives stood by this exceptionally privileged, refined, and feminine leader of the Communist Labor Party. Represented by Jane Addams, Norman Hapgood, Fremont Older, and Rev. John A. Ryan, the Progressive Party formed a delegation and lobbied the governor for her pardon. This group of politically and socially connected Californians united to help Whitney, a dedicated clubwoman, social activist, and Communist, avoid serving a prison sentence at San Quentin. Whitney's gender- and class-based support from progressives, suffragists, Christians, and Republicans alike demonstrates how and why she transcended many political and ideological boundaries during the first half of the twentieth century.

Whitney's unique role as an elite leftist suggests several far-reaching conclusions about early-twentieth-century politics and society as well as the nature of the California Communist Party from the 1910s through the 1940s. Whitney lived in both the privileged world of benefit dinners and summer vacations and the radical world of late-night Communist Party meetings and soapbox corner protests. Both worlds embraced and admired her. Even after the Red Scare of 1919 legitimized Americans' hatred and fear of Communists, Whitney's old friends in the world of establishment liberalism continued to support her. Whitney's case suggests that radical movements and liberal organizations had many overlapping concerns, most often coalescing on single-issue campaigns that frequently culminated in courtrooms and on ballots. Furthermore, the divide between radical and non-radical worlds emerged over time, but it never proved to be completely insurmountable, in part because of the way that Whitney's supporters used her gendered identity to mollify any deep concerns about liberals supporting revolutionaries.[2]

Several women's historians and historians of the Left have written of the crossover that occurred between social welfare concerns and radical causes.[3] In spite of what some saw at the time as competing and contradictory interests in their organizing efforts, radicals united with liberals in campaigns, suffrage movements, social welfare platforms, and court cases. Most significantly in Whitney's own life, liberals united with radicals over free speech rights, as exemplified in her criminal syndicalism case. Whitney's movement in the worlds of social welfare and social activism must be framed in the context of the unique moment of early-twentieth-century California, one that was socially fluid and politically open.

In addition to documenting this sort of activism, a few writers have attempted to capture the particular significance of Whitney's life and career. The Communist Party itself built something of a cottage industry around constructing narratives about the lives of its most valued members; these publications arguably served the interests of the Party's recruiting directives above all else. In its strongest attempt to document the deeply patriotic and radical life of its western matriarch, the Communist writer and editor Al Richmond published *Native Daughter* in 1942.[4] More historically descriptive, Lisa Rubens's 1986 article in *California History*, "The Patrician Radical: Charlotte Anita Whitney," seeks to explain Whitney's life story as it illuminates the relatively fluid boundaries between radicalism and liberalism during her trial years. And more theoretically, legal scholars have scrutinized Whitney's famous 1920 criminal syndicalism conviction and 1926 appeal to the U.S. Supreme Court because of a concurring opinion written by Justice Louis Brandeis regarding the importance of free speech.[5] This account of Whitney's life aims both to amplify the debate surrounding the significance of her activism and to contextualize her within the political and social climate of early-twentieth-century California. Although this narrative of Whitney illustrates why she, a native-born elite activist, was uniquely situated to facilitate coalition building, it also exposes the limits of cooperation between radicals and non-radicals. It was often Whitney's gender and class background that enabled liberals to support this Communist, not to mention the Communist Party's own emphasis on her conventional femininity and privileged class identity, which prompted the Party to label her as its domestic matriarch and thereby gain greater legitimacy. In short, rigid understandings of gender roles—cast by both radicals and liberals—overtook her self-proclaimed identity as a revolutionary and allowed supporters to rally around a wealthy woman, albeit a Communist. Indeed, this gender identity effectively reveals the limits of the porous boundaries between mainstream and radical worlds in California during the first half of the twentieth century.

Born July 7, 1867, to Mary Swearingen and George Edwin Whitney, a lawyer and state senator, Whitney grew up in a privileged household in Oakland, California. Her father's brother-in-law, Stephen Johnson Field, brought the family its highest regard when President Lincoln appointed him to serve on the U.S. Supreme Court. As an associate justice on the high court who later became famous for his advocacy of laissez-faire economics, Field hosted his young niece, Anita, in Washington DC for several summers throughout her childhood. Because of this relationship and those with a number of other family members, Whitney came of age in a well-connected yet conventional family. Whitney's immediate family had come to California from Maine in 1861 because of her father's poor health. Throughout the 1860s and 1870s George Whitney worked to formulate state policies and garner aid for the elderly and the criminally insane in Alameda County.[6] This distinguished family background made Anita Whitney a cause célèbre in later years, when the Communist Party cherished her as an indigenous American Communist. The Party, for example, proudly traced her paternal lineage to the *Mayflower*. In fact, one of her ancestors, Thomas Dudley, served as the governor of the Massachusetts Colony in 1634.[7] And Whitney's mother traced her ancestry to equally distinguished origins. Migrating to Maryland in 1640, her ancestors came to colonial North America from Holland. This side of the family even claimed a major and colonel in the Revolutionary War.

Continuing the family tradition of earning distinguished credentials, in 1885, following her father's suggestion, Whitney left the West Coast and enrolled at Wellesley College in Massachusetts. Here she immersed herself in the normal course of study; she learned the sciences, Latin, philosophy, and the Bible.[8] Beyond the religious, social, and intellectual experience she first encountered at Wellesley, Whitney found a community of similarly privileged and socially conscious women, with whom she stayed in contact for the remainder of her life. These young women welcomed her into a burgeoning environment of like-minded, refined, and progressive women. College inspired Whitney to develop strong Christian and democratic convictions as an Episcopalian; she later recalled, "I was, for the first time in my life, surrounded by a distinctly religious atmosphere and I had my first realization of a spiritual life within."[9] The ties that Whitney developed at Wellesley brought her to her first job as a social worker and supported her throughout her tumultuous years as a Communist and criminal syndicalist. These Wellesley connections also constitute a key part of Whitney's legacy because nearly every year for the rest of her life she penned a letter to the Wellesley class of 1889 alumnae book. In writing to the Wellesley community for more than a half century, Whitney gave her friends, fellow alumnae, and future historians a priceless window into how she wanted to be remembered.

Like many members of the first generation of college-educated women, Whitney seemed lost after graduating in 1889. In her 1894 class letter she admitted: "My record for the past year makes such a small showing that I dislike to put it down in black and white. Home life, with some club work among the boys and girls of West Oakland, and a course in Philosophy at the University of California, is all I have to show."[10] The dissatisfaction that Whitney felt in the years immediately following her graduation was not at all unusual for college-educated women of this era. Jane Addams, for example, upon graduating from the Rockford Female Seminary in Illinois, moved back to her parents' home and later recalled a sense of aimlessness and purposelessness. Similarly, Lillian Wald graduated from a woman's college in Rochester, New York, in 1889, only to find herself alone in a world of stylish married women.[11] On the one hand, because so few career opportunities presented themselves and they had no precedent to follow, many first-generation college-educated women spent several years feeling alone and frustrated. On the other hand, significant numbers of these women found fulfillment in their work as social welfare activists.

Whitney's conversion happened in 1892, three years after graduating from Wellesley. That summer Whitney traveled east for a class reunion and stopped in New York to visit some former classmates who worked in the Lower East Side at a settlement house. After one week the staff invited her to stay and work as a social worker at the College Settlement, the same place Eleanor Roosevelt would find work in the coming decade. Located in the slums of Rivington Street, this settlement house was one in which "educated people tried to help the poor, through various social and educational activities."[12] Working among the poorest immigrants in New York City gave Whitney firsthand experience with the unrelenting poverty that plagued urban slums. In the house Whitney organized activities for neighborhood children and helped out in the homes of some of the most impoverished residents, leading her to proudly declare to her Wellesley community, "It is a splendid school, where a resident learns and receives much more than she can give out."[13] A close friend many years later, Elizabeth Gurley Flynn, recalled the impact of this experience on Whitney: "The sights and smells of the squalid slums, the sweat shops, child labor, the crowded living quarters of the poor with rats and roaches, the prostitution, crime and terrible fires were appalling revelations. Such mockery of the promise of life, liberty and the pursuit of happiness haunted her on her return to her pleasant California home."[14] Decades later Al Richmond, her official Communist Party biographer, suspected that "the terrible revelations" that Whitney had in the settlement caused her to question the Christian democratic principles that she had developed in college.[15] Although these comrades wrote their assessments long after the fact, at the time Whitney's letters reveal that she was convinced that she could best treat widespread urban suffering through settlement and charity work. In fact, after her father's illness and death later in 1892, Whitney returned to Oakland, where she opened a settlement house on the east side of the city and a Boys' Club in West Oakland.[16]

After spending eight years engaged in California social work, Whitney began to use her budding public reputation to organize other social workers and raise money for settlement houses through the Associated Charities of Oakland, a philanthropic group of primarily Christian residents that sought to help the most vulnerable of citizens: children, the disabled, and elderly. In 1901, at age thirty-four, Whitney became secretary of this organization, where she remained until 1908.[17] Although she was not well compensated for her efforts, working on the charities board gave her experience in confronting the city administration. A fellow social worker remembered, "She worked long hours at $85 a month, dyed her suits, economized on her luncheons, and gave more generously than she could afford from her own funds."[18] Between 1901 and 1903 Whitney also served as an unpaid probation officer for Alameda County, and in 1903 the Oakland Juvenile Court appointed her to be the city's first youth probation officer.[19] In this capacity she fought for and achieved separate detention facilities for child offenders. Altogether, throughout the first decade of the twentieth century, by working within and alongside governmental structures, Whitney honed a strong liberal identity as a social and political reformer. She hoped that by working as a reformer inside charity and governmental organizations she would effect direct and relevant changes in the lives of the most impoverished Californians. Moreover, the connections she established through this work gave her a sturdy foundation as a mainstream reformer that she parlayed into later activism. Still, despite her flourishing career, Whitney admitted doubts. As she noted in a 1905 letter, "Work all day long and six days in a week—though it be most absorbing and interesting—does leave something in life for a woman to desire."[20] This charity work did not deliver the personal fulfillment Whitney sought, though at the time the culture of American political radicals certainly would not have been an obvious place for her to look.

Nevertheless, when the San Francisco earthquake struck on April 18, 1906, Whitney did not hesitate to volunteer for several months to aid the victims, all the while becoming a devoted prohibitionist. And after an extended stay in the East, where she familiarized herself with Boston's charity department, Whitney returned home to California to embark on a new venture: suffrage.[21]

In turning her attention toward the woman's suffrage movement, Whitney found herself surrounded by familiar company. It was quite common for progressive women who had been active in settlement houses and protective labor legislation to become suffragists. Many suffragists argued that women had proved their worth in social welfare work and that as voters they had something fundamental to offer. Across the country in statewide suffrage campaigns, activists asserted both "natural rights" and "expediency" arguments for the vote. Initially, in the post–Fourteenth Amendment years through the 1890s, suffragists reasoned that women deserved the vote because of their inherent equality with men and natural rights as human beings. By the early twentieth century, however, women began rallying around a different argument based on expediency: women deserved the vote because they were more moral than men. Emphasizing women's differences from men, its advocates asserted a connection between earlier reform work and women's morality. They linked their progressive tradition of confronting urban problems such as housing, sanitation, and education with their value as voters. As Anna Garlin Spencer declared at the 1898 National American Woman Suffrage Association (NAWSA) convention: "So long as the state concerned itself with only the most external and mechanical of social interests, the presumption that men should rule was inevitable, natural and beneficent. The instant, however, the State took upon itself any form of educative charitable, or personally helpful work, it entered the area of distinctive feminine training and power, and therefore became in need of service of women."[22] In other words, in addition to protecting their distinct maternal interests, according to Whitney and other like-minded reformers, suffrage would privilege female morality and pave the way for broad-based Progressive Era reform, something the country, especially California, desperately needed.[23]

These expediency suffrage arguments certainly resonated with Whitney. She stood alongside other suffragists of the era because of their shared conviction that if given the vote, women would permanently eliminate the social ills that she had thus far spent her life trying to eradicate. In her 1911 class letter Whitney wrote: "We are making the fight for Woman's Suffrage in the California Legislature and I've had my first experience with legislators in Sacramento where I went as a member of the College Equal Suffrage League. Nothing but my sincere conviction of the justice of the cause would have led me to enter the arena, but I do believe so heartily in the movement that I must work for it."[24] At the same time, neighbors teased Whitney for being a suffragette. A friend amusedly remembered, "They called her a woman lover or something like that."[25] But this criticism certainly had little impact on her convictions and politics. She managed to become the president of the College Equal Suffrage League of Northern California, president of the California Civic League, and eventually the second vice president of the National American Woman Suffrage Association. Speaking in 1911 for the statewide suffrage campaign, Whitney commented, "The world has recognized the mind of women in schools and colleges, and her political identity must be the next phase of her expression."[26]

In addition to working for suffrage alongside other educated elite women, in the early 1910s Whitney also supported trade unions' efforts to recruit workingwomen to the suffrage campaign. By deciding to align herself with workingwomen, Whitney entered into a different realm of suffrage activism. Originating with Fabian Socialists in England in the 1890s and brought to New York by Harriot Stanton Blatch a few years later, suffragists who had a working-class focus reconsidered the traditional narrative that wealthy women uplifted and educated the poor. Instead, Blatch, who personally came from a privileged family, wrote, "Every workingman needs the suffrage more than I do, but there is another who needs it more than he does, just because [her] conditions are more galling, and that is the working woman."[27] Recognizing the centrality of wage-earning women to the future of suffrage campaigns, Blatch and other activists, including Whitney, expanded the scope of organizing. In fact, as Ellen Carol DuBois has argued, socialist feminism "has consistently been a radicalizing force in the larger history of feminism."[28] Linked with European socialist feminists such as Clara Zetkin, American suffragists such as Maud Younger, a San Francisco trade union activist, organized the Working Women's Suffrage Society. Comprising a significant, albeit underestimated, portion of suffragists (and their overall arguments), these leftist activists played a substantial role in pushing the movement into broader class populations. Still, a division emerged: while the leadership of mainstream suffrage organizations found that the popular expediency argument built more momentum for statewide amendments, socialist feminist arguments did persuade many workingwomen of the value of the vote for their own livelihoods.

Still, in the end, while the suffrage organizations that Whitney led accepted the membership of working-class women, most of her pre-1911 activity occurred in the realm of middle- and upper-class suffragists. Whitney had yet to fully embrace the significance of class in her vision of equality. In California (in part because the amendment passed earlier there than in other states) the two sides of the statewide suffrage campaign—the middle-class progressives and workers—operated more or less separately.[29] Although Whitney sympathized with the arguments of working-class suffragists, she did not personally organize workers in her leadership of California suffrage campaigns. Rather, her activism focused more exclusively on clubwomen and educated Californians. In her post-1911 national activism, however, Whitney embraced some of the arguments put forth by Blatch and the more militant wing of suffragists. This early familiarity with socialist feminism certainly reminded her in future years of the importance of workers in broader political struggles.

After the suffrage amendment passed in California on October 10, 1911 (alongside other progressive reform laws such as the recall and workmen's compensation), Whitney sought to give female voters more influence in the government, and she proceeded with her own political activism. In 1912, for example, she campaigned to put women on juries, to police red-light districts, and to regulate racetracks. But Whitney continued to be active in the suffrage movement by becoming the second vice president of the NAWSA, serving under Dr. Anna Howard Shaw. This national leadership role also brought her into a close relationship with Jane Addams and led her to travel across the country campaigning for suffrage amendments in Connecticut, Nevada, and Oregon. In 1912 she spent a month in Oregon, where she "went with the hope of stirring up the college women of that state to some sense of their responsibility to the equal suffrage movement."[30] While there, Whitney visited with fellow Wellesley alumnae and spoke to suffrage leagues at Reed College and the University of Oregon. Her 1912 class letter detailed the regions throughout Oregon in which she hoped to have effected change.[31]

By the time she became a leader in the suffrage movement, Whitney's tone had shifted from that of a charity do-gooder to a politically motivated and focused suffragist. Engulfed in politics, she urged her Wellesley friends to "bestir yourselves, my eastern sisters, and don't wait for this great movement to come triumphantly upon you from the West. Don't you want it to come because of you rather than in spite of you?"[32] Whitney became a more determined activist when she made the transition from charity worker to ardent suffragist. In 1913 she wrote, "Once a suffragist always a suffragist, and though we women are voting in California, we want all the women of our country to have the same duty, responsibility, privilege, or opportunity—whichever you choose to call it."[33] Whitney's more focused support of suffrage stemmed from her interests both in enacting social welfare reforms as well as in supporting equal rights for all Americans, regardless of gender or race. But in terms of organizational affiliation, Whitney still had not officially aligned herself with socialist feminists; in the early 1910s her commitment rested with the more moderate middle-class-minded organizations.

Ultimately, Whitney's suffrage activity turned her into a feminist, though in 1913 she certainly would have shunned the label because of its radical connotations. Many years later a friend recalled that Whitney, while trying to galvanize women labor organizers, "used to tell us how much she did, what she did, and how come she started organizing these women to make them understand how important it was that they were not subject to what a man had to say."[34] In other words, she lived as a feminist in that she called for women's independence and equality with men. Positioning herself as a strong but moderate leader of the suffrage movement, Whitney explained in her many speeches and directives as vice president of the NAWSA that she had joined the suffragists to lift the status of women in society. Organizational, class-based, or even theoretical tensions in suffrage arguments did not plague Whitney's unwavering devotion to the cause, although she scorned women who sought lavish attention and gifts from men. A friend remembered her having said: "Just because you are a woman you shouldn't feel that you want the men to kiss your hand. . . . We are looking for equality on all bases."[35] During the peak suffrage campaign years Whitney employed many arguments supporting a woman's right to vote. As with a number of other diverse suffragists, the higher good of women voting persuaded Whitney to remain committed to recruiting suffragists above all else. For Whitney, however, the fight all the way to the national amendment would not keep her attention.

After finally succeeding in getting the vote, Whitney, like many suffragists, felt let down and disillusioned when having this right seemed to accomplish very little. Although it was said many years after she had joined the Communist Party, and possibly with its agenda in mind, Whitney confessed to friends in the 1920s that "she was very much disappointed after women got the suffrage."[36] Once women had the vote, they simply did not mobilize as a group of progressive-minded voters in California. She expressed sharp frustration that women seemed to be happy with their husbands telling them whom to vote for. Speaking at an International Women's Day meeting, Whitney professed, "After we got it they should have known what to do with it better."[37]

Whitney also witnessed "this great movement" become divided after 1920, though since the mid-1910s she herself had radicalized and came to identify with the more radical wing of the suffrage movement. Long before Congress ratified the national amendment,

Whitney had left her leadership position in the NAWSA and shifted her sympathies toward the more radical wing of suffrage organizations. She enlisted with the Congressional Union for Woman Suffrage, predecessor to the National Women's Party (NWP), the more militant group that oftentimes stood in opposition to the moderate League of Women Voters (LWV).[38] Led by the renowned feminist Alice Paul, the NWP radicalized its theories and tactics by issuing broad critiques of American politics, especially asserting its opposition to U.S. entrance into World War I and the government's employment of anti-sedition laws. As several historians have documented, the war ultimately handicapped the women's rights movement, and eventually the NWP became a single-issue organization pursuing the Equal Rights Amendment. Yet by the time these national debates came to the fore in the late 1910s, Whitney had departed altogether from women's rights organizations to pursue larger radical endeavors.[39]

In the context of the 1910s, Whitney's support of a more radical cause—namely, racial equality—also took her down a more radical, and more controversial, path of activism. Simultaneously with her suffrage efforts, she started working for racial justice. She was a charter member of the National Association for the Advancement of Colored People (NAACP), which gave her a platform to travel the state publicly denouncing racism, Jim Crow laws, and lynching. Among her many speeches against the state's racist legislation, in 1926, for example, she spoke to the National Women's Party at the Fairmont Hotel in San Francisco calling for "the abolishment of all laws forbidding inter-racial marriage." Opposing California's antimiscegenation laws, she argued, "If a full-grown man and woman wish to live together as man and wife it is only decent to allow them to do it, no matter what their color."[40] For Whitney to take this position in California, a state that had adopted strong antimiscegenation laws in 1850, when it was in its infancy, shows just how far she had moved from more mainstream social norms about the racial order.

Whitney took an even more politically radical stand in 1913, when she came out in support of the anarcho-syndicalist union the Industrial Workers of the World (IWW), or Wobblies, and specifically the participants in the Wheatland Hop Riots in Northern California. When IWW leaders arrived at Durst Ranch and attempted to organize the workers because of reports about harsh labor conditions there, the town sheriff and ranch owner showed up at a union meeting intending to disperse the crowd of two thousand workers. A deputy fired a shot into the air, and the room erupted in violence; in the end, two workers, a sheriff, and a district attorney lay dead. As a result of the riot, two Wobblies were tried, convicted, and sentenced to second-degree murder.[41] By early 1914 Whitney had become active in the campaign to release the two men from prison. In addition to supporting these particular prisoners' releases, Whitney sought to protect the free speech rights of all IWW members.

In her advocacy of free speech Whitney lent her support to an issue that held appeal beyond radical circles. Free speech united vastly diverse organizations and interests. Progressives had been longtime defenders and promoters of free speech rights. And in the case of labor activists who were often unfairly indicted or convicted, free speech became a rallying point around which many radical and reformist organizations could construct coalitions. These coalitions would become important for Whitney's own livelihood in the coming decade and would continue for the next half century.[42]

Meanwhile, as Whitney worked to defend the two anarchists, she continued to pursue other progressive work. In 1914 she worked on saloon reform, helped to establish a state institution for the "feeble minded," and started an industrial farm for convicted adult female criminals. For several years Whitney managed to blend her charity-minded reform work with her radical sympathies, as she transcended seemingly rigid social and political boundaries. In part her unique social position enabled Whitney to become an activist in many realms. She had the financial privilege, education, community reputation, and leadership experience to work for real change.

Moreover, the particular political and social environment of California in the 1910s created an atmosphere in which women often participated in a diverse set of organizations, many of which were involved in long-standing feuds. The state's fluid and tolerant political climate enabled women to run in local elections, publicly decry low wages, contribute to temperance crusades, and belong to the Socialist Party at the same time.[43] In this sense Whitney's elite background, combined with California's unique circumstances, made it possible for her to cast a large net of activism.

Over time, however, despite her constant organizing activities, Whitney's friends recalled a growing pessimism in her faith in the effectiveness of reform work. She increasingly felt that "the basic problems could not be solved by women alone."[44] Consequently, Whitney became more interested in the labor movement and its politics. In particular textile strikes on the East Coast and individual labor organizers such as Eugene Debs and Elizabeth Gurley Flynn convinced Whitney of the value of a broader class-based approach to problems. Flynn felt that Whitney "finally resigned from her profession because she felt a fundamental change of a political character was necessary to affect poverty."[45] Even as early as 1913, Whitney's tone had changed. When speaking on the situation of women, her language appeared to have hardened; it was now less rooted in morality and more based in political and social struggles. She publicly declared, "The double standard of morals is frayed and worn out," signifying her abandonment of progressive-minded arguments that instructed social reformers of their moral obligation to aid and uplift the needy.[46] Instead, Whitney bitterly criticized the morally grounded calls for action and sought an alternative form of social activism. The passion and conviction of working-class struggles had piqued Whitney's interest. Progressivism, suffragism, and charity work remained Whitney's causes, but in the mid-1910s she began to seek alternative methods of activism.

In 1914, at age forty-seven, she publicly embraced the Socialist cause. She proudly decided to join the Socialist Party of America, less than two years after Eugene Debs's remarkable run for president, in which he took 5.9 percent of the overall vote. In California he polled over 10 percent of the total vote. When Whitney enlisted with the Socialist Party, it was in its heyday.[47]

Whitney's decision to join the Socialists appears to have posed a conflict with her other allegiances; national suffrage leaders were generally opposed to socialism. Throughout the 1910s many of the middle-class, genteel women in Whitney's charity and progressive organizations distrusted the Socialist Party. In 1912, for example, controversy erupted because Miss Ashley, a San Francisco Socialist sympathizer, ran for the office of treasurer in the NAWSA at the same time that Whitney successfully sought the vice presidency of the organization. Problems emerged for Ashley when fellow NAWSA activists accused her of "using the stationery of the association to send out appeals for the socialists on trial for murder at Lawrence." The NAWSA refused to allow Ashley on the nomination ticket when it came out that her "socialistic proclivities were frowned upon by many members."[48] Aside from disapproving of the radical nature of the Socialist Party, suffragists felt that the broad programs and campaigns of Socialists detracted from their single issue. Rather, suffragists asserted that they needed to maintain focus on a more paramount yet feasible goal.

In 1913 Whitney published an instructive and reflective book on behalf of the College Equal Suffrage League in which she appeared to officially agree with the national position. In her introduction to the book, released only one year prior to her becoming a Socialist, she insisted that "equal suffrage and equal suffrage alone" should be the sole issue of suffragists. "If your association allows itself to become identified with Socialism, Women's Christian Temperance work, Prohibition, reforms for working women, or any other measure," she explained, "it will be at the expense of alienating the interest of some of the friends of your own cause."[49] In an official capacity Whitney denounced the alignment of suffragists with Socialists, but one year after publishing the book, she joined the Socialist Party. This decision, however, should not be understood as a break with the past if one looks beyond her organizational affiliation and toward the platforms and issues that concerned her most.

Although many suffragists shunned them, the Socialists embraced suffrage as one of their most significant goals. Staking a claim to natural rights suffrage arguments, Socialists tried to connect the need for the vote as part of women's overall class struggle, which, they said, had become all the more urgent in industrializing economies and societies in which women labored in the public sphere. In other words, suffrage would help the proletariat begin to challenge its subordinate status. This working-class feminist argument resonated with Whitney's increasingly class-conscious understanding of the world.

A regular column in the *Socialist Woman*, for example, "Why Women Should Be Socialists," offered vivid, if contradictory, testimonials of women's reasons for supporting a political system that would abolish private property and class inequality. In the June 1907 issue May Wood Simons, a prominent national Socialist, confirmed the necessary connections between suffragism and socialism, writing that a woman "can never better her condition until she has both the ballot and is free from wage bondage." By extension, she insisted, a woman's "interest as a citizen, as an individual, as a worker, as a mother, as one possessed of unquenchable enthusiasm or right," obligated women everywhere to join the Socialist cause. In other words, Simons framed her argument to highlight socialism's relevance to uniquely female concerns—domestic and otherwise. Women had their own decidedly separate reasons to support a system that would abolish the economy of wage labor under which all women suffered.[50] Yet a later article in the same issue of the journal celebrated Simons for embodying the ideal Socialist woman traits. The article praised her as "slight, refined, cultured, [and] thoroughly feminine in appearance and manner," but also as someone who was learned as a doctor, writer, homemaker, philanthropist, and of course Socialist. As a role model who might attract a wider array of cultured and political middle-class women, Simons personified the duality that the Socialist Party ascribed to women: she was simultaneously distinct because of her maternal status and united with men and citizens everywhere because of her economic concerns.[51]

Moreover, in California suffragists were much more inclined generally to cooperate with Socialists. As Mari Jo Buhle describes,

"In many localities, particularly in the Plains states and California where ties to the woman's movement were still strong, Socialist women collaborated freely with their suffrage sisters."[52] While eastern urban Socialists had a difficult time forging coalitions with suffragists because of the suffragists' opposition to immigrants, diverse western Socialists worked more closely and effectively on local suffrage campaigns. The 1911 California suffrage campaign, in particular, established an effective suffrage-Socialist coalition. California Socialist women set up an independent Women's Socialist Union that worked hand in hand with the WCTU, women's clubs, and suffrage societies in coordinating parades, local campaigning, fundraising, and strategizing over "swing" districts. Although Whitney had shunned Socialists in her publications as president of the College Equal Suffrage League and vice president of the NAWSA, it is clear that the multiple organizations worked together, giving her some familiarity with leftist causes, leaders, and strategies.[53]

In light of the multitude of arguments and the diversity among members, Whitney's decision to enter the Socialist Party should not necessarily be understood as a dramatic break with her past, in spite of her public opposition to it a year earlier. Instead, joining the Party was a logical and practical step that she took in her increasingly radical quest to find ways to alleviate class-based suffering in society. Perhaps an equally insightful question is why Whitney did not join the Socialist Party earlier, given that three thousand like-minded members belonged to the statewide branch at the turn of the century. Ultimately, it was the Socialist connection with suffrage and a broader women's movement that convinced Whitney to consider joining her more radical counterparts. Moreover, as Buhle has noted, many California Socialist women shared Whitney's privileged, educated, and progressive background: "California women were generally less apocalyptic and more genteely sentimental . . . in short, more comfortably middle class than their counterparts in the Midwest. But they shared a common heritage of Christian Socialism. . . . They tended to be middle-aged or even older, veterans of the WCTU or women's clubs."[54] In other words, California

Socialists' personal backgrounds, theoretical orientations, and particular activism became framed in a way that made them heirs to an indigenous radical tradition that, they said, stretched back to the American Revolution.

But Whitney did not join the Socialist Party because of its ideology. Although she developed a strong Marxist ideology later in life, in 1914 she did not demonstrate a sophisticated understanding of economic theory, as her simultaneous membership in reformist and radical groups suggests. Instead, she simply sought to make society more just and fair through participating in specific activities. Historians of the Socialist Party have emphasized similar characteristics among the many women who had been active in women's rights movements (such as Ella Reeve Bloor, Florence Kelley, Margaret Sanger, and Anna Louise Strong) and went on to join the Socialist Party. These women asserted that democratic and Christian values were implicit in the party. Yet many of the women had little, if any, knowledge of Marxism or Leninism.[55] Even Whitney's Communist biographer later acknowledged, "Prior to the Bolshevik advent to power, California Socialists, with few exceptions, and those consisting almost entirely of immigrant workmen, had never heard of Lenin, let alone any of his writings."[56] In other words, observers, activists, and historians alike understood that when Whitney joined the Socialist Party in 1914, she did not necessarily read or theorize about the teachings of Marx and Lenin; her decision to join was prompted by her desire to effect political change.

Even as late as 1915, Whitney characterized herself in her annual class letter first and foremost as a suffragist, commenting, "The duties of citizenship are interesting and can be onerous, but I am more of a suffragist than ever."[57] She purposefully combined her suffragist and Socialist interests and resolved them in such a way that she could be involved in both simultaneously. The feminist leanings she had developed as an activist were effectively framed through the Socialist Party's multiple analyses of industrialization's impact on women.

At the time, the Socialist Party embraced a wide variety of mainstream reform-minded liberals, radicals, and feminists. The famous

New York union organizer Rose Schneiderman, for example, mediated between the two worlds of the working class and the middle class. The first she organized; the second she befriended. Transgressing these class boundaries enabled her to draw support for protective labor legislation among two different pools of activists. Schneiderman saw no tension in calling upon middle-class women to organize workers in radical political movements.[58] Likewise, Crystal Eastman, journalist, labor advocate, and renowned radical feminist, embodied similar tensions. In addition to devoting her life to leftist political radicalism, Eastman considered herself to be an extreme feminist, arguing that communism alone would not fundamentally alter gender relations. Instead, "for Eastman, the creation of a communistic society based on sex equality was the task of the organized feminist movement."[59] Conversely, Emma Goldman, the legendary anarchist and union organizer who moved in the same political, social, and intellectual circles as Eastman, felt that feminists were misguided in their efforts to make society more egalitarian by uplifting women. American socialism included many different types of female activism. Thus, Whitney found plenty of freedom to express her own version of socialism.

Indeed, upon joining the Socialist Party in 1914, Whitney focused her activities on political problems that could be solved through electoral politics and the courts, illustrating that little had yet changed when she decided to join the Party. In 1916 she helped to raise money to pay the bail of IWW members, including her friends Warren Billings and Tom Mooney.[60] Billings and Mooney, two notable labor organizers and pacifists, were falsely accused and imprisoned for plotting the San Francisco Preparedness Day Parade bombings. They spent twenty-two years in prison. Radicals spent years galvanizing support for their release, often having Mooney's mother speak publicly about the unfair imprisonment of her son.

Coinciding with her efforts to free IWW members, Whitney became an ardent pacifist and participated in groups opposed to U.S. involvement in World War I.[61] She was, however, something of a confrontational pacifist. In her 1917 Wellesley letter she wrote, "I always have a punch ready for the militarists when they cross my path."[62] While her former classmates' letters of 1918 professed faith and devotion to the Allied nations, Whitney's note brewed with pacifist conviction. Even despite the sorrow in her tone over the death of her sister, Mary, and the anxiousness about her new role as caretaker of her young nephew, Whitney Henry, Whitney focused her 1918 letter on a strong antiwar message. Choosing to align with pacifists appears to have taken Whitney another step farther away from her politically mainstream life as a progressive reformer, at least from the outside.

Whitney was not unusual in moving among progressive, suffrage, Socialist, and pacifist organizations. In particular the Woman's Peace Party formed in 1915, headed by Jane Addams, Harriet Stanton Blatch, Carrie Chapman Catt, Anna Howard Shaw, and Anna Garlin Spencer. Driven by many, often contradictory, impulses that argued for both humanitarian and nationalist noninterventionist justifications for their pacifism, many Women's Peace Party leaders believed, "Only through women, somehow free from the combative instinct, could our man-made militarism be eliminated."[63] The Women's Peace Party reasoned that maternalist arguments would underscore its criticism of the war—and the American government's imminent decision to enter it—and resonate with a broader pool of potential supporters. This stance of the Peace Party and the radical and reform-minded members that took up its cause underscore the increasingly diverse context in which Whitney was becoming more radicalized. By this point Whitney had clearly chosen to side with the more radical faction of female pacifists. Yet within these pacifist groups, Whitney claimed the role of a moderate. After the war ended, she refuted charges that she had worked against the Food Administration, recalling, "I agreed with Jane Addams when we discussed the matter during the war, that food should be administered for the benefit of the starving peoples of Europe."[64] Nevertheless, as progressive and suffrage organizations fractured over support or opposition to the war, possibly as a way to show their patriotism, Whitney enlisted with the more radical factions. Within a few years this decision proved to have important consequences for her; the breadth of supporters, ranging from pacifists to clubwomen, was essential in building a coalition around her well-known character and the issue of free speech rights.

Still, while Whitney was criticizing the war, she maintained her mainstream leadership role in California. As chair of the NAACP and the Women's Irish Educational League, Whitney hosted notable political meetings through 1919. She invited the president of Mills College in Oakland, Dr. Aurelia Reinhardt, for example, to speak to the Women's Irish Educational League on the debate over joining the League of Nations. Whitney's continued leadership of the NAACP and Irish League while staunchly opposing war and holding membership in the Socialist Party highlights California's generally more accepting environment toward activists who would have been marginalized in other states because of their politics.[65]

Ultimately, however, Whitney's refusal to back away from pressing social and political concerns led her down a more radical path. In 1919 she was forced to make a choice when the Socialist Party fractured. At the beginning of that year the new Communist leader of Russia, Vladimir Lenin, had invited members from 390 worldwide organizations to form the Communist International (Comintern). Four left-wing members of the American Socialist Party attended the Moscow meeting and agreed to join the association. Upset over their perceived defection to Lenin and their submissiveness to his direction, in May 1919 American Socialist Party moderates expelled the entire left wing that had voted to join the Comintern. At an emergency Socialist Party convention convened in Chicago on August 30, 1919, attendees sought to resolve the dispute. Instead, eighty-two left-wing Socialists walked out of the meeting, defected, and formed the Communist Labor Party (CLP). Ultimately, four thousand members of the Socialist Party (two-thirds of its entire membership) left the organization and joined the Comintern-aligned Communist Labor Party. As John Earl Haynes and Harvey Klehr have explained, "The Communist Labor Party proclaimed undeviating loyalty to the Comintern and its policies, although the delegates only partly understood what those were."[66]

International and national divisions hit home in October 1919, when the Oakland Branch of the Socialist Party voted eight to one to adopt the constitution of the Communist Labor Party.[67] Whitney cast her vote in favor of the new Communist Party's title and principles, alongside Max Bedacht, the CLP leader who had recently returned from defecting from the Chicago Socialist convention. Also, at this local October meeting leaders scheduled a statewide convention of the new CLP to be held at the city's Loring Hall on November 9. Organizers later reported that 145 delegates attended the November meeting, where Whitney volunteered to serve on the credentials and resolutions committee; she was also chosen to be an alternate on the statewide executive committee of the CLP.[68]

Whitney's decision to join a Communist organization made her vulnerable to government prosecution in 1919. The Red Scare that followed World War I had ushered in an era of unprecedented government repression of radicalism. Widespread anti-Bolshevism, rampant labor unrest, race riots, and a series of mail bombs prompted the heated response of Attorney General A. Mitchell Palmer to order the raids, arrests, and deportations of more than six thousand Americans and immigrants, including leading labor figures such as Alexander Berkman and Emma Goldman. On top of these sweeps, federal and state governments rapidly passed laws prohibiting certain acts of free speech that they deemed seditious, marking the first time that "government officials became the leaders of the [antiradical] movement, [and] national and state policies the instruments of repression."[69] California's version of these restrictions became effective on April 30, 1919. The California Criminal Syndicalism Act made it illegal to belong to any organization that advocated the violent overthrow of the government. The law included a clause that "defined as any doctrine or precept advocating, teaching or aiding and abetting the commission of crime, sabotage ... or unlawful acts of force and violence or unlawful methods of terrorism as a means of accomplishing a change in industrial ownership or control, or effecting any political change."[70] By the end of 1919 the state had charged 108 people with violating the law, most of whom were Wobblies.[71]

Twenty days after Whitney voted to become a charter member of the CLP, Oakland police upset socially prominent and active women everywhere by setting their sights on her. On November 28, 1919, Whitney was scheduled to address a crowd of 150 California Civic League women at the Hotel Oakland on the topic of lynching in the South. Her speech had been contentious for several days leading up to the planned event. Immersed in the Red Scare fury and fear, the "100 percent American" section of the league had suspected that Whitney, though not explicitly her speech, would be too radical to address its group. These women wrote letters of complaint about her planned appearance. They found it worrisome that she held the position of treasurer of the Labor Defense League of the IWW, claiming "that by such association she gives aid, comfort and encouragement to their disloyal and murderous propaganda."[72] Reports even circulated about police pressuring the press and attendees to prevent Whitney from delivering her speech. And because of these concerns, the Civic League polled its members about her appearance; ninety-four voted in favor of hearing Whitney speak, while forty-eight were opposed. Although her speech did not relate to Communist ideas—rather, it called for "a square deal for negroes by means of the orderly processes of law"—Whitney's speech about racial violence was set against the dramatic backdrop of the Red Scare. An attendee recalled that in Whitney's speech "statistics were quoted in regard to lynchings and it was shown that less than one-fifth of the lynchings were in any way associated with the crime of rape." After concluding with a pamphlet's slogan that "the negro was safer in No Man's Land than he was in Texas," Whitney exited the stage, left the hall, and started down the steps of the building. Several police officers met her outside, placed her under arrest, and escorted her to the police station. Although this was her first arrest, the charges came as no surprise to the seasoned activist. Three close friends accompanied her to jail.[73]

Taken to the Oakland County Jail and put in a cell on the eleventh floor, Whitney faced her first criminal charges at the age of fifty-two. The Oakland district attorney indicted Whitney on five counts: teaching violence; advocating violence; justifying violence; committing violence; and organizing people to advocate, teach, aid, and abet criminal syndicalism. Ironically, on the day that Whitney spoke out against lynching (and the government's failure to protect its African American citizens from terrorist violence), she herself was indicted for advocating violence against the government. With most mainstream newspapers besieged with articles about Bolshevik plots in America and planned deportations, the irony generally went unnoticed. According to police, she was arrested because of her affiliation with the IWW, although her connections to the union had been well documented for five years. She insisted that her affiliation with the IWW related solely to the free speech defense funds of its members. Furthermore, her arrest resulted from her close affiliation with the CLP, which, according to many newspapers, was "under fire for alleged disloyal utterances of its members."[74]

Reportedly, a half hour after her arrest friends paid her bail of two thousand dollars and the police discharged her until the trial concluded. Nevertheless, upon her release Oakland police raided Whitney's family home, searching for "correspondence and literature dealing with the supposed radical movement." As they searched, Whitney simply told inspector Fenton Thompson to "go to it."[75] In the midst of her own legal troubles Whitney continued to post bail for her fellow Communists, who also faced charges of violating the California Criminal Syndicalism Law. Following their publicized returns to the state in March 1920, she secured the release of fellow radicals Max Bedacht and John Reed.[76]

Between her 1919 arrest and 1927 pardon radicals, reformers, politicians, writers, and workers alike lined up to support Whitney's freedom. Her travails produced some of the most wide-ranging coalitions of Californians ever forged for a Communist. Portraying Whitney as all things refined, cultured, honest, educated, and moral, this vastly diverse group of prominent Americans launched a free speech movement around her trial and pardon campaign that they maintained for nearly eight years. At no other point in Whitney's life and career did liberals and leftists construct stronger coalitions.

Whitney's gender certainly affected the sentiment and vigor of her supporters. Her arrest let loose an outpouring of support. But ironically, not only did this coalition reveal the porous boundaries among class, political, and theoretical allegiances; her pardon campaign also reflected the rigidity of gender, class, and racial identity. Whitney's liberal and radical supporters alike characterized her as a wealthy social do-gooder incapable of inflicting harm. Her mainstream supporters argued that a woman this cultured and domestic could not actually have become a real revolutionary; thus, they downplayed her self-proclaimed radical identity and supported her right to free speech. As one editorial in the *Oakland Examiner* noted, "Never was the law intended to reach far afield and entrap a soft-voiced, refined, gentle little woman, with a wonderful record for doing good."[77] Similarly, her radical counterparts attempted to manipulate her gender identity for their own purposes, asserting that Whitney's virtuous and charming personality reflected the Party's overall identity, thereby legitimizing its own reputation. Operating on every level—grassroots leafleting, public relations campaigning, letter writing, and legal maneuvering—Whitney's supporters built a coalition that agreed on one legal issue and one character issue: supporters consistently backed her right to free speech and agreed that her feminine characteristics nullified any threat she posed to society.

Whitney's initial trial commenced on January 27, 1920, with Thomas O'Connor serving as her lawyer and J. E. Pemberton as his assistant. By the time he took Whitney's case, O'Connor already had considerable experience with Red Scare trials. He had defended Reena Mooney and Israel Weinberg, who had been accused in the July 1916 Preparedness Day bombings. Despite the experience of her legal team, from the start Whitney's trial turned into a melodramatic spectacle for the entire state to monitor. Daily newspapers closely covered both the drama and the details of Whitney's case, regularly highlighting the "fashionably gowned society women, who have been attending the trial in large numbers as friends and supporters of Miss Whitney."[78] On the most bizarre day in court Edward Condon, a seventeen-year-old student and newspaper reporter for the

Oakland Enquirer and the *Oakland Tribune*, took the stand because he had attended the infamous November 9 charter meeting of the CLP. O'Connor began by asking Condon, "From what you observed there, did you feel that a crime had been committed?" Condon initially replied that the sale of *The Communist Manifesto* at the meeting, "if anything, establishes it as a Syndicalist organization."[79] But the testimony became more peculiar when Condon spoke of a red piece of cloth that had been draped over an American flag that sat at the front of the meeting room. He recalled how no one had noticed or stood up to remove the red cloth, which horrified him because it signaled the deep Communist—and un-American—conviction of the members. But in testimony later that day, when Whitney's attorney pressed Condon about the draping of the red cloth, he revealed a different side of the story. Condon admitted that police inspector Fenton Thompson had confided in him that one of his subordinates at the police department had planted the red cloth over the American flag to implicate the Communist Labor Party. After much squabbling between the lawyers and judge, Condon's earlier testimony about the red cloth was not admitted as valid evidence but still made its way to the front pages of newspapers across the state. This red cloth anecdote took on a life of its own in later years, as Whitney's supporters cited the incident to illustrate the unfairness of her initial trial.[80]

During the short trial the prosecution tried to link Whitney directly to advocating the overthrow of the U.S. government through her CLP membership. When Whitney briefly took the stand, the prosecutor, Deputy District Attorney Myron Harris, asked her to characterize her idea of a class war or political prisoner. She replied, "I should not consider class war prisoners necessarily men that had broken any law; I should say a class war prisoner was a person who was in jail in an attempt to better the working conditions of men and the families of working men." She continued to assert that Eugene Debs and Kate Richards O'Hare, those opposed to the selective draft law, and John G. Wieler, a former clergyman accused of sending threatening bomb notes, exemplified "class war" prisoners.

Using her own testimony, the prosecution sought to demonstrate that Whitney's extreme criticism of the U.S. government stemmed from her belief that the government "knowingly imprisons people who are not guilty of any crime," according to Harris.[81] The prosecutors also used rhetoric from the Third International to brand the CLP as revolutionary. They focused on one passage to prove the group's revolutionary potential: the Comintern directed the Party to "disarm the middle class of Americans at the proper time and to arm the laborers for the formation of a huge communistic army as the protector of the rule of the proletariat and the inviolability of the social structure." Whitney insisted, however, that she did not approve of violence and that the Party "was not to be an instrument of violence, nor was it to violate any law of the United States." She went on to explain, "If we had intended to violate any laws, the meeting [founding the CLP] would not have been open to the public." Yet prosecutors shaped their case on the importance of her membership alone.[82] In response her lawyer endeavored "to show this jury, that never in her life did Anita Whitney ever say or do a single thing . . . which can even by the wildest of flight of the imagination be construed into an act of violence or a suggestion of violence."[83]

Outside the courtroom Whitney's supporters argued that the state should not imprison a person of such strong moral character. Liberal friends and radical comrades alike circulated pamphlets and articles to establish her virtue. Her progressive allies even secured the services of a renowned journalist and publicity expert, Franklin Hichborn, to disseminate messages about how this model citizen, who "has stood always for clean living, for law enforcement, for order, for good government, for even-handed justice," could not have committed such a crime.[84]

Her radical allies sounded a similar note. As John D. Barry, a self-described philosophical anarchist who had organized San Francisco's International Radical Club in 1912, asserted: "Miss Whitney belongs among the rapidly increasing number of women who, in spite of being favored by fortune themselves, nevertheless understand the plight of those who are not so favored and who, in consequence, often find themselves in positions of extreme hardship. For example, she is an almost fanatical believer in the idea that the poor ought to get the same rights in court as the rich."[85] A sweeping range of Whitney's supporters argued that her education had led her to care for the poor, which translated into her willingness to stand up for their rights. Nevertheless, these pronouncements did little to aid her defense in January and February 1920.

Halfway through the trial O'Connor, Whitney's leading attorney, fell ill with that year's notorious and virulent flu strain, but Judge Quinn insisted that the trial proceed. When one of the jurors also became ill and delirious, Quinn allowed for a three-day postponement. On the third night of the hiatus, O'Connor's condition worsened, and he died, only to be followed by the death of the juror that same evening. But Quinn nevertheless insisted that Whitney remain on trial with the alternate juror and only the counsel of J. E. Pemberton, O'Connor's assistant. Observers believed that Pemberton's lack of preparedness and resulting performance in the courtroom would doom Whitney's case. Pemberton apparently agreed with this low opinion of his legal skills, and he attempted to delay the trial in order to hire an attorney who had been versed in free speech trials. Yet the judge insisted on finishing the trial that month. In the days that Pemberton served as Whitney's defender, he watched as the prosecution highlighted her visits to the iww San Francisco office, linking her radical affiliation with the clp to the iww's violent record.[86] The prosecution even put on the stand Florence Johnson, a clerk at *The World*, to confirm that Whitney subscribed to the newspaper and that she was a member of the Socialist Party. According to the district attorney, these pieces of evidence undoubtedly added up to Whitney's guilt in violating the California Criminal Syndicalism Law.[87]

After a nearly four-week trial, on February 20, 1920, Whitney's case went to the jury, which, in less than a day, decided to convict her. While the jurors could not agree on the other four counts, they convicted her of organizing and belonging to a group that advocated criminal syndicalism.[88] In other words, the guilty verdict applied not to her "personal utterances but for her membership in an organization allegedly created to advocate criminal syndicalism."[89] Upon hearing the guilty verdict, many newspapers depicted Whitney as "unaffected either by the sobs which came from a number of women in the crowded courtroom lobby or the rising demonstration which greeted her arrival."[90] With her conviction in hand, critics once again inserted her gender as a way to further condemn Whitney for stepping so far outside appropriate norms. Throughout California newspaper editorials affirmed Whitney's guilt and described the particularly grave danger she posed. "The urge of these wealthy, well-read but really ill-educated women," an anonymous critic decreed, "is the urge of idle restlessness, the crave for adventure, the lust for power—even if it be the leadership of the lawlessness in the assault upon the citadels of civilization."[91] Thus, according to this and many other observers at the time, Whitney's crime of violating the California Criminal Syndicalism Law took on a different dimension of subversion because she had violated gender norms. Her real radicalism, in other words, came not simply from her political affiliation but also from her transgressing of traditional gender roles, first with education, second with power, and third with anti-Americanism.

The public spectacle of Whitney's escort to the Alameda County Jail hinted, however, at the inventive and resolute protest campaigns to come. Nearly fifty of her closest friends showed up at the jailhouse and demanded the opportunity to shower Whitney with bouquets of flowers. "Laden with blossoms taken to the courthouse earlier in the day for the purpose of strewing them in Miss Whitney's path," according to the *Oakland Examiner*, these women insisted on getting them to Whitney, even if it meant tossing them up to her cell window.[92] Other, more conventional support also surfaced in the weeks following the trial. Coming out in her defense through more conventional means, for example, the Alameda County Labor Union immediately established a special committee to "intercede on behalf of Miss Anita Whitney in her application for bail."[93] Thus, despite the jury's verdict, Whitney's supporters refused to accept her as a convicted radical criminal.

Whitney's sentencing took place three days after her conviction, on the morning of February 23. After denying a motion for a new trial, Judge Quinn sentenced Whitney to one to fourteen years in San Quentin State Prison. As one supporter noted, the sentence was more severe than the term for manslaughter.[94] But the judge freed Whitney eleven days after her conviction on ten thousand dollars bail, apparently because of ill health. Her appeals began immediately.

Despite being freed on bail, Whitney's freedom was restricted. She could not travel freely, and she could not continue to address or represent her organizations. The Intercollegiate Socialist Society had scheduled her to speak at a Los Angeles meeting, but the city's district attorney ordered the chief of police to prevent her from giving her address.[95] Throughout the appeals process the threat of prison loomed over her. But in late spring of 1920 she put up a brave front to the Wellesley alumnae. Somewhat cynically, she began, "Since the press has given my case so much publicity I am sure that you all know that I have been convicted." Yet her tone quickly shifted when she asserted satisfaction over the fact that the Californians have "been much aroused as to the dangers of the law . . . under which I was convicted, which has really gagged our constitutional rights of free speech, free press and assemblage."[96] With an equally dogged tone, in a newspaper interview she explained that if she went to prison, she would "be able to tell the world, after it is over, what conditions are like for a woman in San Quentin."[97] Contrary to her bold pronouncements at the time, however, Whitney conceded years later that she had a real fear of going to prison and giving up material comforts. In private moments with close friends Whitney showed cracks in her brave and hardened facade. A close friend remembered: "She was afraid that she would be in prison for a long time so she made a list of things. And she wanted some of those things to go to certain people that she loved."[98]

The California District Court of Appeal heard Whitney's first appeal in 1922. After the court upheld the conviction, she decided to bring her case to the U.S. Supreme Court. Although Whitney's lawyers first approached the high court in June 1922, the court delayed hearing her case for three years. In the meantime the State of California retried her case in 1925, and again a jury convicted her. By 1926 Whitney finally succeeded in having her case argued in front of the U.S. Supreme Court. In her annual Wellesley letter Whitney's personal tone shifted to one of hesitant optimism. She confidently reported, "I am very well, very busy, very happy, and doing everything I can to show up the hollow mockery of our present system of civilization."[99]

Months after being argued in front of the same high bench that her uncle had served on decades earlier, on May 15, 1927, the Supreme Court decided unanimously to uphold Whitney's conviction of having violated the California Criminal Syndicalism Act. The majority opinion held that Whitney's membership in an organization that proposed to teach the practice of criminal syndicalism had directly led to her violation of the state law, which the court declared constitutional. The court cited the "clear and present danger" test that had been set in 1919 by Justice Oliver Wendell Holmes in the case *Schenck v. United States*, enabling the government to infringe on a citizen's First Amendment rights in some cases. Whitney's lawyers had argued that the California Criminal Syndicalism Act violated both the due process clause and the equal protection clause of the Fourteenth Amendment. But this argument did not persuade the majority on the court. Led by Justice Edward T. Sanford, seven justices felt that states possessed the fundamental right to punish those who abused free speech. The court also felt that "the defendant had failed procedurally to raise the issue of imminency of danger" in having free speech restricted under the law. Rather, the justices decided because of the "vagueness and uncertainty of definition" in the act, it did not inherently restrain "free speech, assembly, and association."[100]

Although Justice Brandeis and Justice Holmes agreed to uphold Whitney's conviction, Brandeis disagreed with the court's reasoning, and his concurring opinion introduced one of the most famous defenses of freedom ever handed down from the high court. "Even advocacy of violation [of law breaking], however reprehensible morally," he asserted, "is not a justification for denying free speech where the advocacy falls short of incitement."[101] In his opinion Brandeis made an important connection between free speech and the democratic process. He argued that because citizens possess an obligation to take part in government, "if the government can punish unpopular views, then it cramps freedom, and in the long run, will strangle democratic processes."[102] Several legal scholars have since argued that Brandeis's "time to answer" test, which he developed in his concurring statement, promoted maximum free speech and in fact clarified the clear and present danger test. Effectively, Brandeis's time to answer test proclaimed that no danger could stem from free speech if there was full opportunity for free discussion. His opinion came to be cited in support of free speech cases of the civil rights movement of the 1950s and 1960s, though at the time it meant that Whitney was headed to jail.[103]

By the spring of 1927 it appeared that Whitney was fated to go to prison. She clearly felt a sense of immediate threat to her freedom in the plans that she set in place for her future.[104] Nevertheless, her correspondence offers an insightful reminder of how her personal life endured during the tumultuous and precarious trial years. Her nephew, whom she had raised, married and left her Oakland home, only to return a few years later with his wife. Whitney also built a summerhouse in Carmel, which she sensibly planned to rent out in the winter and in case of her imprisonment.[105] And continuing to remain faithfully committed to the Communist Party and increasingly devoted to the study of Marxism, Whitney opened a Workers Bookshop on Telegraph Street in Oakland.

Yet as she planned for prison, hope for her freedom still lingered. It rested upon a long-term campaign her friends had conducted to secure a pardon. Long before her conviction was upheld in 1927, Whitney's friends had pioneered a massive campaign throughout the state to pressure Governor Friend Richardson and then his successor, Clement C. Young, to issue an executive pardon. Initially, Whitney reacted reluctantly to the efforts of her friends (headed by the distinguished Aurelia Reinhardt, president of Mills College) to organize so extensively on her behalf. She insisted, "I have done nothing to be pardoned for," even initially refusing to request one on the grounds that she "should receive no favors because of my sex." Indeed, Whitney never personally signed the petition in favor of the pardon on the basis that she believed she had committed no crime.[106] But in October 1925 Alicia Mosgrove, a prominent California progressive and former suffragist, formed the statewide Citizens' Committee to Appeal for Whitney's Pardon. Revealing Whitney's crossover appeal between radical and non-radical worlds, Mosgrove also directed the Children's Hospital in Oakland and served on the national board of the Campfire Girls.[107] With similar activist backgrounds, members of Whitney's pardon committee gave public speeches, issued pamphlets, and wrote several opinion pieces in major newspapers. They argued that the state had carried out a vendetta against Whitney because no other member of the Communist Labor Party had been sentenced to long prison terms for violating the California Criminal Syndicalism Act. They detailed that nine other members had faced prosecution but that seven of the cases had resulted in hung juries. The remaining two CLP members were convicted, but one had already been freed after serving fourteen months in San Quentin; thus, Whitney's case and sentence were exceptional. In hopes of framing and disseminating their message to the largest audience, Franklin Hichborn, the publicity expert, used multiple strategies and media to convey Whitney's innocence.

In 1925 Whitney's pardon campaign reached the highest ranks of state government when it sparked a heated exchange between California governor Richardson and Dr. Aurelia Reinhardt. Richardson sent a scathing letter to Reinhardt in reference to a speech made by one of her professors. Mary Roberts Coolidge, a former suffragist, noted feminist academic, and professor of English at Mills College, repeatedly lambasted the governor for allowing a "travesty of justice" to occur in the state. In several public speeches Coolidge denounced the governor for upholding Whitney's conviction. According to Coolidge, "The issue is not Anita Whitney only, but whether citizens by threat, arrest misrepresentation and suppression of truth may be sent to prison for taking the part of the poor and lending them aid."[108] Outraged by what he perceived to be an indefensible insult, the governor fired off an angry letter to Coolidge's superior, Reinhardt. "If she enjoys flaying governors without rhyme, reason or investigation of the facts," Governor Richardson wrote, "she can go ahead with her fun."[109] Although she did not directly respond to this letter, Reinhardt supported Whitney and Coolidge personally and repeatedly issued statements denouncing the law and disapproving "of the definition of membership in any organization as an overt criminal act."[110]

Some of the most prominent figures in the nation worked alongside Whitney's longtime friends to vehemently defend her. Supporters circulated petitions all over the state, collecting thousands of signatures for her pardon. While most of the arguments for Whitney's pardon rested on her own outstanding character and how that was inextricably connected with her right to free speech and open expression, each group had different primary reasons for supporting her freedom. Many lawyers pleaded for a pardon on the basis of the trial technicalities, such as the red flag draping testimony. Attorney William J. Locke, for example, wrote, "It appears that some of the evidence had been 'framed' and the jury willfully deceived by over zealous policemen."[111] Alternately, the lawyer and former state senator who had introduced the syndicalism act into law, William Kehoe, emphasized Whitney's exceptional character, contending: "Punishment of offenders has several purposes: To reform the offender, to deter others from committing crimes and to create a wholesome respect for the law. Not one of these can be accomplished by the imprisonment of Miss Whitney."[112] And author Upton Sinclair voiced criticism about the entire era and support for pardons for all seventy-two Californians convicted under the Criminal Syndicalism Act. "The mood of hysteria on the part of our propertied class has now passed," he maintained, "and it is time for statesmen to realize the crudity and cruelty of what was done five years ago."[113]

Pleas for Whitney's civil liberties united the most diverse groups of supporters. A social welfare activist, Mary Van Kleeck, wrote:

"Miss Whitney's experience is an illustration of our failure to preserve American liberties.... It seems to me an unthinkable state of mind that would convict a woman for no crime except a protest against what she considered social injustice."[114] Groups as diverse as the Housewives Club of Santa Clara, the Los Angeles Labor Council, the Pioneer Farming Company, and thirty professors from the University of California and Stanford University agreed with Van Kleeck's assessment and also "expressed bitter indignation at the failure of the Supreme Court to grant Miss Whitney's appeal and pledged their earnest support."[115] While each of these groups had different reasons for supporting her pardon, ranging from her unfair conviction to the unconstitutionality of the law itself, they preferred to center their arguments on Whitney as an exceptional woman. In this case Whitney's unique personal appeal stemming from her prominent reputation, leadership experience, and passion for free speech encouraged diverse interests to coalesce around her pardon campaign.

Yet when Governor Clement Young initially remained steadfast on upholding the Supreme Court's conviction, he received praise from several conservative groups throughout the state. The Daughters of the American Revolution and the Republican Women's Study Club, for example, wrote letters commending him "for upholding the law of our state."[116] Bolstering its own position, the state even issued a pamphlet outlining the facts of the Whitney case that made it necessary for her conviction to be upheld, emphasizing once again that the Communist Labor Party supported the radical overthrow of the U.S. government and that because Whitney was a founding member, she must be punished.

Ignoring that detail, Whitney's supporters countered that such a civic-minded, upstanding, well-known woman from a respectable family could not have committed such a crime.[117] Another lawyer pleaded, "It is altogether improbable that this cultured lady, who for many years served as head of one of the charitable organizations of Alameda County and whose forebears occupied such a conspicuous place in the history and upbuilding of this nation, would approve of the use of violence for political ends."[118] Oakland's mayor John L. Davie creatively stated that the middle-aged woman's syndicalism "is only the revolt of the younger generation against too much paternalism."[119] The range of support and analysis surrounding the campaign reflected how Whitney's personal identity and professional experience played a significant role in making the broad coalition possible. Yet in embracing her well-respected gender and class-based identity, supporters effectively avoided addressing the issue of radicalism altogether. They could frame her as politically naive and unwilling to endorse revolution if they characterized her as properly cultured and feminine.

In addition, many of the support letters sent to the governor aimed to show that Whitney would not have even been tried, let alone convicted, in the peacetime political climate of 1927. William Randolph Hearst's *San Francisco Examiner* argued that the law, "passed under the spell of war hysteria, is extremely severe in its terms, placing a mere inactive membership in radical organizations on the same par of criminality as an active leadership in syndicalist activities."[120] In the official petition for her pardon John Francis Neylan, Whitney's lawyer, contended that the extraordinary circumstances of 1920 had changed so drastically that by 1927 she never would have been brought to trial. He backed up his claims by emphasizing her lifelong dedication to pacifism, remarking, "It seems to be a queer prank of fate that Miss Whitney, an outstanding pacifist, should be sentenced to a term in prison for identity with a political party which was alleged to advocate violence."[121] Neylan used this irony, along with all of the other free speech arguments, to press the governor to reconsider the conviction.

Governor Young finally bowed to the pressure and pardoned Whitney on June 20, 1927. In a five-hundred-word statement informing the public, the governor declared that imprisoning a sixty-year-old woman "is an action which is absolutely unthinkable." Young asserted: "Because I do not believe that under ordinary circumstances this case would have ever been brought to trial. . . . Because I feel that the Criminal Syndicalism Act was primarily intended to apply to organizations actually known as advocates of violence, terrorism, or sabotage, rather than to such organizations as a Communist labor party.... Because whatever may be thought as to the folly of her misdirected sympathies, Miss Whitney, lifelong friend to the unfortunate in any true sense, is not a 'criminal.'"[122] In issuing this statement, Young did not disagree with the Supreme Court; rather, he skirted its decision about the legality of the Criminal Syndicalism Act by focusing on Whitney's personal identity as a self-avowed revolutionary. Yet as editorialists on both sides of her pardon debate recognized, "the Governor took into account the age of the defendant, her sex and her undoubted good works in other fields than that which brought her into conflict with the law."[123] Because of the widespread mainstream support for this woman, which hinged on her feminine identity, the governor decided to pardon her. Thus, her gender, age, and class made Whitney's pardon possible.

Upon hearing of the governor's decision, Whitney's supporters flooded Young with letters expressing their appreciation—and reiterating the themes of the pardon campaign. The American Civil Liberties Union, trade unions, and members of the state assembly wrote letters of affirmation for the issuance of Whitney's executive pardon. The *Locomotive Engineers Journal* erroneously contended, "A highly cultured and gentlewoman and granddaughter of a famous justice of the U.S. Supreme Court, she attended a radical labor meeting and used her influence there to prevent the adoption of a policy of force."[124] Whitney, of course, had not attempted to change the CLP's policy of force. Perhaps the journal's decision here to twist the facts highlights the triumph and transcendence of her personal appeal throughout the state beyond the legal facts of her conviction. But in any case the united coalition to clear Whitney brought an unprecedented number of Californians together for her fundamental right to free speech and association.

Many Californians expected Whitney to fade away from political activism after receiving her pardon. They felt she should have been appropriately scared and then saved by the state and that she would not want to jeopardize her freedom again. But she did not fade away; her legal battles did not appear to undermine her commitment to radical activism. In the years following the trial Whitney became more of a determined political radical yet at the same time continued to maintain her connections to upper-class communities and liberal reform work. In 1927, for example, Whitney focused some of her attention on non-radical social welfare programs. She worked with the Pioneer Farming Company to help handicapped people and foreigners find more opportunities for work. But she also pursued more radical endeavors, attempting to organize Filipino farmworkers and African American communities in West Oakland. Even her Wellesley class letter in early 1928 contained a strong critique of the government and defense of free speech. "After seven years and a half," she wrote, "I have had wiped out, by executive clemency, a penitentiary sentence for having believed that the United States Constitution meant what it said and that we were guaranteed in this country the right of free speech and free assembly."[125] Whitney's dedication to free speech above all else in this letter demonstrated her commitment to persuading Wellesley alumnae to support the existence of the California Communist Party. Furthermore, her nearly eight-year-long legal crusade had strengthened Whitney's resolve. To her the Party was the only oppositional force that could challenge the corrupt capitalist democracy that had convicted her and stripped her of freedom.

Free from legal troubles, Whitney soon rededicated herself to radical politics. Although a malfunctioning thyroid gland left her with overwhelming fatigue for many of these years, she nevertheless maintained a frenzy of organizational activity well into her seventies. The Workers (Communist) Party of America, a product of the 1921 merger between the CLP and Communist Party, nominated Whitney to run for the U.S. Senate in 1928. Alongside Ella Reeve Bloor and Gertrude Warwick, two other notable radical organizers, she worked continuously throughout the Great Depression years as part of the International Labor Defense Committee.[126] During the heyday of 1930s labor organizing, Whitney became a committed, fearless, yet polite speaker who climbed atop soapboxes on crowded street corners to rouse the attention of all passersby. A friend remembered: "She was not what you would say a fiery speaker. She spoke in a calm voice. She did raise it a little bit when it was necessary. But every word that she said had facts. . . . She didn't have any idle words."[127] The corner of Tenth and Broadway in Oakland became Whitney's haven of leafleting and soapbox activity. She focused much of her activity on raising money for agricultural and industrial strikers who had been arrested.[128]

In addition to her seemingly endless labor organizing and Communist activities, Whitney continued to maintain close ties with Wellesley friends in the East and clubwomen in the West. In the summer of 1931, for example, Whitney attended a class reunion and enjoyed the company of the "Dear Old Girls" (the nickname coined to represent the class of 1889). She also lived the majority of her later years with her nephew, Whitney Henry, who remained at his aunt's side for decades. In the midst of her Party activities, family visits, and illnesses that plagued her for many years, Henry stayed devoted to his aunt. They lived comfortably together trying to "settle down to a quiet life" according to Whitney, "that is, as quiet a life as an ardent and active a Communist can live in a world so full of maladjustments and social wreckage."[129]

Whitney even remained an ardent antiwar activist throughout the late 1920s and 1930s. In 1929, for example, she protested the escalating war in China. When Mao Tse-tung began to ignite Communist activism in China by organizing peasants in opposition to the ruling Nationalist Party, Chiang Kai-shek ordered their swift suppression. The authoritarian actions of the Chinese Nationalist Party led Whitney to label China's government as an imperialist aggressor. In July 1929 San Francisco police arrested her for refusing to obey a mandate to leave a demonstration in front of the Chinese consulate. Whitney and the nine others with whom she faced arrest insisted, "The demonstration was against imperialistic wars and in defense of the Soviet Union."[130] Her arrest in 1929 was for violating a local version of a criminal syndicalism law. Specifically, the city charged her with violating penal code 403-A, which "made it a felony to carry banners in opposition to organized government, of disturbing the peace . . . and the distribution of pamphlets on the street."[131] The similarities between this and her 1919 case brought significant attention once again to her political activity. But less than two weeks later, Whitney and the nine others received minimal sentences of only thirty days in jail or a fine. No record exists indicating that Whitney served this time in jail; in all likelihood her nephew paid the fine against her wishes, as he did on a couple of other occasions. Regardless, the fury of the earlier episode of anti-radicalism had clearly subsided, and the aging Whitney carried on with her activism.[132]

In the early and mid-1930s Whitney's class and gender continued to inform her Communist identity. During these years she belonged to a number of Unemployed Councils, helped lead the local branch of the Women's International League for Peace and Freedom, and held membership in the Women's League. Characteristic of her prior organizational record, the economic and social status of each of these groups' members varied widely. Many members in the Women's League, for example, came from middle-class families, whereas other groups aimed to recruit specifically working-class women. Even the Communist Party reached out to middle-class Americans. In 1938, for example, the Party estimated that 22 percent of its new recruits came from the middle class. Moreover, "young Communist women were working in business offices, social agencies, publishing houses, government offices, and trade union offices."[133] This breadth of membership, as Kate Weigand has explained, for a short time allowed women's internal networks within the Party to thrive. In carving out this gender-specific space within the Party, many of the women vocalized a need for stronger Party support, such as day care during meetings, and conceptualized a broader critique of women's opportunities in the workplace, which, Weigand has argued, planted the seed for feminist activism in later decades.[134] By this point, however, Whitney was in her senior years, and it was up to Healey and the next generation of female Communists to join and steer this growing dialogue among Party women.

Nevertheless, a friend of Whitney's recalled the intensive demands of organizing in the 1930s. "We nearly every second night had meetings on corners of the streets, speaking to people, to the unemployed, to let's get together and march to the city hall and demand work or wages," she said.[135] On multiple occasions during these marches the police beat, gassed, and imprisoned Whitney and other women. In 1935, for instance, police arrested Whitney on charges of "falsely attesting signatures to Communist election petitions."[136] Found guilty and convicted on these counts, the court sentenced Whitney to serve either three hundred days in jail or pay a six-hundred-dollar fine. Whitney chose to go to jail; that same day, however, Whitney's devoted nephew paid the fine against her wishes and took her home.[137] Also during the early 1930s, she continued to organize textile unions, succeeded in forcing a three-month minimum maternity leave into women's contracts in one shop in San Francisco, and collected money and supplies for women's auxiliaries of local unions.[138] In 1932 Whitney collected money and spoke on behalf of the Bonus Army march to Washington DC. She, along with several of her female friends, spoke on the corner of Ninth and Broadway to encourage people to donate and join the trip.

Also in 1932, Whitney moved across the bay from Oakland to North Beach in San Francisco. Her Communist Party biographer, Al Richmond, proudly declared that upon her move to the city in 1932, Whitney promptly joined the North Beach branch of the Workers (Communist) Party and became the only woman and native-born member of the local branch. In spite of a "serious illness that was [her] undoing for many months," Whitney appeared to have become even more active in organizing labor.[139] Throughout the tumultuous year of 1934 Whitney helped to organize the maritime strike and the general strike in San Francisco. Her North Beach home even became the San Francisco Party headquarters for a time during the strike.[140]

By now in her late sixties and ailing with arthritis, Whitney continued to work diligently on behalf of the Party. Her recruitment efforts benefited from her considerable charisma. In her years speaking on soapboxes, she not only roused the attention of her audience, but she turned soapbox corners into friendly endurance (versus ideological) competitions with her union or Communist comrades. A friend fondly remembered: "Anita always used to get off when she was finished and she would put her arms around me and say, 'Which one of us spoke the longest?' It was sort of a joke with us."[141] The same spirited dynamic also applied to her leafleting activity. She loved to talk sincerely with people about working conditions, representation, and unemployment; her success lay in her own genuine interest in all related topics.

By the 1930s Whitney translated this deep concern into a public political career. In 1934 she ran on the Communist Party ticket for state treasurer. This famous election featured the gubernatorial candidate and Socialist author Upton Sinclair with his End Poverty in California (EPIC) platform. Although the popularity of Sinclair marginalized the Communist Party candidate, Sam Darcy, surveillance papers reported that the EPIC campaign endorsed Whitney's candidacy for state treasurer. An undercover informant, "A.X.," also indicated that not only did the EPIC campaign support Whitney, a Communist candidate, but the CPUSA, led by Earl Browder, secretly favored Sinclair's candidacy for governor. Browder felt, however, that the "capitalists must never know that the Communist Party has a soft spot for Sinclair and the Press and Publicity Committee must keep publishing articles against Sinclair." These points did not stifle Whitney's popularity.[142]

At age sixty-nine Whitney's political electoral career peaked in her astonishing election campaign. In her run for state treasurer she received 100,820 votes, more than double the number of votes of any other Communist Party member in that election. Whitney's vote total even earned the Communist Party a slot on the next election ballot. The *Western Worker* declared, "This is by far the greatest Communist vote ever polled in this city and shows the protest of the workers and sympathizers against the armed force used to break the general strike."[143] Drawing support from the nearly four thousand actual card-carrying Communists, plus union members and liberals, Whitney's vote illustrated her crossover political appeal during the unique economic conditions of 1934.

Throughout her life Whitney viewed herself as an independent American Communist, though the Party clearly used her reputation and status for its own purposes, all the while keeping her ignorant of its underground activities. No evidence exists that suggests that Whitney involved herself in the Party's attempted spying, nor did she participate in the Party's international operations. Twice invited to travel to the Soviet Union, Whitney refused, arguing that the money and time for the trip could be better spent organizing at home. Still, this attitude did not allay any of the government's concerns about her popularity or about her status as an agent for international communism. In the years surrounding her electoral political activity, the FBI and other government investigation agencies stepped up their surveillance of her.[144]

Amid her state and national electoral activity, the National Committee of the Communist Party selected Whitney to serve as its California representative. By 1936 she even held the prestigious post of state chairman of the national branch of the Communist Party. She proudly reported this information to the Wellesley alumnae in the 1937 letter. She also excitedly claimed, "There is never a lull in these days when such large numbers of workers and young people are becoming economically alert and politically conscious and are looking for interpretation and guidance."[145]

In 1938 Whitney made another run for public office in the election for state controller. She received nearly as many votes as she had four years earlier. The 98,791 votes that Whitney earned as a candidate were attributed at this point to her personal fame more than to her Communist affiliation.[146] Throughout the 1930s Whitney had also maintained her activity in the Women's Civic League of San Francisco, whose members typically came from the opposite side of the class divide from the workingwomen whom she spent so much time organizing.[147] Perhaps it was her rapport with individuals from varied backgrounds that convinced Whitney to run for national office again. In her 1940 run for U.S. Senate, Whitney polled 97,478 votes statewide. By this point the FBI monitored the precise sources of her votes, noting that 16,468 came from San Francisco County, 41,000 from Los Angeles County, 10,387 from Alameda County, and the rest were evenly distributed throughout the state.[148] Her continuing popular appeal as a Communist candidate illustrates how long-lasting coalitions could be sustained when they centered on popular figures such as Whitney.

Throughout that decade free speech rights continued to dominate Whitney's political agenda. Radicals repeatedly faced arrest into the 1940s under the Criminal Syndicalism Act, and Whitney supported and frequently posted bail for those charged with what she deemed offenses by the state. In 1937, for example, Whitney wrote an op-ed piece in the *San Francisco Chronicle* criticizing the governor for maintaining the California Criminal Syndicalism Law and defending eight comrades who had been recently convicted in Sacramento. Although the International Labor Defense League mounted an elaborate and expensive defense campaign, leading to the release of the eight charged, Whitney bitingly charged that the newspaper had failed to defend the free speech rights of the eight, observing, "Some hint of regret that they have no redress for their unwarranted conviction might well have come from the pen of your editorial writer instead of the wanton slap offered these victims of your capitalist justice."[149] Whitney's characteristically vituperative opinion did not go unnoticed. Her column sparked a heated response in the following day's editorial. Condemning her Communist and Soviet sympathies, the writer contended, "Can Anita Whitney visualize any Russian being free to write and have published in Russia as frankly a critical letter as this one of hers in a 'capitalist' newspaper?"[150] Californians clearly understood Whitney's prominence as a statewide political figure and Communist. She had firmly established herself as a leading dissenter in the public, legal, and political realms.

Although she had shown little interest in political or theoretical dogma early in her career, by the 1930s and 1940s Whitney appeared to have embraced Communist ideology.[151] Confirming her deepening commitment to the Party, in 1940 Whitney made the list of "Distinguished Notables" in the *People's World*.[152] Also that year, she, along with William Schneiderman (the future brother-in-law of Dorothy Healey), opened the national convention of the CPUSA in New York.[153]

Remarkably, Whitney still received almost a hundred thousand votes in the 1940 campaign for Senate, even though the Soviets had made a pact with Hitler the previous year. Whitney did not publicly endorse the Nazi-Soviet Pact, although she remained an active member of the CPUSA during the pact years. Declining to leave the Party at this juncture took Whitney down another path of supposed domestic subversion; unlike the thousands of American Communists who left the Party in the wake of the Nazi-Soviet Pact, Whitney determined that the Soviets needed to make this strategic alliance to protect themselves. Into her seventies Whitney, who had been fully immersed in the American Communist community for many years, lived within the Party's internal world and thereby absorbed and adopted the official Soviet explanation of the Nazi-Soviet Pact.

When on June 22, 1941, Germany broke the pact and invaded the Soviet Union, triggering an immediate alliance between the United States and the Soviet Union, Whitney became an ardent war supporter. Coincidentally, on the same day as the invasion, Whitney had attended a meeting of the national committee of the CPUSA and helped draft the Party's response, "The People's Program of Struggle for the Defeat of Hitler and Hitlerism!" The invasion brought Communists in the United States into complete support of their country's aid for the Allies. Thus, World War II officially signaled Whitney's retirement from pacifism. She consistently decreed support for the war effort against fascism. After the bombing of Pearl Harbor and America's entrance into the war, Whitney volunteered at a local firehouse in San Francisco as part of the "civilian defense effort." She also wound surgical bandages with the American Red Cross and offered to volunteer with the American Women's Volunteer Service, an interracial group of women dedicated to supporting soldiers, though her offer was rejected because of her age.[154]

Throughout the 1940s Whitney tried to maintain an identity as an independent American Communist, but the Party leadership and the FBI both appear to have determined that she followed the Party line. When, for example, the Kremlin dissolved the Comintern in 1943, claiming dissatisfaction over the structure of Communist Parties around the world, Whitney told an American audience, "This action may break down the absurd suspicion of Russia held by some people in this country."[155] While she maintained a level of absolute dedication to the Soviet Union, Whitney simply did not concern herself with the debates surrounding the Soviet Union's relationship to the Comintern and its relationship with the CPUSA. Rather, she focused on organizing workers and running for office. Her direct relationship with the national Party headquarters in New York and with the Soviets was distant. She openly refuted allegations about the extent to which the Soviets controlled American Communists; she apparently saw herself as an autonomous American Communist who simply worked in tandem with the Kremlin. The Kremlin also embraced this image of Whitney through the funding it spent on her campaigns and through its continued support of her leadership position.[156] It may have been this component of her activism that led the FBI to report in 1941 that Whitney was "still active in Communist Party affairs in Bay Area, but has little or no authority. She spends time, principally, in giving speeches at meetings and rallies and . . . soliciting funds for the Party. The CP dictates the topics of her speeches, as well as the place and time of delivery. . . . It seems that she is merely being 'tolerated' by the Communists in San Francisco, and they are merely using her because of her reputation and background."[157] Yet despite the benign labels the FBI applied to Whitney, they closely monitored each local and national meeting, transaction, and appearance she made throughout the 1940s. J. Edgar Hoover himself even suggested on December 1, 1941, that Whitney "be considered for custodial detention in the event of a national emergency."[158]

The Party leadership regarded her as one of their most prized members well into her senior years. When Whitney's seventy-fifth birthday arrived, in 1942, for example, the CPUSA formed a national committee to celebrate and commemorate the life and activities of this remarkable woman. Elizabeth Gurley Flynn participated in the event, boasting, "Anita Whitney keeps house for herself and her nephew and is active daily in routine party work and in defense work."[159] On a personal level Whitney maintained the charm of a conventional woman in her home. She frequently invited guests over, which was quite a treat because "she always had tea and cookies," according to a close friend. "Not only that, but [Whitney] always proudly remarked that, 'I baked them.'"[160] The Party portrayed Whitney as the perfect woman and continued to celebrate her distinctly gendered identity. Flynn, for example, in highlighting Whitney's domestic pursuits, sought to celebrate this idealized woman Communist. By imagining Whitney as utterly feminine and not at all subversive or interested in transgressing professional boundaries, the Party managed to disseminate an image of itself that was much more mainstream. Leading radical women accepted these gendered arguments as a way to highlight the Party's dedication to traditional gender roles and to show that Communists posed no threat to femininity and domesticity.

Despite her age and failing health, Whitney continued to battle for free speech rights in the state courts. When, for example, she ran for state controller again in 1942, the registrar of voters rejected her nomination because of accusations over signature fraud. She filed a lawsuit and won the right to be nominated for the post.[161] A similar effort to bar her from the state ballot in 1946 led to another lawsuit that Whitney's lawyers successfully argued at the California Supreme Court.[162] In 1947 Whitney wrote to her group of Wellesley alumnae with indignation but also with a trace of hope, "I think it unfortunate to have our political life so completely controlled by brass hats and Wall Street financial interests, but I have faith that the American spirit of democracy will prevail."[163]

In 1948, at her eightieth birthday celebration at Friendship Hall in Berkeley, Whitney continued her lifelong commitment to organizing by encouraging her guests to do the same. Tearfully responding to speeches paying homage to her years of service and friendship,

Whitney mustered the poise to say: "That's enough about me.... I'm eighty and there isn't very much more that I can do on my own two feet unless I sit home and do something. So why don't you people organize people like me to see what we can do after we've reached a certain age."[164] Not only did the strength and quality of her character inspire her friends and admirers, but Whitney's energy for the cause of alleviating human suffering also brought massive broad-based recognition and admiration. Her support came from friends, comrades, and recruits but also from anonymous onlookers who noted and respected her decades of selfless community service. Two years later she made her last run for public office, again for the U.S. Senate.

Whitney died of a heart ailment at her San Francisco home on February 4, 1955, when she was eighty-seven years old. The fierce Cold War anti-Communist tone of 1955 tainted most of Whitney's obituaries. The *San Francisco Examiner* reported, "She evidently held her illusions about communism and Soviet Russia through every act of aggression, every diplomatic move and every twist in the party line."[165] But viewing her from a different angle that acknowledged her unique identity, the *San Francisco Chronicle* wrote, "To her revolutionary flair she lent a glittering aura—wealth, social position, culture, a distinguished family background."[166] Whitney was a radical, but she never publicly supported the violent overthrow of the government. In fact, while she remained a leading figure in the Communist Party throughout most of its existence, all her life she championed the democratic spirit. If asked, she probably would have asserted that her vision of utopia included democratically elected Communists. Her ability to maintain an identity as an American woman radical confirms the distinctly indigenous roots of radicalism in American society and demonstrates how fluid political and social boundaries remained for her over the course of her lifetime. While the next generation of American Communist women would face a different set of domestic and international challenges—challenges that certainly made Whitney's fluid world harder to sustain—the same organizational structure and similar assumptions about gender would continue to guide this most radical of American political organizations.

3 Red Queen of the West

*Dorothy Ray Healey and the Grounding
of California's Old Left, 1914–2006*

In 1928, less than a year after Anita Whitney received her pardon, a determined fourteen-year-old named Dorothy Ray Healey joined the Young Communist League in Berkeley, California. Although there was considerable overlap in their involvement in the years that Healey belonged to the Party that Whitney had helped to birth, their activism over these two decades appears to have occurred in separate worlds. Healey ushered in the generation of California Communists that constituted the Party's most successful era, one that has since earned the most attention in Americans' and scholars' collective memories of the Communist Party. In part because the Great Depression made the rapidly expanding and increasingly desperate workforce across the state more willing to consider radical alternatives, Healey's activism and leadership, which evolved during this period, has been the most thoroughly documented. But the struggles of those years eventually became the seed that sprouted into the century's second decade-long anti-Communist hysteria.[1]

Healey started her career as a Party revolutionary by taking jobs in factories and fields throughout the state. As a very young organizer of cannery women workers, lettuce growers, garment laborers, and workers in a multitude of other agricultural and productive industries, Healey never hid her Communist membership. But this did not matter to most of the workers she attempted to organize in the 1920s, 1930s, and 1940s. Coalitions between Healey, the Party representative, and labor organizations protected and advanced the interests of California's working class. Moreover, as an extension of her advocacy of the rights of labor, Healey promoted civil rights and civil liberties. While Jim Crow laws governed the South, western states still practiced a number of legal and de facto discriminatory traditions. At a time when housing segregation and employment discrimination plagued much of Healey's home state, the Party's long-standing dedication to racial equality and the rights of labor appealed to some of the most oppressed and vulnerable populations across the state.

This commitment to civil rights, similar to that of the California Communists from the earlier generation, facilitated coalition building with other radicals and liberals. But in contrast to the coalitions formed by Whitney's generation, Healey's alliances seemed to come more easily and spread across different political boundaries. When Healey's Party took up a campaign or topic, it started to tackle the issue within the government and worked through the organizations that supported it. This approach helped to build a Communist Party that was much more visible in the 1930s and 1940s than it had ever been before. Yet because it had established such a public face—in Los Angeles characterized by Healey—the California Party took on an independent spirit quite distinct from the national Party by the late 1950s and 1960s. Furthermore, because the Party had become so visible in the 1930s, its members and leaders were susceptible to persecution when the tide of the postwar world shifted against

Joseph Stalin's Communist Party, as it was viewed in the United States. Yet Healey's Southern California Communist Party weathered the Cold War and even survived the devastating year of 1956, when Soviet premier Nikita Khrushchev exposed Stalin's years of terror. Indeed, what became the final blow for many committed American Communists empowered Healey to stick with the Party because she could finally build a truly autonomous national Party; like Whitney, she hoped to channel her political and social activism through this nearly half-century-old embattled organization. Nevertheless, Healey's long tenure in the Party ultimately came to an end in the early 1970s, when she determined that the Party's national structure inhibited her own revolutionary agenda and methods of activism.

Throughout her nearly half century in the Party, Healey, like other Communist women of her generation, lived in multiple worlds with more than one allegiance and identity. Many seemingly personal decisions—marriage, sexual relationships, children, birth control, gender roles in the home—were shaped both by American gender norms and by Party directives. Healey's personal life exemplified the tensions that abounded for female party leaders. Thus, giving gender a more central place in this study of Healey reveals the complexities of her life as a leading American woman Communist in the middle decades of the twentieth century.[2]

Healey's career was marked by fluidity, ambiguity, relevance, and even fame. California—and Los Angeles in particular—played a key role in sustaining her status as a leading American Communist. As with Whitney, her distance from the East Coast and independence from the national Party helped Healey build a western, grassroots Party. Her geographic space allowed her to pursue local campaigns alongside national Party goals, ultimately creating a local Communist Party that was visible, proactive, and more acceptable to non-Communists. Perhaps its wide appeal is what prompted the FBI to name Healey "The Red Queen of the West," a label she surely snickered over with her countless friends and supporters in her Los Angeles haven.

Born on September 22, 1914, in Denver, Colorado, to Barbara

Nestor and Joseph Rosenblum, Healey was the fourth of their five children. Without access to adequate birth control, Barbara also induced several additional miscarriages. Both Healey's mother and father were born in Hungary in 1884 and came to the United States in 1889 and 1890, respectively. Raised in Jewish families that spoke Yiddish and regularly observed the Sabbath, Barbara and Joseph had similar family backgrounds. Barbara had first migrated to St. Louis, Missouri, before her family moved to Los Angeles in 1894 and then to Denver in 1897 in search of work.

Dorothy Healey's mother influenced her politics and life more than her father did. As a young woman in Denver, Barbara developed an antireligious and staunchly atheist stance, though her Jewish cultural heritage stayed with her, particularly in her cuisine preferences. In 1915, a year after Anita Whitney joined the Socialist Party and one year after Healey's birth, Barbara officially became a member of the Socialist Party; she had heard a mesmerizing speech by the famed Socialist Kate Richards O'Hare a few years earlier. Barbara's own politicization strongly influenced the upbringing of her children, though during the anti-Communist Red Scare years following World War I, she lost track of her radical contacts. She also dropped out of political involvement because she married Joseph Rosenblum, an apolitical traveling salesman, and became a mother. With a love and talent for playing the mandolin but never able to make a living as a musician, Joseph committed himself to business. The Rosenblum children remembered their father as a hardworking but generally absent provider until his death at age forty-six. Joseph did not wholeheartedly support Barbara's activism because he feared it would jeopardize his job, though to her knowledge it never did. Still, as his wife and children became more committed to radical activities—certainly when they faced prosecution for them—Joseph stood alone in the family in criticizing them.[3]

Growing up a red-diaper baby in Denver, Healey's consciousness was formed by her mother, who once took her children to preparedness parades to shout: "I didn't raise my son to be a soldier! I raised him up to be my pride and joy."[4] These sorts of political anecdotes featured prominently in Healey's and her siblings' memories of their childhoods. Healey's sister Carol Jean Newman recalled Barbara's constant criticism of materialism and fashion in particular, remembering, "She told all of us those were bourgeois things, we shouldn't want them, we shouldn't crave them, and she herself wore this straight haircut, maybe it was fashionable, but it didn't help her face any."[5] Healey came to share in her mother's values about clothes but only to a degree. Throughout her childhood and adulthood she was plagued by insecurity about her nose and physical appearance; much later in life she had plastic surgery to reshape her nose.

On November 27, 1921, the Rosenblum family arrived in Northern California from Denver hoping there would be more work for Joseph and that the weather would suit the habitually flu-stricken Dorothy. She enrolled at Garfield primary school in Berkeley and became friendly with several other students, some political and some wealthy. Devouring books became her preferred pastime during her youth. By the time she was ready to enter secondary school, her older brother, Bernard, had enrolled at the University of California–Berkeley in 1928 and made friends among the city's extensive radical community. Under the influence of Bernard and his friends, Barbara decided to formally join the Communist Party that year, and she maintained her Party membership well into her eighties. Dorothy, meanwhile, stood on the sidelines, waiting to be invited to a meeting so that she could confirm her sympathies to her family.

By December 1928 friends of Healey's older brother who were members of the Young Communist League (or YCL, the Party's arm for its younger adolescent-age members) took the fourteen-year-old girl along to a meeting and invited her to join. Less than a decade old, the YCL was a fledgling organization with mostly young, inexperienced, foreign-born members. But Healey was not among the very youngest of Communists because the Party also operated a children's group, the Young Pioneers. Despite the fact that she failed to understand even the discussion topics at her first meeting, Healey nevertheless felt an overwhelming sense of purpose in enlisting with the YCL. At her first meeting the staff marked her membership card as "paid in full for the whole year" so that she would be able to vote for William Foster for general secretary in the Party leadership. A longtime Party member and union organizer, Foster's devotion to Stalin and nomination as general secretary meant that the Communist Party in 1929 would follow more closely directives from Moscow, especially those that called for new unions such as the Trade Union Unity League. This approach of organizing Communist-sympathetic unions resonated with Healey and her blossoming interest in working on the ground with workers and the unemployed.

Healey developed a strong personal identity as a young Communist. She went door to door selling the YCL's newspaper in west Berkeley. Some of her early favorite activities included leafleting at a 1929 Army-Navy football game, demonstrating in front of factories where workers had walked out on strike, and selling papers on street corners. Her radical activities quickly became all-encompassing. Although later she was somewhat regretful that full-time activism had diverted her attention away from pursuing a college degree, at the time her experiences made her feel contempt for "bourgeois education." Remembering the central role the Party had played in her teenage life, she said: "That was my real life; that was the real world; that was all that mattered. . . . The school was a kind of a shadow existence that I had to go through, but it had no particular meaning."[6]

Less than a year after Healey joined the Party, the stock market crashed, and the country lurched into the Great Depression. The Party attempted to respond to the faltering economy by framing itself as the rational alternative to a capitalist system that fostered so many inequalities and so much suffering. To implement its plan, by early 1930 the YCL regularly organized demonstrations of the unemployed at the central intersections of Tenth and Broadway in Oakland (surely alongside the legendary Whitney) and at University and San Pablo in Berkeley. At these rallies each YCL member took a turn to speak. "It didn't make any difference whether you were prepared or unprepared, a speaker or not," one participant remembered; every member had to muster the composure and volume to address the crowd of unemployed workers.[7] Healey remembered the power of the moment when individual workers, who had blamed themselves for their job loss, began to recognize their common identity. She loved "watching the change of consciousness, watching unemployed men, almost entirely . . . start to feel a consciousness that it was not an individual thing, that it was social, that they did have rights which were being neglected."[8] Planning these street protests took an enormous amount of coordination, which led Healey, for practical reasons, to focus much less on Marxist theory and philosophy and nearly exclusively on coordinating and publicizing events.

These well-known Oakland protests even led to her first arrest, fittingly on May Day, in 1930. Holding a stack of *Daily Workers* in her arms and shouting headlines from a soapbox at the infamous Oakland intersection, Healey was immediately spotted by police. She recalled, "The police watched me for a few minutes, and then one of them gave a signal to the patrolman, and they just picked me up in their arms and very ignominiously carried me off to a police wagon."[9] Taken to juvenile hall, Healey first created an anonymous last name for herself, Ray, when booked by police for protesting unlawfully because she feared endangering her father's job through her radical affiliation. She stayed in the juvenile detention facility for about two weeks, during which she tried her hardest to "agitate" the girls around her, which ultimately made the judge concede to her early release so that they would be rid of her.

Healey's arrest was not at all unusual during these years of protests, when police did not allow any demonstrations, pickets, or protests. Consequently, police routinely rounded up hundreds of participants during the large rallies, which made Healey somewhat cavalier about the threat of arrest. Indeed, her mother, Barbara, was once arrested as a regular Party member and was aided in her defense by Anita Whitney. Still, these run-ins with the authorities did not sit well with Joseph Rosenblum. In letters she wrote to him, Healey regularly defended her activities and attacked her father for his criticism, specifically with regards to his opposition to the Party's egalitarian racial attitudes. She heatedly charged: "I, for one, would dance or talk to a Negro at any time, and I am proud of it. And you send us an article ... hoping that 'we will come to our sense, and stay with our own people.' God, it gets me sick, to see and hear someone who ought to know better talk the way you do."[10] In future years her relationship with her father would fracture even more because of his contempt for her dedication to the Communist Party.

Long before Healey turned sixteen, the Young Communist League had become Healey's central focus. By 1931 leaders suggested that Healey commit herself even further by leaving school to get a factory job in order to organize workers. She first found work pitting peaches in the spring of 1931 at the California Packing Corporation. A San Jose cannery hired Healey and paid her twenty-five cents per hour to work on the assembly line. Working among primarily Chicana women gave Healey important insights into the community and operations of a factory and the components needed to organize the workers. One of the first things she did was spot the workers who appeared to be popular with other workers and stood out as leaders. She would visit them at their homes to discuss the poor working conditions—the regular speedups and low wages—and then address the need to form a union. Although Healey always remained open with her fellow workers about her Communist affiliation, she recalled: "The paradox is the fact that to convince workers to join the union was as hard as it would have been to convince them to join the CP or YCL .... The fear of joining a union was even stronger because they knew the boss would take immediate action ... they knew they could lose their job if they joined a union."[11] Yet she got her opportunity when in the summer of 1931 the workers spontaneously walked out at the San Jose cannery over the unjust firing of one of their colleagues. Soon all of the cannery's workers walked out and came together to strike outside the factory. At sixteen Healey took the formally designated title of "Youth Activities Director" and managed her first strike, setting up committees to mobilize, publicize, and educate the workers.

One of the central meeting places for Healey's striking cannery workers was St. James Park, a central public space in downtown San Jose. For the first several days of the strike, police greeted the strikers and organizers with brutal attacks. In response the groups of strikers would then organize new rallies to protest their treatment by the police in addition to their usual cannery picketing. During these weeks in the summer of 1931 Healey also came to work closely with the International Labor Defense League (ILD) and Labor's Non-Partisan League (LNPL), which both regularly defended workers who had been arrested. The ILD had initially formed in 1925 out of the various organizations that worked on the Sacco-Vanzetti defense and then went on to represent the unemployed and underprivileged in California. The LNPL, a newer group, functioned as a political and lobbying organization. The professional and institutional relationships with the ILD and LNPL that Healey formed during this strike would continue to support her during the next several years as an organizer.[12]

Ultimately, the San Jose cannery owners succeeded in breaking the strike by the late summer of 1931, and the effort to organize the workers "dribbled out," according to Healey. While they failed to win union recognition, strikers made modest gains in bettering their working conditions, and as Healey recalled with delight, women gained political and organizational skills in setting up the protests. Healey defended the significance of this and other strikes, insisting that the YCL organizers were "providing the most important kind of service . . . the ability to understand the society in which that one lives . . . to understand the capacity of organized people to fight and win, to win those people to an understanding of why they should join a revolutionary party."[13] This strong commitment to rousing worker awareness drove Healey to become even more devoted to the YCL.

Healey strengthened this Communist Party relationship when, just shy of her seventeenth birthday, she married Lou Sherman on August 15, 1931, the same year that she participated in her first strike. Sherman was a YCL member who was three years her elder and also the brother of William Schneiderman, the future chairman of the California Communist Party. On the morning of her wedding Healey bought a used green and white wedding gown. Her younger sister remembered thinking "there was something funny about buying your wedding dress at a rummage sale the day you were getting married, something poignant about it."[14] Yet given the context in which Barbara had raised her children, Healey's wedding and marriage makes sense; Barbara had always taught her children to both shun materialism and value romantic relationships. Healey later wrote that one of the main factors driving her to marry at such a young age was that "you didn't feel that you had made it if you didn't either have a boyfriend or were married."[15] Even taking into account her youth and innocence, it is telling that as a young Party activist she not only valued traditional marriage but felt as though her relationship status defined her. Moreover, she did not feel obligated to reconcile the social and cultural meanings attached to marriage in the United States with communistic theories defining marriage as a capitalist, unequal arrangement. Young women seeking traditional marriages simply fit into Party culture.

Soon after marrying Sherman, however, Healey became pregnant because she had used an ineffective birth control foam. She never doubted that she would end the pregnancy (and two others over the next decade), remarking, "Who could think of a revolutionary having a child?"[16] Healey deciding to pursue a traditional marriage while refusing to have a child illustrates the complexities of gender within the Party. She chose marriage for personal reasons but rejected motherhood because of her professional obligations. Healey and Sherman soon divorced. Later she said the failure of her first marriage had left her indifferent toward romantic relationships, though this sentiment would only last a short time.

Before they separated, Healey and Sherman moved to the Hollenbeck Park section of East Los Angeles, on Soto Street, at the request of the YCL. As a new resident, she worked for the YCL to recruit members and sympathizers for the organization and for the Unemployed Council. Except for a stint working at a Sears, Roebuck department store in Fullerton, she remained officially unemployed, which enabled her to spend long hours organizing workers and attending meetings.

The most visible signs of radicalism in Los Angeles during the early 1930s were the public rallies attended by scores of the city's unemployed and the immediate and violent responses to them by Police Chief "Red" Hynes and his "Red Squad." Hynes's particularly vicious practices and notorious corruption dominated Los Angeles for nearly a decade. One Communist later remembered, "He achieved dubious fame by his brutal tactics against union workers . . . [he] posed as an 'authority on Communism' which he claimed to study zealously. . . . He also took $50 per day from the Street Railway Company in the 1934 strike, for leading a goon squad that slugged and gassed strikers and citizens."[17] At unemployed meetings across Southern California, and especially at the ones in downtown Los Angeles at Pershing Square and the Plaza, which were intended to be "free speech zones," police under Hynes's direction regularly threw tear gas canisters into crowds and beat participants at will. They would typically arrest anyone suspected of leafleting, an illegal activity in Los Angeles, and then testify at their trials.[18] Moreover, Hynes's influence in Southern California's political climate in the 1930s reached well beyond the borders of Los Angeles. At Communist Party conventions held outside of the city, police often raided the meetings and arrested dozens, simply as a show of force. Often charged with unlawful assembly, disturbing the peace, inciting to riot, vagrancy, and even criminal syndicalism, those arrested would eventually be released but only after the Party's activities had been interrupted.[19] During the desperate times of the Great Depression, Los Angeles authorities did not receive protestors kindly. Ultimately, Hynes became such a problem for the Los Angeles Police Department that in 1938 leaders in his department disbanded his squad and demoted him to patrolman.

But during the doldrums of the Great Depression, violent anti-communism among Los Angeles authorities still reigned supreme. During the 1932 presidential campaign Healey tried to host Communist Party presidential candidate William Z. Foster, who had nominated as his running mate James Ford, an African American Party member from Alabama. Foster traveled to Southern California to speak at the Plaza in downtown Los Angeles. But the Red Squad refused to allow Foster to hold his planned rallies and even refused to let him step foot in the city. Squad members met Foster at the train station and physically escorted him away from Los Angeles. At the time newspapers and civil libertarians alike widely noted, as one newspaper explained: "Foster spoke in Oakland and San Francisco, with no interference. In Los Angeles, our police dictator broke up his meetings."[20] Because of this widespread intimidation, near certain harassment, and fear, Healey found it challenging to convince workers to join unions and become active in the labor movement. Beyond the police repression, Los Angeles had a reputation as one of the most antiunion cities in the country.

Yet in spite of these challenges in Los Angeles, outside the city's limits Healey managed to organize several large strikes. December 1933 marked the start of one of her most notable labor efforts. That month a delegation of Mexican and Mexican American workers traveled to Los Angeles from California's Imperial Valley to discuss their recent failed lettuce strike and to ask for assistance with their new strike plans. The Communist Party's Cannery and Agricultural Workers Industrial Union (CAWIU) sent two representatives, Stanley Hancock and Healey, to help them organize. Early the following month the two of them departed for Brawley, the Imperial Valley town that housed the union headquarters. When they arrived, Healey remembered there being "absolutely no resistance on the part of Chicanos to our presence."[21] She figured that these workers might have been comfortable working with Communists because they had some familiarity with the IWW and the Trade and Union Unity League (TUUL), which had organized in the region a few years earlier. Healey also recalled sensing a genuine comradeship and common political identity with the workers from the beginning.

Upon arriving in the Imperial Valley, Healey sent groups to notify workers of the plans for labor activity and to draw up their demands. After facilitating hours-long debates and meetings among the workers about how to prioritize their demands—ranging from clean drinking water to the end of labor contractors—Healey found herself in the middle of this vibrant movement. She also set up committees and chose workers to serve as shoppers, cooks, or educators. Although most of the workers who took part were Mexican Americans, others—including Filipino, black, and white laborers—agreed to come together to protest their conditions. Their renewed lettuce strike started in January 1934, when five thousand workers walked off their jobs.[22]

In Brawley the winter of 1934 was an overwhelming, busy, and dangerous season. Together the striking workers and the Communists set up a structure to run, coordinate, and survive what they imagined would be an extended strike. During these weeks Healey grew personally and professionally close to the workers, all the while confirming for herself the value not just of the labor movement but of radicalism in general. Interviewed in the 1970s, she reminisced: "That strike more than anything else in my life ... demonstrated to me what is meant by the potential of the working class when there is a channel by which it can express itself, when it starts to acquire consciousness. In the first place I watched semi-literate people become great speakers and organizers and administrators. I watched bigotry break down.... When one talked about the question of the role of workers when emancipated from social and economic oppression as the leading factor in society, it was not an abstract thing to me, it was a real thing. I watched that happen."[23]

There are two explanations that account for Healey's positive experiences in Imperial Valley. First, the unprecedented economic desperation of the Great Depression seems to have fostered a relatively more accepting climate for Communist organizers across the country. But just as important, the specific environment of California's rural agricultural regions showed the potential for radical activism. Just as decades earlier, when the IWW members determined they could have the most success organizing and radicalizing the least-skilled and least-powerful workers, Communists found that the low-paying agricultural work during the Depression, the relatively isolated location of the farms, and the ethnic and political identity of the workers provided a welcoming atmosphere for their organizing efforts.

Healey also fondly recalled the dynamics of the workers' community. As opposed to her experience with the hierarchy of the Communist Party later on in the decade, Healey did not "have any memory at all of there being any reaction to the fact that I was both a youngster and a woman, then or later in the 30s, as far as workers were concerned. Nor do I have any memory of any particular male supremacy attitude towards the women who were on strike."[24] While this recollection may have only applied to Healey and may have been colored by the distance of nearly forty years, she clearly developed a strong respect for and attachment to the agricultural workers she organized in the heyday of activism. This close relationship extended well beyond official organizational coalition building and played a significant role in shaping her overall experience with communism in California in the 1930s. In addition to working to organize the laborers, Healey also exchanged political views with them, many of whom were veterans of the Mexican Revolution and had been willing to consider anarchism as a means to gain rights for workers. Still, for Healey the most important legacy of the Brawley strike was the memory of worker unity and the role of the Party in achieving that goal.

Nevertheless, in terms of practical success the strike itself did not benefit workers in agribusiness. The organizers were forced to travel to anonymous, far-off locations to avoid the predatory growers—who soon organized into the Associated Farmers—making it very difficult for them to communicate with one another.[25] The growers met every picket line and demonstration with tear gas and police attacks; they also mobilized vigilante forces across the valley to prevent any sort of relief from reaching the workers. During one parade, on January 9, 1934, vigilantes threw bombs at the marchers and knocked down Alvaro Sanchez, a two-year-old boy, who later died as a result of the tear gas.[26] After one week of the strike, the deputy issued a warrant for Healey, forcing her to operate in secrecy by slipping away from meetings and escaping police by hiding in labor camps. The town sheriff even issued a ten-thousand-dollar reward for her arrest, but none of her neighbors took the bait. Yet less than two weeks later, on January 18, the police finally tracked her down hiding in a pit underneath a bed in a worker's house and took her to the El Centro Jail. Charged with inciting to riot, unlawful assemblage, vagrancy, and rout, Healey sat in the Imperial Valley jail and refused to leave until all the other female workers had been bailed out. Helen Marston, a wealthy department store heiress and leftist sympathizer from San Diego, finally paid Healey's bail.[27] While temporarily released, Healey stayed in the area and met with those involved in a pea pickers strike, activity that posed a grave threat to her safety and independence. She routinely found threatening notes on her car windshields and at one point learned of bounties placed on her head.[28]

During the spring of 1934, when Anita Whitney was starting her electoral bid for the Senate, Healey faced the Imperial Valley judicial system. Her Brawley trial started and ended that March. She volunteered to represent herself because defense lawyers had long been harassed during the Imperial Valley labor trials. ILD attorneys had frequently been arrested or even kidnapped, robbed, and beaten upon arriving in the region. And just as Healey had anticipated, her trial and sentencing offered no exception to this animosity toward labor activism. After deliberating for only ten minutes, the jury sentenced Healey to serve 180 days in jail, the maximum penalty for her crime. She did not appeal the decision. In fact, when she started serving her sentence, she did not complain, explaining later that for her "jail was a time in which I could do two things which I always loved to do anyway: read and talk."[29] She fondly recalled the friendly conversations she had with other female prisoners there, most of them having been charged with prostitution, and her efforts to explain what a proletariat-led revolution would mean for them and how it could improve their lives. She regretted missing the wave of general strikes that had erupted up and down the West Coast in 1934 and wished that she could have participated in the gubernatorial election in support of Upton Sinclair and his EPIC campaign and presumably in the election of Anita Whitney, by this point the Party's elder stateswoman, who was running for state treasurer.

Although the Party officially opposed the EPIC program and branded it "social fascism," Healey always supported unity with EPIC supporters. This attitude accorded with her practical desire to pursue concrete leftist goals rather than Party supremacy: Californians who supported the EPIC campaign also agreed with stances taken by the Communists. Their substantive positions on topics such as state-sponsored enterprises and safety nets for workers were similar. In Healey's mind, then, political divisions were arbitrary. "One of the big lessons we learned," she reflected, "was that the people we were uniting on the issues that we were fighting about—antifascism, the right of workers to organize, the fight for unemployment insurance—that these were the same people who were in the EPIC movement. Here we had been condemning them, and yet we found that they were the ones who were immediately joining with us on the issues that we were organizing."[30] In this case, as in many others in the years to come, Healey embraced political coalition building around specific issues that concerned workers, the unemployed, and the oppressed in California. These alliances, though often temporary, spread across multiple organizations and political boundaries. They created a space in California in which the Communist Party influenced diverse and often popular campaigns.

At the time Healey's experience with coalition building was still in its infancy and became stalled because of her jail sentence. In the autumn of 1934, when Healey was finally set free, the ILD coordinated her safe transportation home because in recent months attacks on labor organizers had intensified. At nineteen years old Healey had just served six months in an Imperial Valley jail, and in the meantime her name had become so widely known among opponents of organized labor that the ILD asked for federal protection for her by an order from the attorney general. Citing the "hangman's noose, threat note, and steel-studded knout with which Stanley Hancock (a codefendant) was threatened," the ILD felt it was of utmost importance that the local police be kept away from Healey's release. Taking these precautions worked, and Healey returned home safely and rejoined the activist world of Southern California.[31]

During Healey's prison sentence and in the years to come, the Communist Party worked hard to expand its membership base. Nationally, Healey estimated that the Party had grown from twenty-five thousand members in 1934 to seventy-five thousand in 1938, with at least three thousand people in the Los Angeles chapter.[32] Beyond the desperation caused by the Great Depression and Americans' willingness to consider radical political alternatives, several additional factors account for this rise in membership. For one, the Party's Popular Front position, which it officially adopted at the Seventh World Congress of the Comintern in 1935, directed Parties across the globe to align with non-radicals inside and outside of the government to promote the rights of workers and oppose the power of fascists. As a result, although the CP had failed to officially support Upton Sinclair's EPIC program, in 1938 it made an about-face by implementing the Popular Front Program on orders from the Soviet Union.[33] Healey maintained that in California Communists had already ushered in a "premature People's Frontism" two years prior to the Seventh World Congress. Soon she and other Communists began working with the newly formed unions of the Congress of Industrial Organizations (CIO).

A second way the California Communist Party expanded its base was through its communication efforts. As labor historians have observed about the Party during these years: "One of the manifestations of the Party's strength . . . was its conviction that it now had a solid enough base in the labor movement and in the liberal political community to launch a western daily newspaper."[34] The *People's World* debuted on January 1, 1938, and endeavored to align itself with mainstream figures such as labor leader Harry Bridges, political activist and writer Upton Sinclair, state assemblyman Sam Yorty, future lieutenant governor and congressman Ellis Patterson, and state senator Jack Tenney. While some of these leaders would later go on to become staunch anti-Communists, at the time each wrote editorials in the paper expressing words of encouragement for the new western enterprise.[35] Thus, across California the mid-1930s really did appear to be the heyday for Party popularity.

Although its tactics and coalitions changed markedly in the mid-1930s, the Party's demands and agenda remained much the same as they had been for nearly a decade. For workers Communists called for a universal minimum wage, the abolition of child labor, a decrease in income taxes for low-wage employees, equal union opportunities for all races and genders, and an abolition of the sales tax. To aid farmers, the official Party position also demanded that banks and the government halt farm foreclosures and utility shutoffs as well as decrease income and property taxes for farmers stuck in poverty. To help the unemployed, Communists supported implementing an unemployment insurance program that would give payments of ten dollars per week for each unemployed worker, with additional sums for family members, and the end of evictions. Toeing the international Party line, the national Party proposed that the American government also take steps to eliminate all relations with Nazi Germany. In taking these positions, American Communists seemed to be advocating policies that resembled New Deal programs. What is more, the Communist Party seemed more oriented toward reforming rather than ending capitalism.

In the mid-1930s American Communists even gave lip service to workingwomen's concerns, despite the fact that the male leaders did not truly embrace gender equity. The Party press published and circulated pamphlets showcasing Communist positions on maternity and unemployment insurance and on food and housing assistance. In the 1932 and 1936 campaigns Party leaders appeared to believe that pressing issues of gender equity would earn them votes in statewide elections. Applauding the Soviet model of gender equality, the Party pamphlets insisted, "When a woman can put her baby in a cradle at the factory . . . when factory kitchens and cooperative restaurants provide the meals . . . when housework is reduced to a minimum . . . a woman has a real possibility to take part in productive work and to participate fully in political and social activities."[36] Besides helping women who were suffering under the ailing American economy, the California Party insisted that the government allow more freedom of speech in public spaces to promote the rights of labor, minorities, and immigrants. Unsurprisingly, the Party's general positions on this broad range of topics overlapped with many pursuits of non-Communist union and political activists. Consequently, coalition building became even more feasible than during Whitney's trial, when supporters were simply lining up to oppose her conviction.[37]

Healey's leadership role in this strategically reformulated Communist Party did not change significantly once she returned from jail in late 1934, though she did for the first time sense the way her gender affected her organizing abilities. She worked in San Pedro as a YCL organizer and later in San Francisco for the Alaska Cannery Workers' Union office. Then in the middle of the decade Los Angeles's United Cannery, Agricultural, Packing and Allied Workers of America (UCAPAWA), the seventh largest CIO union affiliate, drew Healey into its ranks.[38] Unique because it allowed Communists, and particularly women, leading roles, UCAPAWA had trouble finding organizers because most professional labor activists viewed female workers as too vulnerable to employer retaliation because of their gender. But Healey's gender helped her to rise to power within the union in 1938; the members elected her to serve as their international vice president. They chose her based on her reputation but also because she was a woman. Thus, her gender became a strategy to organize the union in important ways. At the time this decision made her resentful. She thought: "What the hell difference does it make that I'm a woman? Am I qualified or not?"[39] Although many years later Healey reflected more critically on her position on gender and politics, in the late 1930s her hostile response to privileging her gender was typical for protofeminist Communists.

In fact, this hostility exposes a central tension of the female Party experience. Healey and other female members rejected special treatment because of their gender and refused to consider the ways that gender prevented other professional opportunities for them, but Healey did indeed become a career woman in the Party and a leader with the UCAPAWA because of her gender. The Party and the union, in other words, facilitated greater workplace and leadership opportunities for her. And the UCAPAWA proudly highlighted this fact in its bulletin: "Dorothy Ray was the first woman member of UCAPAWA to be elected to the International Executive Board at the second national convention held in San Francisco last December.... Since she has come to the UCAPAWA she has accomplished great things for the International."[40] Clearly, the political and union work provided Healey with opportunities for professional advancement that would have been nearly impossible to find elsewhere in the 1930s. At a time when most unions excluded female members and leaders and mainstream political parties reluctantly accepted token female representation, Healey embraced the professional feminist identity that labor activity afforded her.

Under Healey's tenure the UCAPAWA emerged as one of the largest women's unions, as Vicki Ruiz has explained in *Cannery Women, Cannery Lives*. With seventy-five thousand women working in California canneries and packinghouses, these female workers sought raises and union protection from their employers. Racial and ethnic diversity also characterized the large union: Mexican American women dominated numerically, but they worked closely with their Jewish, black, and Anglo counterparts. Once Healey took the new post as vice president, she quickly established a solid reputation within the union because of her "flashy" and articulate speaking style, according to union publications. On the ground her initial activity in the UCAPAWA included responding to spontaneous strikes that often erupted at Farm Security Administration camps when workers lost their jobs and the camp administrators threatened to expel them. But overall, Healey's quick wit and willingness to be at the center of messy situations easily earned her a well-respected position on the executive council of this union.[41]

Serving in this leadership position enabled Healey to help coordinate one of UCAPAWA's largest strikes. On August 31, 1939, the 430 workers at the California Sanitary Canning Company (Cal San) walked off their jobs and started a round-the-clock picket line. Topping their list of demands, the workers sought recognition for their union, Local 75 of the UCAPAWA. In the weeks leading up to the walkout, Healey enrolled employees in the union, planned the practical operations of the strike, and traveled to members' homes to speak about the importance of the union. Harking back to San Jose strike-planning experience, Healey organized workers into committees and created a schedule.[42] Each day workers stood outside the Cal San plant holding picket signs, and they boycotted and protested in front of stores that sold Cal San products. Yet even when the National Labor Relations Board encouraged owners of Cal San to bargain with the union, the employers resisted. Only when the children of striking workers showed up and picketed on the lawns of the homes of Cal San's owners did the owners agree to meet and negotiate with the union.

Ultimately, the two-week strike secured a five-cent wage increase and, most important, recognition for Local 75, which became "the second UCAPAWA affiliate (and the first on the West Coast) to negotiate successfully a closed shop contract."[43] Key to Healey's success with the union was her ability to appeal to workers on a personal level, to work within government agencies to promote the rights of workers, and to administer the day-to-day operations of a strike. Over the several months following the strike, Healey stayed with the union in a business capacity, protesting the owners' racially discriminatory hiring practices and coordinating regular marches across the city. Throughout these years as a labor activist, Healey still maintained her leading role in the YCL, focusing her radicalism on incorporating the most unskilled and unrepresented workers into the thriving labor movement.

Her broader agenda, of course, aimed not only to organize labor but also to recruit members for her increasingly visible Communist Party. One of the ways Healey did this was by spreading a Communist culture. It became commonplace, for example, for the Party to host an annual May Day Carnival and Picnic, where political statements, sporting events, and dancing would all mix in a public area. Columns in the *People's World* and *Western Worker* spread the message. Moreover, wedding receptions, youth-specific social activities, and bazaars all characterized the California Communist culture.[44] Constructing a Party culture helped local Communists both legitimize their own radical lives and recruit others during these tumultuous years.

Although the Communist culture tried to integrate Communists with mainstream communities, one component of it deliberately kept the Party on the fringes—their inclusion of racial minorities. The Party attempted to politicize the working-class minorities who had been long overlooked by more moderate political and labor organizers in Southern California. LaRue McCormick, executive director of the ILD in Los Angeles, recalled that the county government calibrated relief payments based on race. "There were three sets of standards for the unemployed. If you were black you got a certain amount to live on; and if you were Mexican you got the least of all, because it was presumed that the Mexican people could live on beans and tortillas and they didn't need as much as either blacks, or of course, the whites."[45] The ILD, supported by Communists and community activists alike, worked vigorously to oppose these racist practices used by the government and employers. Healey helped lead the way in recruiting radical sympathizers among racial minorities, particularly African Americans, in Los Angeles.

Communists boldly courted the attention of those fighting for racial and class equality by running James Ford, an African American man, as the Party's vice presidential candidate in the 1932 election. At their nominating convention Communists directly appealed for a multiracial working-class alliance, pleading: "We call upon the colored and white toilers to stand shoulder to shoulder in the fight to win such equality for the Negro people now! A solid, unbreakable fighting front of all toilers, Negro and white, can smash the vicious, white ruling-class system of Jim Crowism and lynch terror."[46] Calling for diverse working-class unity, the Communist Party placed blame for the poor living and working conditions of African Americans squarely on the capitalist system rather than on a vague notion of historical racism. The Party also published articles by prominent African American intellectuals including W. E. B. Du Bois, Pettis Perry, and Doxey A. Wilkerson outlining how the Party could solve their problems better than any other political group. Wilkerson, for example, spoke and wrote widely about the need for African Americans to align with white workers in the CIO to gain broad support for abolishing Jim Crow laws in southern plants. With African Americans and whites working together in unions, Wilkerson maintained, they could struggle for improved salaries, job security, working conditions, and racial equality.[47]

On a daily basis the Party focused on fighting employment discrimination and housing segregation. Attempting to recruit African Americans to the Party, Communists regularly issued pamphlets detailing their positions. In 1935, for example, two theoreticians wrote "The Negroes in a Soviet America," in which they asserted: "The fundamental policy of a Soviet Government with regard to the Negro generally would therefore be to create even relatively greater opportunities for advance and progress for the Negro than for the white. Special emphasis would be placed upon training more Negro skilled workers, upon technical and other forms of education, upon inducing larger numbers to take up engineering, science, etc. . . . the Negro will be playing a prominent part, just as Georgians, Tadjiks, Ukrainians . . . are today among the leaders of the Soviet Union and its Communist Party. The horrors of segregated, over-crowded ghettos will disappear."[48] Linking poverty, racism, and revolution made the Communist Party appear to present a comprehensive alternative to reformers who simply sought to eliminate racism. This class-based approach also enabled the Party to openly criticize the NAACP for working primarily with wealthy African Americans, which, Communists insisted, took public attention away from the enduring issue of poverty.

In spite of the Party's criticism of the NAACP, Healey's California Party successfully created coalitions in pursuit of a common race-focused agenda, just as Whitney had managed to do through her membership in the NAACP alongside the Communist Party. The 1931 Scottsboro case played a key role in galvanizing diverse support from civil rights and leftist organizations across the country. In this case the ILD, NAACP, American Civil Liberties Union (ACLU), American Federation of Labor (AFL), and Communist Party worked together to defend nine black youths who had been falsely accused of rape in Alabama. The case made headlines when the state of Alabama charged nine young boys, aged twelve to nineteen, for the rape of two white women on a freight train. As was typical with these and other civil rights trials, an all-white jury swiftly convicted them and then sentenced eight of the boys to death for the crime, even though one of the alleged victims had recanted her accusation. All of the defendants were ultimately freed but only after spending years behind bars and in and out of courtrooms. Leftist organizations from across the country lined up to provide legal advice and public support to the black youths. Communist support played a key role in their defense. The Communist Party strategically seized on the national popularity of the case, asserting that the trial shed light on racism in the judicial system.[49] Communists further used the Scottsboro case to illustrate what it meant to be black in the southern judicial system and also more broadly to bring attention to what they called "white chauvinism," or racism. During and after the Scottsboro Boys' trial, the Party regularly hosted the defendants to speak around the country at public rallies and appealed to all Scottsboro supporters to wage their struggles for racial equality through the Communist Party. Thus, with the Scottsboro case the Party effectively allied with each organization that sought justice and racial equality for the boys.[50]

Healey's Los Angeles Party worked to extend interest and sympathy for the Scottsboro Boys to issues of local concern. Concerns about police brutality that reached beyond Hynes's Red Squad ranked high on the agenda of the Party, the ILD, and the ACLU in the 1930s and 1940s, creating the potential for even broader coalitions on the local level. The local Party directed a committee to collect and circulate reports of beatings and violence inflicted on African

Americans and Mexican Americans by white police officers. Other groups then disseminated the collected reports. In one publication, for example, the ILD detailed the case of Alex Spinoza, a seventeen-year-old boy arrested after a traffic accident on November 14, 1938. According to the report, Spinoza disappeared within the county jail system for days, and when his mother finally found him, "he told her that police had struck him in the face many times and had hit and kicked him in the stomach. He fainted and when he came to, the police were dragging him by the hair. He said they were trying to make him confess he had stolen a new pair of trousers that were in the car when he was arrested."[51] In part because of the ILD's publicity and legal expertise, the juvenile court agreed to investigate the mistreatment of Spinoza. Thus, Healey's Party and the ILD worked together to focus the community's attention on the widespread violence and intimidation that law enforcement directed at minorities.

Moreover, local chapters of the ACLU worked alongside the Communist Party to draw attention and support to the battles for racial and labor equality in the 1930s. These shared concerns appeared to broaden both the ACLU's and the Communist Party's popularity in Southern California. Healey often spoke of the overlap between the interests of the Communist Party and of ACLU chapters in her region. The Southern California branch of the ACLU in particular focused on labor activism more so than other chapters, a tendency that gained the local branch many CP allies. In 1938, for example, the director of the Southern California branch of the ACLU, Clinton J. Taft, reported how city councils from Beverly Hills to Riverside to Ventura "have been stampeded into passing ordinances practically preventing peaceful picketing."[52] These new limitations on free speech united radicals and liberals in Southern California. The Los Angeles ACLU also frequently worked with the longtime Communist Party allies, the ILD and the LNPL. In choosing to defend the civil liberties of leftist organizations, as opposed to choosing more moderate causes such as censorship laws or political corruption, the Southern California ACLU (SCACLU) established a definite leftist orientation by the 1930s.

The SCACLU was so independent in part because it was the first "affiliate" of the national organization. Somewhat apart from other branches, "affiliate leaders pursued their own versions of success, much to the dismay of the national organization," as historian Judy Kutulas has explained.[53] Indeed, local branches had so much autonomy that members even had a choice of whether to pay dues to their local group, the national group, or both. Frequently, the result was local inactivity or subordination to the national group's goals. In 1923, however, Upton Sinclair offered significant funding for the new SCACLU to monitor Los Angeles's police department. With continued financial backing from this famous leftist writer and other wealthy Southern Californians, local activism thrived around specific campaigns, including a statewide one to repeal the California Criminal Syndicalism Law (though the repeal of this law ultimately did not happen until 1991). Thus, throughout the 1930s, because of this increased funding, the SCACLU, with its own paid staff, had more resources and in turn pursued more publicly and vigorously labor and free speech cases than other regional branches.[54]

By contrast, both the national ACLU and its Northern California branch had a much more limited set of goals and less sympathy for radical labor. In 1940 the national ACLU went so far as to expel from her leadership post longtime radical labor activist and close friend of Whitney, Elizabeth Gurley Flynn. According to historian Judy Kutulas, Flynn was expelled because "she was the only self-identified Communist director and she was female, with a trail of ex-lovers in high places."[55] The controversy over Flynn's ousting led to the loss of nearly one-fifth of the national membership and had significant consequences for the national organization and for Healey's region. As the 1940s progressed, the nation's "premier civil liberties organization" pursued its more conservative agenda and ended up equating communism and fascism. Yet despite this conservative turn within the national ACLU, the organization in Southern California remained more sympathetic to the Left. Ultimately, Southern California's exceptionally fluid political environment—represented by Healey—enabled the region's unusually independent Communists and independent civil libertarians to thrive and cooperate on the local level, despite the antagonism of their national leadership. In the early Cold War years this solidarity would come to play an important role in the Southern California Communist Party's ability to sustain tenuous coalitions with other radicals and some liberals.

Anti-Communists grew increasingly alarmed by the Party's relationships with other labor activists. In 1937, still in the midst of the Great Depression, the state Peace Officers' Association issued a dire report on the growing threat of Soviet-led American Communists, which grabbed the attention of statewide representatives from across the political spectrum. Fearfully noting that thirty thousand people had attended a rally for Earl Browder in San Francisco during his 1936 presidential campaign and that the Communist Party continued to build its young population by opening Workers' Schools across the state, the Peace Officers' Committee warned that "we have thus far been unable to stay the menacing advance of Communism."[56] The report appealed to readers' cultural and racial prejudices by highlighting the "subversive" tendencies of the Communist Party, repeatedly asserting that the Party encouraged racial mixing. "The prohibition of the practice of white Communist girls," they insisted, "living out of wedlock with young Negroes is the solemn obligation of every citizen, black and white, who is interested in preserving the purity of race."[57] Indeed, the peace officers claimed that in attempting to rally race and class consciousness among both African Americans and workers, the Party aimed to destroy American culture. The report also detailed alleged Communist front groups, arguing that these groups used deceptive practices to secretly spread communism throughout the state.

Despite the growing concern of those on the Right, many California leftists—and even a few Communists, including Healey—acquired positions of influence in city and state government in the 1930s and early 1940s. In part this heightened level of mainstream political involvement grew out of leftists' leading roles in labor activity and broader Popular Front policies. In 1937, for example, when Healey began organizing walnut pickers, she had developed a close relationship with Sam Yorty, the future mayor of Los Angeles who went on to become a staunch anti-Communist. At the time an assemblyman in the California state legislature, Yorty came to two of Healey's union meetings to convince workers to join the union. Healey recalled Yorty exhorting workers to "fight the masters of monopoly and the princes of plenty" by joining together.[58] Healey also worked through the recently formed National Labor Relations Board (NLRB) to file charges of unfair bargaining practices against the walnut growers. The NLRB members sympathized with the union and did everything they could to advance the union's right to bargain. Over time these interactions with government officials and bureaucracies taught Healey "that this picture we had of the state apparatus as always representing the ruling class wasn't true." Through her labor activity Healey, an open Communist, played a key role in building coalitions with various government agencies.[59]

In California politics Healey's Communist Party participated with other leftist organizations in attempting to encourage the Democratic Party to push forward a number of programs both parties supported, thus illustrating the potential efficacy of the Popular Front. Together the radicals and liberals promoted consumer cooperatives, low-cost housing, universal minimum wage and maximum-hour laws, and subsidies for tenant and farm laborers.[60] In 1938 the CPUSA officially adopted a position opposing third-party political candidates. The Popular Front had fully come of age when the Central Committee declared: "The socialist reorganization of society is not the immediate task. Yet the education of the people into the true meaning of socialism is always the task of Communists. The fact is that the working class and the toiling people generally are turning ever more in the direction of socialism, toward the example of the Soviet Union, as their greatest hope and ultimate solution."[61] In the short term, because of the Popular Front, Healey's Party pursued a political realignment, incorporating youth and peace movements, civil rights groups, labor organizations, and even members of the middle class. Bringing these diverse interests into one cohesive Democratic bloc of voters would, according to the Communist plan, give their interests a stronger role in the operations of the government. In fact, throughout the 1940s the Party and Healey continued to work with government agencies, primarily to pursue their labor and relief goals.

Healey's relationship with government agencies became even stronger when Democratic governor Culbert Olson took office in 1939. Healey openly endorsed Olson in his run for governor, and Communists collectively supported him by forming the Federation (or Conference) for Political Unity, an umbrella organization that united Sinclair's older EPIC supporters, progressives, labor activists, and Communists alike. Indeed, in 1938 Anita Whitney hosted then candidate Olson at her home, where he accepted the Party's support for his election campaign.[62]

For her part, Healey worked on the ground in Los Angeles as a CIO organizer and as county organizer for the LNPL, where she watched as California's governing officials came to the aid of some of the most impoverished workers and also appointed leftists to various government posts. Working with the LNPL gave Healey the opportunity to construct even more diverse coalitions with churches, parent-teacher associations, and single-issue groups. For her the Popular Front coalition became a reality through these groups. Moreover, with Olson's Democratic coalition in office, Communists as well as other leftists found ways to influence reform for labor within the two-party system. "For a moment," she wrote, "in the early days of his administration, we had the highest hopes, particularly since one of his first acts as governor was of great symbolic importance to the Left and the labor movement."[63] That act was to pardon Tom Mooney, imprisoned since 1916 for the preparedness day bombings.

In a dramatic example of the success of Healey's strategy of building coalitions with liberals, in August 1940 Governor Olson appointed her to serve as the state deputy labor commissioner. In this post she held hearings about labor code violations and visited workplaces to inspect health and safety conditions. For her, working as part of state government on behalf of labor made the ideals of the Popular Front come to life. She was initially enamored with the job because, she later recalled: "I was officially entrusted with the authority to enforce the state's quite progressive labor code. I was given a huge police badge, with the authority to arrest employers—they were the only people I could arrest."[64] Nevertheless, after a year on the job she felt that beyond helping a few individual laborers, her larger mission had been relatively fruitless.

Healey's frustration stemmed from the assaults against her and other leftists within Olson's administration. The year she took office Jack Tenney, a former leftist assemblyman who had swerved rightward in his politics, decided to form a state senate committee to investigate Communists within state government. Tenney's committee forced Healey, a government employee, to testify. When finally pushed into speaking in front of the government committee, she admitted to having been a member of the Young Communist League for years but said she was no longer a Communist. It was a lie; later she explained, "I had no qualms about denying membership when my inquisitors were only asking to serve their own partisan motives." The governor asked Healey to resign, but she refused, telling him to "go to hell."[65] For the remainder of her tenure as state deputy labor commissioner, her responsibilities were severely restricted.

Healey's attempt to build alliances with liberals was also challenged by the Nazi-Soviet Pact. Like Whitney, Healey supported the twists and turns in the Communist Party line before, during, and after the war. In 1939 she believed that "the Soviet Union was justified in signing the [Nazi-Soviet] Pact." She felt that the Soviets had no other alternatives and they could not face Hitler alone; thus, they conceded to the Pact.[66] Yet when the Nazis invaded the Soviet Union in June 1941, thus bringing the United States into an alliance with the Soviets, the Party and Healey once again fell in line with the Soviet model, openly demonstrating their American patriotism and Communist politics simultaneously. American Communists volunteered for war service in droves and wholeheartedly supported the wartime policies of Roosevelt. The Party even dissolved itself during the war years, insisting on the need to support the American government and military leaders beyond pursuing their own political goals.[67]

American Communists supported the war effort by helping the U.S. government to recruit able-bodied people into the wartime workforce, including women. To shore up support for women's wartime work, the Party employed arguments developed by the government's famed "Rosie the Riveter" campaign. It likened the repetition in ironing clothes, for example, to a machinist job. Acknowledging the difficulties in adapting to paid work, Party publications explained to the female members how "most plants now have women counselors to consider the special problems of women employees."[68] American Communists were so unquestioningly supportive of the government's war policies that the Party failed to object when the government sent prominent Party members (and American citizens) Elaine Black and Karl Yoneda to Japanese relocation camps and even followed suit by firing a Japanese American employee at the Party newspaper.

Healey personally fulfilled her American wartime patriotic duty by supporting her husband, Don Healey, who was drafted into the military. She had married Don in 1940 and bore her only child, Richard, with him at the height of the war in June 1943. Healey originally met Don in the late 1930s, when he joined the Party and became the local head of the LNPL. He went on to establish a strong reputation as a leading organizer in the CIO. During the war he was stationed in Alabama because he was not allowed overseas due to his radical politics. After he returned home from military service, their marriage began to crumble. In her memoir Healey wrote: "Don would always decide if we would go out in the evening. . . . But I didn't care in the least. On questions that were important to me, I'd make up my own mind."[69] Yet tensions were developing between the two. Healey explained how she tried to cope and accept his open pursuance of extramarital affairs. But her tolerance did not save the marriage.

In a sense Healey's tolerance of Don's philandering fit with longstanding Communist theories about sex and marriage. In theory Communist thinkers condemned both marriage and the sexual double standard implicit in it, and in practice some Party members refused to marry or practice monogamy. As Friedrich Engels wrote about the gender bias inherent in capitalist romantic relationships, "It is the existence of slavery side by side with monogamy, the presence of young, beautiful slaves belonging unreservedly to the man, that stamps monogamy from the very beginning with its specific character of monogamy for the woman only, but not for the man. And that is the character it still has today."[70] Lenin and Marx also understood marriage to be quite unequal at its foundation. "Full freedom of marriage," according to Lenin, "can therefore only be generally established when the abolition of capitalist production and of the property relations created by it has removed all the accompanying economic considerations which still exert such a powerful influence on the choice of a marriage partner. For then there is no other motive left except mutual inclination."[71] In spite of these criticisms about the constructed power differences in capitalist romantic relationships, Lenin and Marx did very little to challenge the perceived natural and social differences between the sexes. In the famously discussed "Glass of Water" theory Lenin maintained about male and female sexuality: "Of course, thirst must be satisfied. But will the normal man in normal circumstances lie down in the gutter and drink out of a puddle, or out of a glass with a rim greasy from many lips? . . . Drinking water is of course an individual affair."[72] Thus, he emphasized the importance of female sexual purity. Ultimately, Lenin asserted that multiple sexual partners—particularly for women but also, though less explicitly, for men—"does not square with the revolution," as it would distract from the hard work and intellectual pursuits of rousing the proletariat. These seemingly conflicting and sexist messages about the appropriate relationship between men and women gave American Communists little guidance for conducting their own personal lives. These long-standing arguments had an impact on how the national Party understood the role of women. Consequently, Healey's attitude toward Don was certainly affected by this broader understanding about marriage and sexuality.

Although she followed Party directives about marriage, Healey made one important exception to her total commitment to American communism. Her son, Richard, altered her priorities altogether. Afraid that he would become an "orphan of the Party," which she believed often happened to children of activist parents, Healey refused to let Richard be victimized by her Party life. At night and on weekends she limited her Party involvement. She recalled how she picked him up at school daily, spent two hours of uninterrupted time with him in the evenings, and always prioritized his needs over those of the Party.[73] Her choices contrast with those made by other leading Communist women. Peggy Dennis, for example, was an international representative for the Comintern, an editor of the "Woman Today" page of the *Worker*, and the wife of Secretary-General Eugene Dennis. In the early 1930s Peggy left her four-year-old son, Tim, at the Comintern's International Children's Home outside of Moscow while she traveled across Europe as a Party representative. The Comintern even convinced her to keep him in the Soviet Union after she returned to the United States permanently. She trusted the Soviets to protect him and serve his interests; in her view this was the way "a woman's independence and revolutionary activity [could] be combined with motherhood."[74] By contrast, Healey's American Communist culture included understanding the Party's importance but also adopting U.S.-style social life and practices. Her priorities, however, did not translate into an enduring marriage; she and Don separated in 1946 and divorced the following year.

In part her marriage came to an end because of Healey's rise to leadership within the Party's ranks. When the Party published Jaques Duclos's famed article in May 1945, in which he criticized Earl Browder and broad political alliances such as the Popular Front, a new generation of Party leaders took the helm. Browder's reformist policies came out of the 1943 Teheran meeting between Winston Churchill, Franklin Roosevelt, and Joseph Stalin. Concluding that the three powers would emerge from the war as allies, Browder denounced the Communist Party's pursuit of socialism and said, "We are ready to cooperate in making Capitalism work effectively in the post-war period with the least possible burden upon the people."[75] Although this strategy proved effective for the Party in the peak war years, when the war ended Browder's "national unity" plan appeared increasingly naive and unrealistic. Therefore, under Moscow's direction new Communist Party leaders came to the fore and changed the national political strategy once again, refusing to continue supporting the two-party American electoral system. At the time of the internal shake-up, Healey had been working as a delegate for the Mine Mill and Smelter Workers Union (known as the Mine Mill union) to the CIO, a post she had been appointed to in 1945. During the first couple of years following the war, Healey's Communist Party maintained close relationships with the labor movement, particularly leaders in the leftist faction of the United Auto Workers (UAW).

But as the Party reshuffled its leaders, Healey was selected to attend her first national convention, at which the Central Committee chose her to be the organizational secretary for her Southern California district. Historically a woman's position in the Party, the organizational secretary did the "housekeeping" of the Party, which meant collecting dues, keeping track of membership, distributing literature, and advancing educational programs. In taking this new post in 1945, Healey found herself for the first time in an in-house Communist Party position rather than working with non-Communists in politics or the labor movement. Comrades regarded Healey as well suited for this new role because, her colleagues observed, "she had tremendous respect for authority. And she was a very modest person.... She was one of the few Communists ... who didn't go around making enemies."[76] Although at the time this change in revolutionary jobs may not have looked significant, it started Healey down a path toward conflict with the Party's national committee and organization that would last for decades.

Unaware of the looming Cold War that came to reshape political radicalism forever, in the few years following the end of the war, many American Communists believed that they were once again poised to wage a viable political struggle. The Party population in California grew in the immediate postwar years: in 1945 it reported 3,200 registered members, which grew to 5,081 in 1948, with the industrial workers sector comprising about 36 to 38 percent of them. Healey accounted for this highest point in Los Angeles Party membership by pointing to coalitions that had been constructed and sustained throughout the region. At the national Communist convention she insisted, "When we reach and involve the thousands of AFL and CIO members in factories, in the communities and in the trade unions and mass organizations, we are doing more than carrying on a campaign around a specific project, we are building the United Front, the coalition."[77] Implementing this Popular Front–style program during the mid-1940s enabled Healey to recruit diverse younger members, including African Americans, skilled and unskilled laborers, and liberals. The Southern California Party openly and willingly reached into the non-Communist masses to find common ground with them on specific topics, ultimately in hopes of recruiting additional members and sympathizers.

These coalitions coalesced most clearly in late 1947 and 1948 around the presidential campaign of the Progressive Party presidential candidate, Henry Wallace. Running on a platform that called for racial equality, an end to the Marshall Plan and the recent Cold War, and a minimum standard of living for all Americans, Wallace's third-party platform pleased Communists, who had sought many of the same goals for years. Healey offered strong support for Wallace's campaign. And in rallying California support for his campaign, Healey regularly highlighted the thousands of Mexican Americans who constituted the "Amigos de Wallace," the crowds of tens of thousands who turned out at large stadiums around the city to hear Wallace speak. The Party reasoned that in California and the nation Wallace faced a fair opportunity to seize the highly coveted labor vote as well as a wide array of liberal voters. Yet on Election Day, Wallace polled a dismal one million votes, in comparison with the five million that his supporters expected. It became apparent to the Communist Party that the labor vote had been lost and co-opted by the Democratic Party, though in California, Wallace still polled more than double his national average, as Debs had done in 1912. But equally devastating for the California Communist was the split within the CIO. Because the state CIO supported the third-party ticket while the national union did not, the national union fractured and ended up expelling many of the more leftist unions, thereby severing the once thriving relationship between the Party and Southern California labor.[78]

This decisive loss of influence for the Party in the broader community of California set the stage for what would become its most devastating decade yet, the early years of the Cold War. Following on the heels of the 1947 House Un-American Activities Committee (HUAC) hearings of the so-called Hollywood Ten, California looked ripe for a widespread government investigation into its long-time leftist climate. By the autumn of 1948 government investigations had heated up, with a federal grand jury issuing a subpoena for Healey in its investigation into the alleged subversive activities among government employees, which she had once been. The grand jury sought to ask known Communist Party members about the status of alleged members, which they flatly refused to do. When the grand jury issued Healey's subpoena, eastern Party leaders directed her to avoid it by fleeing underground. In October 1948 she obeyed the order to live in secrecy. This "was a political decision based on the analysis that we were about to enter a period of fascism and that the Party legally would be destroyed," Healey's attorney Ben Margolis later explained.[79]

Beginning in the autumn of 1948, Healey left her family and friends and disappeared. She remained underground for six months and successfully avoided the grand jury subpoena and indictment. Hiding out at members' houses and being smuggled in and out of secret locations on car floors, Healey escaped the FBI so that she could continue operating her temporarily dormant Communist Party. The goal of hiding was to wait out the session of the grand jury that sought to issue her subpoena. Although clearly hindered, her Party activity continued during these months, and in February

1949 Healey was promoted to the position of chair of the Southern California Communist Party.

One decisive moment, however, forced her to reconsider her Communist obligations. In mid-April she got word that her six-year-old son, Richard, had the mumps. "When I heard that Richard was sick," she recalled later, "I immediately called Ben [Margolis, her attorney] and said, 'This is nonsense. The grand jury will stay in session until they get me. I'm the one they want. It's stupid politically, and it's killing me personally because of Richard. I'm coming home.' I got back to my house on a Saturday night in late April, spent all day Sunday with Richard, and first thing Monday morning a federal marshal came to the door and handed me my subpoena."[80] What compromised Healey's security was not an informant or FBI surveillance but, rather, her personal decision that being with her son was more important than maintaining her power and anonymity as a Communist Party leader. Indeed, even as an underground leader, Healey had to balance being a leader of a radical banned organization with being a mother. Once again, she set aside Party directives and chose to care for her son, illustrating the complex tensions that American Communist mothers confronted.

When Healey was finally served with her subpoena in the spring of 1949, she had to face questions from the grand jury about identifying other Communists. She was asked about the names of members and producing the Party's roll books. As with the Hollywood hearings, "naming names" was the truly contentious issue for these radicals. As Healey's attorney Ben Margolis recalled, those subpoenaed "were perfectly willing to speak about themselves and their own activities, but they were unwilling to give the names of anyone else who was not publicly known."[81] Consequently, the attorneys directed the Communist defendants to refuse to answer the questions based on their Fifth Amendment right to protect themselves from self-incrimination. By the end of June, after weeks of Healey's continued refusal to give the grand jury the information it sought, Judge Pierson M. Hall held Healey in contempt of court because he did not agree that the purpose of the Fifth Amendment was to protect oneself from this particular line of questioning.[82]

When Judge Hall issued his decision holding Healey in contempt of court in June 1949, he allowed her to make a statement pleading for leniency in her sentence. She used the opportunity to make two points. First, she condemned the exceptionally paranoid atmosphere in the nation, which she attributed to corporate America's control over the political system. But second, Healey adopted a personal tone. "I am the mother of a six-year-old child, and like any mother," she stated, "I am heartsick at the prospect of being forcibly separated from him. And yet, my child, young as he is, understands that because of my love and concern for him and the children of all mothers, I cannot and will not compromise now with the forces that would deny him security and decent opportunity in life."[83] Healey evidently felt that appealing to the judge on a maternal level might convince him to allow her to remain free despite her refusal to answer his questions. The plea was to no avail; Judge Hall did not sympathize with Healey's situation. On June 18, 1949, he committed all of the Communist defendants to serve eighteen months in prison for refusing to answer the questions. Healey was released on bail after serving less than two days, pending an appeal. But the grand jury investigation proceeded for the next year, during which time known Party members continued their strategy of refusing to identify or implicate other members.

After more than a year and a half, in February 1951 the Ninth Circuit Court of Appeals reversed Healey's sentence, and the Supreme Court ultimately supported the defendants' rights to use the Fifth Amendment to avoid incriminating themselves. This decision freed Healey to direct many of the Party operations that had been forcibly stalled because of the investigations and widespread anti-Communist atmosphere. Thus, during the early years of the 1950s Healey continued in her new leadership role as Party chair in Southern California. National leaders instructed Healey to establish an underground Party that would sustain itself in the case of total suppression. According to her, it never functioned well. With the exception of the six months she spent underground, Healey operated above ground throughout her entire tenure. In Los Angeles the Party simply did not participate extensively in the underground world. She insisted, "We were determined to preserve as much of open, above-ground, and legal activity as possible, and throughout the early fifties we continued to hold public meetings in the name of the *People's World*."[84] The Communist Party's rejection of secrecy may explain the relatively more accepting atmosphere for the Party in Los Angeles during the Cold War. While other Party branches were permanently excommunicated from broader activist communities, the Southern California branch maintained many of its liberal alliances.

Yet the government paid little attention to this potential difference. Within two years it once again focused on Healey and, on July 31, 1951, indicted her for "conspiring to violate the Smith Act."[85] Passed by Congress in 1940, the Smith Act "made it a crime to conspire to advocate the overthrow of the government by force or violence."[86] Not actively espousing violence in the 1950s but, rather, calling for a peaceful transition to socialism, the Party nevertheless fell prey to the same technical arguments that the government used to convict Whitney more than thirty years earlier in her criminal syndicalism case. The government argued that because American Communist Party members participated in an international Communist movement and followed the dictates of Marx and Lenin, they advocated violent revolution in the United States. As Healey poignantly remembered, "The marvel of the Smith Act was that all the prosecution had to prove was that we did these perfectly legal things in furtherance of an ultimately illegal end."[87] Indeed, just as with Whitney's charges during the First Red Scare, these Second Red Scare charges aimed to prove that one's membership in an organization that indirectly espoused violence implicated the individual Party member as a violent revolutionary posing a threat to the nation.

Eleven other members were also charged on the same day, including Philip "Slim" Connelly, Healey's third and final husband. Healey had married Connelly in 1947, shortly after her divorce from Don Healey. Connelly was the secretary of the Los Angeles CIO Council and then chair of the statewide organization, though once the union began to distance itself from known leftists in the late 1940s, he became the Los Angeles editor of the *People's World*. According to Healey and her friends, from the start this marriage was fraught with tension and turmoil, which was only exacerbated by their Smith Act arrests.

The judge presiding over the Smith Act case refused bail, leaving all eleven defendants in jail for five months. Healey was thus squarely in the center of a wave of anticommunism that was sweeping the nation. As this California Communist sat in jail, Joseph McCarthy intensified his accusations about Communists infiltrating the government, Alger Hiss went to jail for perjury, and Julius and Ethel Rosenberg were convicted and sentenced to death for violating the Espionage Act.

As these controversies gripped the nation, Healey struggled to remain in touch with her loved ones on the outside. The letters she wrote from jail to Richard and her other family members offer important insight into the strained life of this Communist mother. Away at summer camp when police arrested his mother, Richard found out about it in a letter from Healey. "I know you won't worry about me in here," she calmly reminded her young child. "You know that jail won't bother mommy, just as long as I know that my son is happy. Grandma won't give you this letter until you come back from camp; we want you to enjoy your vacation, and not have anything to worry you. I miss you and I know you will miss me, but we know that this short separation is better than not trying to stop a war.... When you get home from camp, you can have your choice of where you want to stay."[88] Healey continued to write letters to Richard nearly every day during these five months, keeping her mother and son abreast of her daily life. Writing about the food, reading material, food poisoning, and clothing, Healey updated her family about the mundane details of jail in order to remain a part of Richard's routine. In addition, Connelly, Richard's stepfather, even put on a brave face in letters to Richard. "It is a very nice jail, so I like it all right," he wrote. Trying to maintain an ordinary tone, he continued: "Wish mother and I could come up in the mountains to see you at camp.... Do you go swimming every day? How is the water?"[89] Caring for Richard made Healey's political persecution even more personally challenging. In fact, in many ways her sacrifices became all the more intense because of her gendered identity. Just as the courts had not shown leniency to Ethel Rosenberg for being a mother, the legal system did not provide for any special treatment, even at a time when female domesticity reigned supreme at home.

Ultimately, when in December 1951 the judge set bail at five thousand and ten thousand dollars, depending on the members' rank, the eleven Party members went home, having served five months. But with the trial starting in less than two months, they faced many hours of preparation—legal, political, and social. Once the trial began, many groups of people assembled to help the defendants. Supporters organized the California Emergency Defense Committee to garner public support from across the political spectrum. Radicals, liberals, union members, churchgoers, ACLU members, and community activists alike joined forces to support these Communists. The coalition, though significantly smaller in number because of the domestic Cold War atmosphere, looked very similar to the one Whitney's supporters had constructed nearly thirty years earlier. In particular, the continued open character of Los Angeles's ACLU branch and the welcoming nature of the First Unitarian Church enabled the construction of solid, albeit small, coalitions. Even traditional liberals did not abandon their old radical allies entirely in the Cold War: prominent liberals—including writers and attorneys—formed a Bill of Rights Committee to defend their right to free speech.

These supporters all lined up behind the unifying issue of free speech for these known radicals. They even borrowed protest strategies from their older counterparts. Healey recalled that supporters signed petitions challenging the legality of their indictments, just as in the 1920s Whitney's supporters circulated petitions on her behalf. In addition, Healey remembered, "every day there were lines of people waiting outside for the start of the trial, to come and observe."[90] The Party connected the broader activist community to the Red

Scare trial and thus succeeded in preventing the Party from becoming wholly isolated from its larger circle of support. And as Healey aptly remembered, the impact of this support made her not only feel less isolated but made her "more willing to continue trying to reach out to a broader, non-Party public."[91] Indeed, these coalitions had somewhat of a self-fulfilling nature; non-Communist support for Communists during the early 1950s made them less marginalized, which in turn created more opportunities for Communists to reach out and continue their organizing efforts once the reactionary atmosphere subsided.

Still, amid the mainstream political climate of Los Angeles, there were many who did not sympathize with or understand the Communist Party. Deliberating for only a few days after a trial that had lasted months, the jury convicted all Party members of violating the Smith Act, and the judge sentenced each of them to serve five years in prison and pay a ten thousand–dollar fine. Temporarily, despite their convictions, Healey and the others remained free on bail. Their appeals began immediately, though the Supreme Court did not rule on them until June 1957.

Ultimately, after eight years spent embroiled in legal battles that threatened to send Healey to prison, the Supreme Court finally cleared her of all of charges in 1957, thirty years after Whitney's pardon. Convinced not by larger theoretical arguments about free speech, the court instead agreed with technical arguments presented by the defense about the evidence used to convict each person. It agreed with the argument, for example, that if a Smith Act conviction were to stand, the prosecution would have had to show that each defendant personally sought to use violence to overthrow the government. As Healey described it, "They would have had to prove instead that I personally had participated in advocating that people go out and, say, buy guns and ammunition in preparation for the revolution."[92] Thus, whereas in Whitney's case the Supreme Court ruled that simply her membership in the Communist Party rendered her guilty of violating the California Criminal Syndicalism Law, with Healey's Smith Act case the court decided that her membership alone did not amount to her espousal of violent revolution. Both of these Red Scare cases brought up the same questions about free speech, but the differences lay in the jurists' interpretations of the respective laws used to convict the women.

In the midst of these legal battles Healey's personal, political, and professional life also underwent extreme turmoil. During the trial Healey admitted that another male Party member had approached her to discuss her husband's affair with his wife. Showing her commitment to the cause, Healey tried to smooth things over to keep the two men loyal to the Party. When she married Connelly in 1947, she had hoped he would be a good father figure for Richard. But despite the marriage's instability, Connelly's infidelity, and his notorious temper, Healey stayed in the relationship much longer than she wanted to because she felt a wifely and professional duty as a revolutionary to keep her husband, a Party member, satisfied. Healey did not speak out against Connelly's infidelity; rather, she tolerated poor treatment from him throughout their marriage.

Healey did not expect an egalitarian marriage from this or any of her romantic relationships. Although she established a reputation as a maverick Party leader, Healey was quite conventional in her approach to personal relationships and even in her sense of self. No record exists that she pursued extramarital affairs, though Healey did have a number of romantic relationships during her unmarried years. Her marriage to Connelly finally ended in the early 1950s, in part, according to her, because of her prioritization of the Party. Her marriage was admittedly a distant third in her life, after Richard and the Party. Indeed, as in other moments throughout her life, Healey's commitment to her son trumped all other matters.[93]

Other Party women had similar struggles with their Communist husbands, who wanted their wives involved with the Party but nonetheless resented the time these women devoted to the Party instead of their domestic lives. Throughout the 1940s and 1950s some of the most progressive Communist male leaders preferred their wives to stay at home and refused to consider them as equals in the Party. And the men who did allow their wives to participate in Party activities still expected their wives to care for the children, find external Party-approved childcare, and do housework on their own before pursuing their Party activities. Historian Kate Weigand has documented the "almost super human effort on the part of the wife to overcome the scorn and ridicule of the type of husband who feels his wife's place is in the home." But despite the hurdles they faced, according to Weigand, in attempting to be active Party members, these women gained opportunities, education, and self-confidence that they probably would not have found in any other organization.[94] Healey certainly found professional opportunities within the Party, but her relationships with men remained very conventional. The internal Party culture accepted distinct roles for men and women, which Healey and other female members accepted.

Furthermore, Healey joined in an era when the Party sought to frame itself as a group clearly within the mainstream of American politics and culture. As Weigand has documented, columns and "household corners" of Communist Party publications replicated what mainstream publications printed for their women readers. Just as popular magazines depicted the latest fashions, foods, and chores, Party papers mirrored these articles and replicated them for Communist women's consumption. Titled "Tips on Beauty," the regular column in the *Daily Worker* instructed women how to use foundation, how to incorporate the latest shirtwaist dress into their wardrobes, and even how to create perfectly rosy cheeks with rouge.[95] Aimed to entertain the female readers, these articles suggested that women should be concerned with feminine pursuits, which only reinforced different—and usually unequal—roles for Party members.[96] Although these gender-specific articles ceased by the late 1940s, while they lasted, they helped to blend American culture with Communist principles.

Healey even decided to sculpt her face to fit into traditional American concepts of beauty. Insecure her whole life about her appearance, Healey's self-perception was shaped by American beauty standards. She had internalized her insecurity about the size and structure of her nose so much that she had plastic surgery soon after marrying

Don Healey. And remarkably, after getting the surgery, she realized a renewed sense of self-worth, admitting, "I discovered that I held my head in a new way." Even more complicated, Healey was well aware of the contradiction because she remembered feeling "vaguely ashamed at having given in to what Mama deemed bourgeois standards."[97] Nevertheless, she managed to reconcile her dedication to end a class-based society with her commitment to capitalist constructed beauty standards. In this respect she replicated American ideas of beauty and femininity, but she did so within the context of the Communist Party. The indigenous Communist culture allowed Healey to subscribe to both ideologies simultaneously.

While it accepted some aspects of American gender roles, during the 1950s the Party did make a genuine effort to fulfill its commitment to women within the working class by attempting to organize them. In 1950 over 18.1 million American women worked outside the home, and one quarter of them had children. In this context, the Party began to recognize that the middle-class ideal of the housewife did not apply to many Americans. Early on in the postwar era Party publications criticized wage differentials based on sex, sought equal pay for equal work, and even espoused workplace-funded childcare facilities. Targeting industrial female laborers, they touted unions such as the United Electrical, Radio, and Machine Workers of America (UE) for proactively giving the same contracts to men and women and refusing to discriminate in its hiring practices. And each March, Communists celebrated International Women's Day, joining in worldwide celebrations to commemorate universal women's rights. Even tracing their roots to the suffrage campaigns of the late nineteenth century, each year Party members commemorated their own heritage in the women's movement and looked to the future, calling "for the advance of women into full political, economic, social, and legal status; and for the protection and education of children."[98] As with so many other campaigns, through its participation in these events, the Party worked to draw attention to larger class-based concerns about gender and family inequalities.

Nevertheless, at the same time that they called for full equality for working-class women, throughout the 1950s the Party forthrightly opposed the Equal Rights Amendment (ERA) on the grounds that "it would mean that neither the federal government nor any state could ever pass a law applying to women and not to men, however urgent and necessary the law might be. The amendment would do away with all the state minimum wage laws now protecting women from notoriously low wages in a number of industries. It would wipe out the laws on shorter hours of work for women, the protection against night work in factories, all labor legislation that protects women against especially dangerous occupations.... The proposed amendment would imperil all the hard-won legislation enacted to prevent the exploitation of women employed in industry."[99]

Simultaneously paternalistic and egalitarian, the Party's opposition to the ERA highlighted its broader ambiguity about gender. Members called for special protection for women who were forced to work because of the financial inequalities brought on by capitalism, and they also espoused workplace equality on all levels. In other words, a double contradiction applied here in the Party's position: capitalism forced women to work to make ends meet (assuming a separate spheres normality), but workingwomen should also be protected from dangerous and onerous tasks because of their natures (which the Party constructed to be physically inferior). Still, despite their inherently tension-ridden arguments, in calling for concrete workplace protections under the law, the Party gave more than a nod to women's rights at a time when mainstream political parties and labor organizations failed to recognize the importance of this issue.

At the same time that the Party started to confront the domestic concerns that arose in the new Cold War world, leaders and members alike were faced with a series of internal and international catastrophes that effectively isolated the national Party. In addition to the losses (both in terms of membership and influence) suffered because of the anti-Communist investigations, the Party reeled from a self-inflicted blow. In April 1956 Healey attended a large meeting of the National Committee in New York, where she heard first-hand from Khrushchev's first secretary of the Soviet Communist

Party that reports of Stalin's atrocities had all been true. She was utterly devastated by what she heard. "Within a half an hour I was convulsed with tears," she later recalled. "It was unbearable. Just this voice going on, piling up facts upon facts, horrible facts about what had happened in the Soviet Union during the years of Stalin's leadership."[100] It hit Healey particularly hard because she claimed to have never given a second thought to earlier reports of Stalin's show trials and executions because in her mind the "capitalist press" had created these stories for propaganda purposes. When she heard of the "wretched, bloody crimes," her world came crashing down: "It was hard to avoid thinking that we bore a significant measure of responsibility for them because we had denied the very possibility that such a thing could happen."[101] Although initially Healey did not know how to react, she decided to take the position that Whitney had chosen at an earlier moment of internal fracturing. This position would effectively sever the strong bonds between American and Soviet Communists and thereby enable a more independent radical movement to thrive in California.

Although personally devastated from learning about Stalin's atrocities, for the time being Healey had to wrestle with questions about how to handle the fallout of these revelations on the Party membership. Weeks after returning from the conference, still thoroughly dispirited by the reports, Healey struggled to write a May Day address to her Party members that would appropriately confront their new situation but also look forward to a new future. Refusing to simply accept the atrocities and move on, Healey searched for explanations about why the Soviet Union had become a haven for such autocratic violence: "We should have stated frankly that the building of Socialism in the Soviet Union was not the establishment of paradise on earth.... We Marxists should not have ever had such illusions for ourselves, nor passed them on, as we did, to others." But committed to moving forward and taking lessons on how to construct a better American Communist movement, Healey proceeded to reorient her Party around domestic struggles. To her the best way for the Party to survive and stay relevant in America was to continue pressing the issue of civil rights, though by the mid-1950s these struggles had taken on new dimensions in both the South and in Los Angeles.[102]

But despite her forward-looking approach, most Party members did not see much use in continuing their radical struggles through this discredited and beleaguered organization. Especially after the Soviet Union's 1956 invasion of Hungary, the California Party lost many prominent longtime members, including Healey's fellow Smith Act defendants. Even in 1956 Healey personally defended the Soviet invasion of Hungary "on the ground that the Communist Party had practically dissolved, and as a result here was both a danger of Western intervention and a restoration of reactionaries and even fascists to power."[103] In spite of her continued and relatively unwavering support for the Communist Party, in 1956 and 1957 Healey's Party confirmed that it had lost a significant proportion of its membership. Spiraling downward from its peak of 5,000 members in 1949 to 3,800 in 1955, by January 1956 only 1,970 people belonged to the California Party. Yet this number continued to fall even further; by July 1957 Party officials estimated a 25 to 30 percent drop in membership from the year before. And according to Healey, by the end of the decade the number continued to plummet; Los Angeles had fewer than five hundred card-carrying Communists. In other words, in little more than a decade the California Party had lost 90 percent of its membership (though in comparison to the national figures the Southern California branches fared slightly better, losing a smaller percentage of members).

This moment of desolation made the Southern California Party look inward and explore what it would take to transform it into a more relevant organization. Optimistically reporting in 1957 that the district still had seventy-five clubs and "to our knowledge no club has made basic changes except for the purpose of consolidation and greater educational opportunities," Party leaders asserted that a new focus on Mexican American affairs, youth, and local politics might reinvigorate the organization.[104]

In once again trying to pick up the pieces of a decimated radical community in Los Angeles, Healey's Communist Party tried to fight its way back to political relevance. Looking forward to a world without an iron curtain, the Party called for peace with the Soviet Union by ending nuclear testing and promoting disarmament. Negotiations over contentious issues such as the division of Berlin, it maintained, would surely bring an end to the stalemate that had nearly destroyed its standing in the past decade. The Southern California Party also became very critical of the Cold War military-industrial complex; especially in the quickly developing and heavily subsidized Southern California regions that Healey organized, the Party argued that the Cold War profited only large corporations. A Southern California Party report asserted, "The Cold War economy is not a good foundation for a prosperous future." Instead, the Party advocated retraining workers that would be displaced from war industries, investing in automation and technology, and increasing unemployment benefits.[105]

Attempting to connect Communists to the broader political and social climate of the 1950s, Healey saw great advantages in working within other activist struggles to bring racial equality to America and ultimately perhaps class equality. Tactically, the California Communist Party continued to build coalitions with mainstream political groups. In the 1958 statewide election, for example, the Party championed the sos (Save Our State) Committee, established by the AFL-CIO to coordinate a voter registration campaign targeting the working class. Politically organized workers, CP members recalled, had successfully forced the Democratic Party to adopt a more progressive agenda in the California elections. Moreover, in again calling for unity among black workers and those of Mexican descent across multiple industries and fields, the Party in the mid-1950s still aimed to work through conventional means to pursue its goals.[106] Healey warned activists that the path would not be easy: "Hell would freeze over before Socialism would come to America if we were to tell the working class that if they keep voting Socialist they can thereby achieve it. . . . It will take mass struggles such as the Montgomery Bus Boycott, plus the solidarity and strength of all

Labor to achieve such an end. This is the path of class struggle."[107] Healey still believed that class inequality was more important than racial inequality in America, but she realized, as Communists had in earlier generations and would again in the future, that significant support could be gained if she connected the two.

But Healey's national Communist comrades viewed her willingness to maintain coalitions with non-Communists with increasing skepticism during these years. Her vision for the Southern California Party appeared to be increasingly out of step with the Party nationwide, which preferred a centralized structure and third-party political strategy. By the mid-1950s national leaders took notice of these differences and became ever more frustrated with the independence of Healey's Party. The national committee placed blame for Southern California's strategies and policies directly on Healey herself. Openly hostile to her independent decision making, Ben Davis, a national leader, declared in 1958: "I don't think Dorothy should be chairman. If I can't speak about it in this national committee what am I supposed to do? Hide it? Not bring it out before the comrades? Well I tell you I don't think she should be the head of the party in California and ... a person with a line and the conduct and the behavior of Dorothy [should be removed]." This particularly heated speech came on the heels of Healey's public criticism of the national committee and of her support for the French Party's backing of the controversial Yugoslavian Communist leader Josip Broz Tito for his embrace of nonalignment in the Cold War.[108]

Although Healey's overt criticism and refusal to follow national orders irritated many leaders in the East, her local members supported her. Even as she decried the lack of internal Party democracy and butted heads with national leaders, she was rising to higher prominence. By the mid-1950s she served on the National Executive Committee and as the district organizer of Southern California. In her 1990 autobiography she insisted, "The internal power dynamics of the Communist Party at the top are more akin to feudalism than socialism."[109] While she was not as outspoken in opposing the Party organization in the 1960s as she became by 1973, when she resigned, at the time the Party clearly recognized that her criticism was a problem that it needed to resolve. But when faced with a decision over whether or how to rein her in, leaders in the East publicly decided to do nothing because she was so popular; she more than anyone else was the face of the Party in California. And because of this, she had a great deal more power than the Party leaders preferred.

As the national leadership continued to chide Healey for leading her Party in unorthodox directions, Southern California did carve out a place for the Communist Party in Los Angeles's rapidly expanding but polarized environment. Throughout the 1950s and into the 1960s Healey's Party made great strides in confronting local civil rights issues such as housing segregation. Keeping track of scholarly and government-sponsored studies about racially segregated housing patterns, the Southern California Party equipped itself for a long local fight for equality on an issue that linked both class and race discrimination. At Party meetings members regularly reviewed statistics that revealed vast income and standard-of-living gaps between black and white families. The Party noted that the median annual income of a white family in 1954 was $4,827, whereas for a nonwhite family it was $2,876, which they stressed was simply a continuation of centuries-long inequalities. The disparity amounted to intolerable racial and class inequality in the eyes of American Communists.[110] Healey also closely read a 1950 study about the racial attitudes of housewives living in integrated versus segregated housing projects. The New York scholars who authored the report found that only 3 percent of white housewives living in segregated projects reported knowing African American women "well enough to call them by their first names," whereas 77 percent of white housewives felt this way within the integrated project. Based on this evidence, the study concluded that "the [white] housewife in the integrated project expects more approval than disapproval from others in the project if she is friendly with the Negro people. . . . In contrast, the [white] housewife in the segregated project expects to be socially ostracized by the other white women if she is friendly with the Negro people."[111] Healey drew on this study to link the perpetuation of racism on a personal level to race-based governmental policies such as discriminatory housing patterns. On a broader level connecting racism to structural housing policies prompted the California Communist Party to mount a grassroots effort to end segregated housing throughout the state.

Indeed, when the Rumford Fair Housing Law banned restrictive housing covenants in California in 1963 (following earlier but less sweeping laws passed in 1959), the Party took it upon itself to ensure that the codes were obeyed and also sought to prevent the highly contentious law from being nullified by conservative lawmakers. By giving out flyers explaining that each resident had the right to file a complaint with the state if he or she suspected discrimination, the Communist Party attempted to take an active role in promoting government-ensured equality. The Party also formed a separate organization, the Fellowship for Advancing Intergroup Relations, or FAIR, which focused exclusively on housing desegregation and discrimination.[112] In addition to working through the government, Party members pursued the business end of housing segregation, compiling a list of real estate firms that pledged to follow fair housing laws. They then mailed the lists to California residents to advise them about which companies to patronize. One branch in Northern California, for example, calling itself the League for Decency in Real Estate, tracked the "sixty-eight companies in the two East Bay counties [that] have pledged themselves to uphold the Fair Housing Code."[113]

California Communists also challenged white Americans' financial sensibilities, which, Party members reasoned, might account for de facto housing segregation. Attempting to construct coalitions with other community activists, Party leaders encouraged all community members to attend a film screening about the myths and realities of property values in segregated and integrated neighborhoods. Produced by the American Friends Service Committee, this film highlighted an economist's study that concluded that there was no truth to the belief that integrated neighborhoods translated to lower housing prices. Instead, "the entry of nonwhites into previously all-white neighborhoods is much more often associated with price improvement or stability than with price lowering."[114] Ultimately, as California became polarized between an increasingly vocal yet oppressed minority population and an equally strident conservative group, Communists discovered they could once again become outspoken advocates for and participants in the state's civil rights movement.[115]

As Communists became increasingly involved with California's civil rights campaigns, supporters boasted and critics conceded that Healey personally had a great deal to do with the Party's persistence during the late 1950s and 1960s. She became something of a community celebrity by appearing regularly on multiple media outlets, particularly her own 1959 radio show on KPFK, *Communist Commentary*. "The most popular part of the show," she admitted, "was when I would take telephone calls and answer questions or get into arguments with the people who called in." Whenever the media wanted to get the opinion of a radical, Healey remembered, "in Los Angeles, it was my face that was shown most often; my voice that was heard."[116] This leading Communist woman's charismatic personality enabled her radical movement to stay afloat during the tempests of the Cold War. The FBI even wrote admiringly of her in confidential reports, noting that Healey was "considered extremely intelligent, capable, theoretically developed and effective as a Party leader. She works easily with other people, as evidenced by her command of the support of most of the leaders and members of the SCDCP [Southern California District of the Communist Party]."[117] Nevertheless, it was precisely at this moment of her ascendance to local fame that national leaders found it increasingly difficult to tolerate her.

In the 1960s Healey had won the admiration of the next generation of activists, baby boomers, but her success prompted fresh criticism from Party leaders in the East. Long before the student movement had fully emerged, Healey decided to reach out to college students across Southern California. Even disobeying the directives of the Party's longtime secretary-general, Gus Hall, Healey openly embraced the New Left. According to her, "Gus regarded the New

Left as a distraction or threat to our own political prospects rather than as a fertile field for our young people to work in."[118] Healey not only supported the chartering of the W. E. B. Du Bois Club, the third generation and Kendra Alexander's method of entry into the Party, but she also proposed working within Students for a Democratic Society (SDS) branches.

Although many New Leftists disregarded Communists as old-fashioned bureaucratic Stalinists, some of these groups made an exception for Healey and the Southern California Party. Socialists, liberals, civil rights activists, and professors alike regularly hosted her to speak on their college campuses. She spoke plainly and connected communism with their lives. In one campus speech Healey said, "I remain a Communist, despite harassment and persecution, because I believe in man's capacity to build a society where all men are free and where, therefore, each individual can freely develop." This core commitment to the Communist theory of universal equality—quite separate from the Party's reputation and operational structure—engendered sympathy and support from many listeners. Healey also distributed pamphlets that were intended to resonate specifically with New Leftists. With sections subtitled "The Joy in Creativity," "Those Who Refuse to Be Intimidated," and "The Right to Dissent," for example, Healey's Party sought to identify with students who were coming of age through the free speech movement.[119] In openly appealing to a new generation of activists, even acknowledging their privileged backgrounds, Healey tried to prevent the Party from becoming isolated and irrelevant in this time of transition from the Old to the New Left.

In reaching out to this new generation, Healey's Southern California Party developed positions and tactics that spoke to the new topics of concern. Her KPFK show served as a forum for Healey to regularly voice the topics on her mind. Connecting the Party's history of fighting class inequalities with the contemporary activist commitment to civil rights, for example, Healey maintained: "Over the years that I have been on KPFK a recurrent theme of my commentaries has been the overwhelming hypocrisy and mythology that permeates every aspect of U.S. life. I have tried to establish that the basic cause for this is the attempt to portray the government, and all our institutions, as being above contending classes; the myth that the working class has equal rights with the capitalist class, that the rich and poor have equal access to justice and equality, and that the institutions of government, education or mass communication ignore class interests and serve equally all sections of the population."[120] While Alexander's generation had started to take the lead in organizing broad-based leftist conventions and protests, Healey certainly did not stay on the sidelines with this new generation of activists. In effect she made their work possible because of the issues her Party pursued and the activists they sought to recruit. Reaching out to minority students became a distinguishing strategy of this branch. Without it Alexander may well have been persuaded to join other black militant groups that were popular with younger radicals.

Healey's name became so synonymous with leftist radicalism that she mounted a campaign to run as an independent candidate for Los Angeles County tax assessor in 1966. Running on a platform that proposed decreasing taxes for low-income and elderly Californians as well as raising property taxes for business and industrial property, she spoke all over the region. In the end Healey polled a remarkable eighty-six thousand votes in this countywide race (more than 5.6 percent of the total vote), reportedly more than any Communist candidate had received in an election since the 1930s, perhaps since Whitney's remarkable electoral campaign. Just as in the earlier decades when Anita Whitney's reputation had surpassed that of the Communist Party, enabling her to receive votes from unlikely supporters, Healey also won votes from many non-Communists. She admitted: "By this time I had become a kind of local institution, and I think I got the votes of a number of people who had simply stopped thinking of me only as a Communist and instead voted for me as Dorothy Healey, the local troublemaker. In this instance familiarity bred a measure of acceptance, or at least an absence of the fear and loathing that is usually elicited by the label 'Communist.'"[121] With her name so widely recognized, Healey's activism resonated with people and organizations well outside the Communist Party. Bridging political boundaries once again proved to be a hallmark of this local Communist.

Healey sought to take this increasingly mainstream outlook to the floor of the national Communist Party. Hoping to pursue topics of concern to her Party's new, younger constituency, Healey's 1966 report to the National Committee criticized the leadership and suggested new methods of activism. Leading the way into Alexander's generation, the Southern California District Convention addressed white America's "colonial occupation" of Watts, the need to promote coalitions with Mexican American labor organizations, and the escalation of the war in Vietnam.[122] Yet many of Healey's positions went unnoticed, as the national leaders felt she had become far too mainstream, or reactionary, in her analysis of politics. But Healey saw herself as reacting to the political circumstances of the day. She felt, for example, that the threat of the New Right, growing out of the John Birch Society in Southern California, far outweighed other political considerations. For this reason she believed that supporting the Democratic Party, as opposed to running Communist candidates on third-party tickets, was the best strategy for fighting the latest conservative movement, calling for a new kind of Popular Front strategy. But Hall had different ideas; he backed only Communist candidates and openly criticized Healey for her support of mainstream political candidates.

Tensions between Healey and the National Committee grew even worse in 1968, when, after she returned from a trip to Czechoslovakia, the Soviet Union invaded that country in August. To Healey the Czech Communist Party had appeared to provide an idyllic open atmosphere, encouraging discussion and democracy in their reformed country. Therefore, when the Soviets invaded shortly after her visit, she immediately defended Czechoslovakia. Dismissing Communist fears about capitalist influence in the country, Healey told her members, "I defended the Czech Communists' right to create their own vision of socialism … if the Soviet Union could guarantee the security of Cuba, half a world away, did it seem likely that

Czechoslovakia, bordered on three sides by Warsaw Pact nations, was in greater danger?"[123] On the heels of her very public criticism of the Soviet Union's decision, many Party members accused her of being anti-Soviet and even anti-Communist in speaking so candidly without the consensus of the Party. After all, she had violated Democratic centralism, the Party's operating structure that prevented public dissent once policies had been determined. According to Healey, this episode was the beginning of her exit from the Party.

Over the next couple of years Healey went further in openly clashing with the Party's national leadership circle. And as she publicly criticized the closed Democratic Centralist structure that prevented her from pursuing her local strategies alongside the national directives, Healey began to lose influence within the Party's ranks. By 1969 she withdrew from her leadership position altogether and retreated to the role of rank-and-file member for the first time in more than thirty years. Yet what finally brought about her formal withdrawal was the Party's criticism of the publication of the auto-biography of her friend Al Richmond, *A Long View from the Left*, who had also authored Whitney's Party-approved biography. When the Party dismissed its own journalist's account of his life because it had not been preapproved by the Party or published by its press, both he and Healey were incensed.

On July 9, 1973, she officially resigned from the Communist Party on her KPFK weekly radio show. She famously declared: "My hatred of capitalism which degrades and debases all humans is as intense now as it was when I joined the Young Communist League in 1928. I remain a communist, as I have been all my life, albeit without a party."[124]

Reeling from her public resignation, the National Party took bold moves both to criticize and distance itself from Healey. In December the Central Committee expelled her from the Party, months after she left, formally forbidding any current Party members from interacting with her. In addition, it countered her public resignation with an equally public press release, which read: "Of particular relevance to the behavior of Richmond and Healey is Article 7, Section 1 of the

Constitution, which declares: 'A member has the right, within the Party organization, to express openly and uphold his or her opinion or differences on any question as long as the Party organization has not adopted a decision. . . . After a decision . . . members have the right to reserve their opinion in the event of disagreement with a decision but at the same time they have the duty to carry out the majority decision.'"[125] When the Party voted to expel Healey, Angela Davis, her close friend and comrade of the third generation of Communists, refused to speak to her officially but phoned her and said: "Dorothy, I'm so sorry. I think you're wrong. But I'm sorry."[126]

By this point the next generation of Communists was in place to assume the lead. Davis and Alexander, for example, while once taking similarly independent positions as Healey, became Party loyalists who in the 1970s denounced her rogue "reactionary" ways. Healey's own animosity toward the Party leadership only deepened in the months following her departure. Likening some of the internal operations of the CPUSA to the Soviet show trials, Healey wrote in a letter, "In essence, there is no difference between . . . what was said and done during the Moscow trials [and] what was said and done during comparable attacks on comrades within our own party."[127] Yet she continued to correspond informally with several former comrades.

Upon leaving the Party, Healey heeded the advice of her son, Richard, who had become an organizer in his own right among non-Communist leftist activists of his baby boomer generation. By the end of the 1970s Healey became part of his New America Movement and ultimately the Democratic Socialist Organizing Committee, serving as vice president for the organization. Her political involvement did continue outside the structures of the American Communist Party, albeit in a more limited capacity.

In 1983 she moved away from Los Angeles for the first time in nearly a half century. She went to live near her son, daughter-in-law, and grandsons in Washington DC. Well into her eighties, Healey continued to participate in the radical community on the East Coast, still regularly hosting a radio show alongside Richard.

Healey died on August 6, 2006, at the age of ninety-one. Her obituaries sounded strangely out of place, commemorating as they did this radical woman from an era that seemed so distant.[128] They all shared their appreciation for Healey's remarkable life on the fringes of legal and political acceptance in California. Many contemporary observers found it difficult to look back at the life of this professional revolutionary woman. She transgressed so many political boundaries, but she also operated within multiple cultural and social constraints of mid-twentieth-century America. She constructed a distinct, indigenous Communist culture that at times flourished and at other times floundered but always endured throughout her tenure in Los Angeles. Indeed, regardless of the exceptional character of Healey herself, she successfully created a space for communism in California that ensured that the Party would last well into the next generation of leaders.

1. Charlotte Anita Whitney, Wellesley College Class of 1889 Alumnae Book. Courtesy of Wellesley College Archives.

2. Charlotte Anita Whitney, ca. 1915, during her membership in the Advisory Council of the Congressional Union for Woman Suffrage and while an officer of the Civic Association of California. Library of Congress.

TRYING TO BE MARTYR

Anita Whitney and Matron Gussie Kennedy
Checking In for 300-Day Stay That Ended in Few Hours

3. "Anita Whitney and Matron Gussie Kennedy Checking In for 300-Day Stay That Ended in Few Hours." *San Francisco Chronicle* / Polaris.

4. Ben Davis Jr., national leader of CPUSA, joins Dorothy in presenting food to Eugene Judd, UAW Local 216 official, during strike in 1946 at the Shrine Auditorium. From "A Tribute for Dorothy Ray Healey," 1983, Dorothy Healey Collection, California State University–Long Beach Library.

5. Dorothy Ray Healey, September 1976. Photograph by Lory Robbin.
Dorothy Healey Collection, California State University–Long Beach Library.

6. Dorothy Ray Healey, early 1980s. Dorothy Healey Collection, California State University–Long Beach Library.

7. Kendra and Franklin Alexander, 1970s. Courtesy of Giuliana Milanese.

8. Kendra Alexander, presentation as Communist leader, 1980s. Courtesy of Giuliana Milanese.

9. Kendra Alexander, personal photograph, 1980s. Courtesy of Giuliana Milanese.

The New Old Left

Kendra Harris Alexander, 1946–1993

On July 9, 1973, Dorothy Healey publicly resigned from the Communist Party on her weekly radio show in Los Angeles. Minutes after she finished her announcement, Kendra Claire Harris Alexander called into Healey's show and spent the remaining on-air hour debating parts of her reasons for leaving.[1] Although Healey had personally recruited Alexander into the Communist Party, in 1973 the national leadership decided that Alexander could represent her generation and speak on behalf of the national Party. Ironically, Alexander's new generation had grown out of Healey's own efforts to rebuild the Southern California Party after it lost most of its membership by the late 1950s, and now they stood ready to lead the organization. Alexander belonged to an African American and baby boomer constituency that Healey had arduously courted at the behest of the national leadership. But ultimately, because of Healey's vision, people like Alexander, who might otherwise have been drawn to civil rights or Black Nationalist organizations, felt compelled to join the Party because of its long-standing commitment to racial equality and workers' rights. Alexander became active in the civil rights struggles of the early and mid-1960s but then went on to become one of the most prominent and high-ranking Communist Party officials in the United States during the 1970s and 1980s. A native of Southern California, Alexander came to believe that true racial equality could only be achieved through the restructuring of the capitalist system, which, she believed, systematically fueled racism and discrimination throughout the country. The Party's concrete actions—ranging from organizing protests to reading groups—in addition to its explanations of poverty and ghettoization, strongly appealed to her generation of activists.

Alexander represented a new generation of Communist Party members and leaders who came of age during the Cold War, became politicized by their participation in the civil rights movement, but then quickly moved on to the Communist Party. This generation shared concern about local civil rights issues such as police brutality; it felt frustration with the limitations of the mainstream civil rights movement and the New Left, Black Power, mainstream political parties; and it was animated by Angela Davis's 1972 trial. This generation, the New Old Left, marks the beginning of the final chapter of the American Communist Party in the twentieth century. Because of the New Old Left, the Party in California, despite its small membership nationally, actively recruited a new core for its membership by focusing on the links between racism and poverty and by trying to unite the working class of all races. The New Old Left actively built alliances with civil rights, Black Power, and New Left organizations, but its members claimed a special foundational position in stimulating these movements and in criticizing them. In carrying forward this class-based understanding of the world, these young Communists sought to unify organizations around issues such as the Vietnam War, the draft, poverty, and police brutality.

Moreover, by the late 1960s, 1970s, and 1980s Alexander's Communist Party looked much different than it had in earlier decades. Not only were the members younger, representative of different class and educational levels, committed to multiple movements, and less obedient to the Soviet Union than ever before, but this Communist Party did not advocate revolution. Instead, its members firmly believed in a united progressive third party and agreed that democratic elections would be the most efficient way to reach this goal. While not entirely new (certainly in harking back to the Popular Front of the Great Depression years), this Party adopted many positions that would have been unimaginable in the revolutionary climate of the earlier twentieth century. By the 1970s the Communist Party changed its focus markedly and made building a "left-center alliance" a principal goal.

Kendra Claire Harris was born to Marjorie Jones and Sidney Harris on June 28, 1946, in Compton, a racially mixed neighborhood in Los Angeles. Her parents' settlement in the area did not follow the typical path of the Second Great Migration initiated by World War II. Wartime and then postwar industry had little to do with this African American family's experience. Instead, Marjorie Jones, a white nurse born to Salvation Army ministers in Canada, moved to Los Angeles in the 1920s and met Sidney Harris, a black working-class man from Compton. Although they could not marry because of California's antimiscegenation laws, Jones and Harris stayed together for more than a decade. Together they bore two daughters, first Patrice in 1943, then Kendra three years later. While Jones and Harris separated when Alexander was three and she lived primarily with her white mother, her father lived nearby in Richmond Farms, a neighborhood in Compton, and maintained a relationship with his daughters throughout most of their childhood. Working as a police officer, post office employee, and bus and truck driver, he lived in an African American community and strongly supported union activism. Similarly, Jones had socially and politically leftist—and often radical—leanings, spending most of her adult life as the single working mother of biracial daughters. While she never joined the Communist Party officially, she supported socialism and became an activist who raised her children in a racially diverse community.[2]

In spite of Alexander's mixed-race complexion, she identified as black. Her community, her friends, and her school all reflected an African American sense of identity, although she lived with her white mother and remembered being acutely aware that her family's biracial composition upset others. As a young girl in Los Angeles, she did what her peers did: attended school, played with friends, and went with her mother to rallies. She attended Centennial High School, where she had an active social life, which included a black boyfriend, Robert Brown. When she graduated high school in June 1964, Alexander enrolled at Los Angeles State College (which in 1972 became California State University–Los Angeles [Cal State–LA]). Here Alexander found the people and organization that stimulated her moral and political consciousness. Early in her first year, one of Alexander's professors introduced her to the Congress on Racial Equality (CORE).[3]

In the fall of 1964 it made sense for Alexander to join CORE, one of the most reputable civil rights organizations in Los Angeles and nationwide. With increasing national attention focused on the organization's successful nonviolent techniques used during the Montgomery Bus Boycott of 1955–56, CORE had quickly earned nationwide recognition by young people. As the civil rights movement sparked national interest in the South, locally, in Southern California, CORE attempted to engage and respond to the concerns of the hundreds of thousands of first-generation African Americans living in California. The Second Great Migration caused Los Angeles's black population to swell from 75,000 in 1940 to 650,000 in 1965. The racism experienced by these new residents looked different than that practiced in the South; California Communists, of course, had experience in identifying this manner of racism and protesting against it. And during the war and early postwar years new chapters of civil rights organizations such as CORE learned to identify and confront these de facto forms of discrimination in California. In Los Angeles, for example, African Americans expressed particular frustration with the scarcity of jobs, inadequate schooling and public transportation, and police brutality. As a strategy to respond to these problems collectively, CORE leaders encouraged participation in both national and regional campaigns.[4]

During Alexander's years with CORE the organization made concrete and locally significant headway in pursuing racial equality. With its mission devoted to "eras[ing] the color line through direct, nonviolent action," CORE certainly appealed to Alexander's budding interest in transcending and obliterating racial boundaries.[5] Like the Communist Party in its heyday, however, CORE demanded time and commitment from its members. Alexander's CORE required its members to join issue-specific committees such as the Housing Committee, the Employment Committee, the Mexican-American Committee, the Police Malpractice Committee, and the Action Committee. At the same time, the local chapter combined entertainment and parties with meetings, which gave the members a sense of community and belonging.[6]

Among its local programs, CORE initiated and administered Operation Jericho. Under the program every weekend CORE members made "door-to-door calls in the Negro community, enlisting support, starting neighborhood actions to tumble down the walls of segregation and discrimination in schools, housing, and employment."[7] Claiming success in the early 1960s, for example, by making Safeway Stores end its racist hiring practices, CORE established a strong reputation for winning local civil rights battles. Furthermore, its members earned recognition for protesting Los Angeles builders' restrictive housing sales policies. In April 1963, for example, CORE confronted Don Wilson, a suburban Los Angeles builder who, according to the organization, "does not like to do business with Negroes at his Dominguez Hills and Southwood Riviera tracts." To protest these practices, CORE members "established picket lines, dwell-outs and sit-ins on the tract," which prompted members of the American Nazi Party to turn out as counter-picketers.[8] These bold confrontations gave CORE and its causes in Los Angeles ample press coverage.

The fall of 1964 was an exciting time in Los Angeles for the young and strikingly idealistic Alexander. Her college experience introduced her to a new group of peers that complemented the activism she had experienced as a child in Compton. Friends recalled that she seemed to come into her own organizationally—if not ideologically—at college. In addition to its activism, CORE introduced Alexander to one of her closest lifelong friends, Marian Gordon, a young black woman from Philadelphia. Gordon was three years older than Alexander and helped to lead her to the civil rights clubs, then ultimately to the Communist Party. Gordon's parents had been Communist Party members, and she had attended the June 1964 founding convention of the W. E. B. Du Bois Club, a student-oriented Socialist youth organization that would later play a pivotal role in Alexander's politicization. In other words, the relationships Alexander established at college helped her to construct and sustain an enduring activist community and identity, in much the same way that the Communist culture captivated Whitney and Healey.

These relationships contributed to Alexander's decision to engage in the national civil rights movement in early 1965, during her first year of college. She first found herself moving toward the center of national struggles when she volunteered for what became one of the largest demonstrations in Los Angeles. Planned in conjunction with Martin Luther King Jr.'s famous march from Selma to Montgomery, Alabama, in March 1965, Alexander sought to identify with southern protestors. In Selma, March 7, 1965, the first day of the attempted march, became known as "Bloody Sunday," when state police and troopers attacked with billy clubs and tear gas the nearly six hundred civil rights marchers. The attack on peaceful protestors at the Edmund Pettis Bridge just outside Selma, which was covered by television reporters, compelled King to call for a second march later that week. In Los Angeles CORE and other local branches of civil rights organizations collectively organized a solidarity protest in which they explicitly criticized the governor of Alabama and the Selma police department's unconstitutional attempts to block black voter registration drives and called on President Lyndon Johnson to intervene to "insure the rights of all Alabama citizens."[9] In addition to petitioning local, state, and national authorities, Alexander's Los Angeles branch of CORE led prayer vigils, marches, pickets, and demonstrations for three days.

The coordinated protest became one of the largest ever in Los Angeles, which resulted in the biggest mass arrest in the city's history. The vast majority of these arrests occurred because of the sit-ins, lie-ins, and kneel-ins held throughout government buildings in the city. Among the 101 arrests Alexander's occurred on Wednesday, March 10, 1965, the second day of the collective sympathy protest. Alexander spent the morning protesting outside of the Federal Building. Police took her into custody and charged her with "obstructing the administration of justice (in the federal courts), interfering with movement of U.S. mail and illegal assembly in a federal building."[10] Activists debated whether to support those arrested. While the Civil Rights Congress (CRC) and both the Western Christian Leadership Conference (WCLC) and the Southern Christian Leadership Conference (SCLC) deplored the participants' illegal actions as violations of their nonviolent commitment, SNCC and CORE leaders stood behind the motives of those arrested and excused their actions as amateur yet passionate.[11] Alexander had thus already landed at the center of a debate within civil rights groups and had positioned herself on the Left side of the discussion.

Alexander's first arrest and her two and a half days in jail turned out to be transformative experiences. Marian Gordon recalled the details of the ordeal. Of the 101 arrested, women numbered between 30 and 40. For both nights in jail the guards herded the women into one cell. The women tried to keep up each other's spirits by singing songs and telling stories. Gordon noticed that some of the more politically advanced women who understood the methods of suppression in jail handled the experience better than the younger women. Alexander did not fit into this category. Despite her emerging political consciousness, Alexander hated being in jail and swore she would never get arrested again. On a personal level she was fastidious about cleanliness, and she found it difficult to shower and maintain her usual standard of appearance in the jail. Furthermore, she faced a very sobering experience when on the last day the guards put the activist women into regular jail cells and mixed the prisoners in with the larger population. Witnessing and interacting with the broader imprisoned population jarred Alexander to the point that she and her other female friends remembered and discussed the incident for decades to come.[12] In the end, however, the protest, the arrest, the jail experience, and the community all solidified Alexander's mounting commitment to activism.

In the spring of 1965, still Alexander's first year at Cal State–LA, she had signed up through CORE to participate in the Council of Federated Organizations' (COFO) summer activities in the South aimed at integrating public facilities. An umbrella organization seeking to unite activists from across the country around specific civil rights campaigns in the South, COFO hoped that a diverse group of activists would converge on sites of the most intense racism. By the age of nineteen Alexander had become a devoted civil rights activist. Because of her commitment to the movement, she attended a charter meeting that formed a Cal State–LA chapter of the W. E. B. Du Bois Club in the winter of 1965. Franklin Alexander, the national coordinator of the club, spoke at the inaugural meeting.[13]

A few years her senior, Franklin Alexander came from a Chicago family with deep activist roots. His older sister, Charlene Mitchell, had joined the Communist Party in Chicago during World War II. After the war the family moved to Los Angeles and worked as union organizers, but Franklin Alexander found his calling in his abilities to appeal to students seeking a more wide-ranging Socialist agenda beyond civil rights. In early 1965, when Kendra first met Franklin, friends remarked that it was his activism and sense of purpose that sparked her attraction to him; she ended her high school romance to pursue the relationship. Indeed, over the next several months this political relationship turned deeply personal.[14] And just as Dorothy Healey had blended her personal and political identities through her romantic relationships, Alexander started down the same path.

At the same time that Alexander found Franklin and the Du Bois

Club in the winter and spring of 1965, she stayed devoted to CORE and her earlier commitment to travel to the South for the summer. Accompanied by Marian Gordon and three other students from Cal State–LA, Alexander had pledged to participate in the summer activities. But before COFO allowed them to go, the leaders required summer participants to attend a two-week-long training session in the Midwest. There Alexander learned the tactics of nonviolence and also how to protect herself from attacks. CORE leaders instructed Alexander to "not show anger by look, speech or manner" and "in case of violence from others . . . remain calm and nonviolent. Do not raise your hands even to protect yourself."[15] CORE's deep commitment to nonviolence also translated into demands that members appear and act "as presentable as possible." Alexander had no problem with this requirement; she always dressed in fashionably appropriate clothes that fit her slim physique and were appropriate to her leadership role. These physical and behavioral characteristics, CORE believed, would deflect criticism from white southerners that accused female protestors of being sexually suggestive. CORE leaders stressed to its members the importance of proper dress and manners as ways to maximize the impact of their integration and voter registration efforts. Furthermore, to create a more diverse collective of activists in the South, COFO separated students from their friends. The organization sent Gordon to Jackson, Mississippi, while they sent Alexander to Jonesboro, Louisiana, with a group of several other mixed-race students from around the country, none of whom she knew.

Alexander spent the summer working to integrate lunch counters, bathrooms, and bus stations and attempting to register voters. Interacting with southerners on a daily basis introduced her to a segregated reality that as a native Californian she had not witnessed before. She also learned about the structures of the civil rights movement in general and the daily oppression and relentless poverty those in the movement and its leaders faced. Several years later Alexander recalled having talked with African Americans in the South about their appreciation for the thriving civil rights movement. She recounted that black southerners understood the importance of maintaining a strong and reputable leadership within the movement, but they also recognized the leaders' fear that they might be discredited. According to Alexander, this tenuous identity prevented activists from developing strong voices on issues that did not directly relate to racial inequalities in the South. In the wake of the 1965 escalation of the Vietnam War, for example, southern members of CORE privately expressed deep opposition to the purpose and conduct of the war. Yet they cautioned their leaders not to take a bold stance denouncing the war, fearing they would be accused of being Communists. She later wrote: "I recall vividly the discussion in the Black community . . . about the war in Vietnam. Most of the older Black people were opposed to the war but were vehemently opposed to leaders of the civil rights movement taking that position. Their argument was simple and to the point: 'If we say we're against the war they'll call us Communist and that will destroy the civil rights movement.'"[16] Thus, they had learned lessons from the Cold War and were determined not to be sidetracked by international conflicts.

This anxiety about red-baiting in the South indeed had a decades-long history. In *Hammer and Hoe: Alabama Communists in the Great Depression* Robin Kelley traces the emergence of a distinctly southern Communist Party in the 1920s and 1930s to show how the Party and its appendages combined their class and racial analyses to attract both desperately impoverished people and industrial and farmworkers to their movement. Organizing through unemployed councils and within mines and rural farming areas, activists dared to cross racial barriers for the purpose of advocating a united relief program during the Depression years. In forging such alliances, the Party even teamed up with the liberal Southern Conference for Human Welfare (SCHW) to promote southern workers' economic interests. In successive decades the Party's decline in the South started with the Popular Front and accelerated during the Cold War, when anti-integrationists condemned civil rights activism as Communist subversion. Nevertheless, as Kelley and Glenda Gilmore, in *Defying Dixie:*

The Radical Roots of Civil Rights, 1919–1950, suggest, the Party's legacy indirectly contributed to the civil rights movement of the 1960s.[17]

Historians David Garrow and Jeff Woods have also traced the ways that opponents of civil rights used the fear of communism to discredit the African American freedom struggle. In *The FBI and Martin Luther King, Jr.: From "Solo" to Memphis* Garrow explains how King's associations with former Communist Party members made him vulnerable to habitual surveillance and blackmail during the 1960s. In particular King's close relationship with Stanley Levison, a wealthy New York attorney with financial ties to the CPUSA in the mid-1950s, drew substantial attention from the FBI. Repeatedly warned by government officials and activists about the suspected Communist ties of Levison and other SCLC officials, King was well aware of the FBI's attempts to connect the Communist Party with the civil rights movement.[18] Similarly, in *Black Struggle, Red Scare: Segregation and Anti-Communism in the South, 1948–1968,* Woods highlights the crossover between Popular Front supporters and members of the liberal interracial social justice organization, the Southern Conference Educational Fund. Members such as Anne Braden, for example, held strong Socialist beliefs but also maintained close ties to SNCC and its famed leader Ella Baker. According to Woods: "It was the tendency among southern conservatives to equate Communism with socialism, socialism with liberalism, and liberalism with an assertive federal power. Thus it was natural for them to portray events in Little Rock as a long stride toward the development of a Soviet-style, collectivist police state in America."[19] These imagined connections remained front and center on the minds of many civil rights activists, especially the church-based leaders who knew how easily the entire movement could be discredited by red-baiting attempts. Yet because of their caution, Alexander felt that movement activists sacrificed broader goals that included a peace agenda for the more immediate causes of legal integration in the South.[20]

Still, while participants in the civil rights movements were keenly aware of the dangers of aligning with Communists, they privately recognized the important contributions of individuals. Alexander claimed that hundreds of Party members traveled south to fight alongside civil rights activists starting in the late 1950s. She followed in the footsteps of Robert Kaufman, for example, a young Jewish Communist from Los Angeles, who started his activism in 1959 and went on to participate in a 1964 Freedom Ride to Houston, Texas, where he faced arrest, beatings, and jail time.[21] Nevertheless, with the exception of northern and western Communists such as Kaufman, who had personal ties to the civil rights movement, the Party as a whole recognized the reluctance of civil rights organizations to accept its aid and in turn stayed away from the public face of the movement, at least in a national official capacity.

On a personal level Alexander's summer in the South not only awakened her to the oppression, the struggle, and the movement, but it also taught her about the intractability of poverty and the value of a broader class-based approach to confront racial inequalities. When she returned from her enlivening summer, she started her second year at Cal State–LA. By this time Alexander's life centered around campus- and community-based civil rights and political activities.

Alexander simultaneously held membership in both CORE and the Du Bois Club, and the year after her summer in the South, in 1966, she officially became a member of the Communist Party. Thirteen years later she reflected: "I was one of those young people who went South in the summer of 1965 to fight freedom's cause. For me it was the startling disparity between our assault on the legal barriers of segregation (the fight to integrate restaurants and toilets) and the minimal impact this had on the terrible poverty most Black people were forced to endure in the South, and in my birthplace of Compton, California. It was this contradiction which led me to seek more fundamental solutions to the oppression of Black people. I found those solutions in Marxist-Leninist theory and within the Communist Party USA."[22]

Whereas many young female participants who became radicalized in the southern civil rights movement tended to join New Left, Black Nationalist, or women's liberation groups, Alexander chose to enlist with the Old Left. Her decision to enlist with the Communist Party seems quite natural given the political and social climate of Southern California; after all, this was Healey's territory. Before leaving for the South in 1965, Alexander already had a connection to the Du Bois Club and had started to develop a Marxist analysis of the inequalities in her world. Both her organizational ties to the Communist Party and her personal experiences with urban racism and poverty allowed Alexander to make conclusions about the Left earlier than other students.[23] Whereas other students from California, such as Mario Savio, who traveled South to participate in the civil rights struggle determined race to be the central contradiction that prevented African Americans from attaining equality, Alexander sought alternative explanations. As a result of the summer of 1965 and her earlier political experiences, Alexander decided that the entire capitalist ruling class, rather than simply elite whites or men, used racial oppression as a tool to maintain class distinctions.

The Party's class-based analysis took on new dimensions in the context of the 1960s. After all, Communists could indeed claim to be the historical heirs of early efforts to combat racism, which struck a chord with some members of this new generation. They proudly and correctly declared that the Communist Party in Los Angeles had confronted white supremacy and agitated for civil rights long before many other organizations came to the fore. Earl Ofari Hutchison has explained that as far back as the 1910s, "Communist Party members could rightfully boast that they broke American racial taboos by supporting social equality and mounting national campaigns against Jim Crow laws and lynching, as well as running black candidates for every office from Vice President to city council."[24] And to demonstrate their own commitment to civil rights, Party leaders encouraged its white members to date nonwhite members. By the 1940s the Communist Party proved its exceptionalism by forcefully pushing for civil rights in Los Angeles, in spite of the broader community's widespread indifference and hostility to the subject. As evidenced by Whitney and Healey's own experiences, racial inequalities remained a top priority of this nearly five-decade-old organization, even in California, a state with comparatively less racial violence than other states. Thus, by the time civil rights became a national discussion, the Party could highlight its early role in local civil rights issues such as demanding swimming pool integration, fielding complaints about police abuse, and picketing venues that refused service or employment to blacks. It was this legacy that made it, in the words of historian Josh Sides, "perhaps the most outspoken and militant advocate for black equality in postwar Los Angeles."[25] Although it was limited in terms of actual African American participants—at the peak of its activity the Southern California Party could claim only 10 percent African American membership—the Party's historic commitment to racial egalitarianism appealed to Alexander. Indeed, when the Party's ideas about the link between class and race seeped into her emergent understanding of the world, they inspired this activist to devote the rest of her life to pursuing them.

The Watts uprisings, as radicals called them, were also an important element in Alexander's ideological conversion, notably occurring the same summer she traveled south. Triggered by the August 11, 1965, public beating and arrest of Rena Frye for protesting the arrest of her son for drunk driving, the ensuing riots led to 34 deaths, 1,032 injuries, 3,952 arrests, and forty million dollars in damage.[26] In all, as many as 10,000 people participated in the protesting and looting, which lasted for seven days. A report issued by the governor's office nearly four months after the uprisings documented the destruction. Rioters, the report said, "looted stores, set fires, beat up white passersby whom they hauled from stopped cars, many of which were turned upside down and burned, exchanged shots with law enforcement officers and stoned and shot at firemen. . . . The disorder spread to adjoining areas, and ultimately an area covering 46.5 square miles had to be controlled with the aid of military authority before public order was restored."[27] While seven major riots had occurred in other non–West Coast cities in the preceding summer, the 1965 Watts Riots inflicted the most widespread damage to people and structures and were followed by many more summers of equally intense uprisings.

As the state later concluded, Los Angeles was a tinderbox ready for the explosion of frustration in August 1965. It had the most inadequate public transportation system of any major American city, a history of failed federal antipoverty programs, and according to a statewide report, "the most extreme and even illegal remedies to right a wide variety of wrongs." In the initial weeks and months following the summer's uprisings, the governor's commission made a somewhat realistic—if not dire—diagnosis and projection for the state. It urged an immediate response lest "the August riots may seem by comparison to be only a curtain-raiser for what could blow up one day in the future." Specifically, the commission encouraged the government to bring employment to the community, to restructure the education system to include preschool education and special vocational courses, and to direct law enforcement to focus on crime prevention and improving community relationships.[28] Despite these explanations of the material conditions that had caused the riots and the commission's indictment of the government and community for allowing such conditions to prevail, the uprisings had only a small impact on regional and national attitudes toward poverty and inequalities. More often than not, official reports and commentaries tended to condemn the violence alone without dwelling on the environment beyond the days of rioting.

Nevertheless, among Watts-area supporters the riots fundamentally affected the character and tone of social movements and activists across the country. Watts changed the geographic axis of the civil rights movement and shifted the focus away from the South alone. It also led people of all races to examine inequalities in their own backyards. Further, it radicalized even more of Los Angeles's residents in the struggle for civil rights and social justice. In the immediate weeks and months following the Watts uprisings, dozens of organizations moved into the neighborhoods seeking to understand its causes and trying to advocate for greater community unity.[29]

The complete shake-up started by the Watts Riots drove the Du Bois Club and the Communist Party to actively promote their ghetto initiatives. The Du Bois Club was primarily a student-run organization that combined a civil rights agenda with a broader class-based critique of American society in the 1960s. Nationally formed in 1964 out of splinter organizations from across the country seeking to unify the causes of civil rights, peace, poverty, unemployment, and social justice, by 1966 the club became relatively popular in California on college campuses and in urban ghettos. Claiming to be an "action oriented multi-issued socialist youth organization," it recruited 2,500 members comprising forty chapters nationwide by December 1966.[30] The organization appeared to work in tandem with other civil rights organization. On the West Side of Chicago the Southern Christian Leadership Conference (SCLC) donated full-time staff to support the blossoming Du Bois Club. And like CORE and COFO, the Du Bois Club instituted summer work programs so that students from around the country could work in cities to organize the oppressed. But unlike CORE and COFO, which sent their workers south, the Du Bois Club focused its efforts on northern industrial cities such as Chicago, Cleveland, Detroit, and Philadelphia. Remaining dedicated to raising awareness among blacks in these industrial centers, the Du Bois Club sent fifty full-time workers to these four cities in the summer of 1967.[31]

The Du Bois Club initially struggled with its relationship with the Communist Party. While the club had a class focus, it was not directly related to the Party—at least not during the first two years of its activism. In the fall of 1965, for example, when Bettina Aptheker, daughter of the famous Communist scholar Herbert Aptheker, publicly announced that she held membership in both the Du Bois Club and the Communist Party, the Du Bois Club had a difficult time deciding how to handle the situation. Knowing that Aptheker's affiliation with the CPUSA would associate the Du Bois Club with the Old Left rather than with the more vanguard New Leftist movements that seemed to recruit more youthful support and members, the national Du Bois Club wrestled with the issue of her mixed allegiances but ultimately decided to send out statements supporting her to all of its local chapters, writing: "Miss Aptheker's action has opened up new opportunities to bring the issue of civil liberties to the American public, and specifically the issue of anti-communism, which is the bulwark of all conservative and anti-democratic forces in the United States. For the movement to seize this opportunity to encourage discussion and defense of Miss Aptheker's statement will be to strengthen all the forces now working for peace, civil rights, and an extension of democracy to all Americans."[32]

The Du Bois Club linked the Old Left to the New by acknowledging the loathsome connotations of the Party for younger activists but also by refusing to accept the stigma and highlighting the joint agendas that all of the organizations shared. Younger activists, particularly students involved with the New Left and Students for a Democratic Society, disdained the Old Left, just as they criticized the "establishment" government at home; both, baby boomers asserted, were concerned with the old Cold War struggles and served to distract from other problems. Yet for Alexander, because of the local focus and agenda of Healey's Communist Party, it still seemed a relevant way to confront inequalities around her. Bridging a perceived divide between Old and New Leftists through coalition building proved to be a centerpiece of the 1960s Southern California Communist Party strategy.

Furthermore, the Du Bois Club, both before and after its publicly acknowledged connection to the Communist Party (in the wake of Aptheker's affiliation), received support from wide-ranging sources. In 1966 Anna Louise Strong, a progressive American journalist who traveled to the Soviet Union and China to report on communism, corresponded with the Venice, California, branch of the Du Bois Club. She expressed interest in its hallmark pamphlet, *The Fire This Time* and voiced support for its numerous publications "on the struggles in Los Angeles."[33] Cesar Chavez also recognized the importance of the organization in his attempts to build social justice solidarity. When the Perelli-Minetti and Sons grape growers and wine producers' workers went on strike, for instance, he notified the Du Bois Club and informally advocated a boycott. Seeking support for the boycott and eliciting sympathy over "whether in good conscience, you should handle the products of a company that refuses to bargain with its striking farm workers," Chavez clearly sought backing from what he envisioned as a broad-based community of support in Los Angeles.[34] His letter highlights that the Du Bois Club constituted a rather far-reaching coalition of organizations that consistently relied on each other and supported each other's agendas.[35] Hoping to create an open exchange of ideas about race, class, and poverty, young Californians from diverse racial and socioeconomic backgrounds expressed a direct interest in hearing from radical groups in the mid-to-late 1960s.

As one of these young hopeful students who bridged organizations, generations, and political ideologies, Alexander solidified her commitment to activism by the time she started her second year at Cal State–LA in the fall of 1965. Her final pledge came early in 1966, when she married Franklin. Their wedding took place at the First Unitarian Church of Los Angeles, a famously progressive church that had once invited Paul Robeson to sing in its auditorium when no other Los Angeles venues would allow him to perform because he had been blacklisted for his political activities. Rev. Stephen H. Fritchman, a "principled" progressive pastor, according to Alexander's friends, performed the small wedding ceremony in his study at the church.[36] Back in 1951 the House Un-American Activities Committee had accused Fritchman of being a Communist. Throughout the intense years of the Second Red Scare, the government repeatedly subpoenaed him to testify, correctly linking him to the Communist and liberal communities of Los Angeles. But despite the heavy surveillance, throughout the 1950s and 1960s Fritchman continually criticized the establishment and made his church a popular haven for those who sympathized with his views.[37] Indeed, Alexander's friends still proudly recount that such a revered man had performed the Alexander's poignant marriage ceremony. Moreover, the wedding reinforced generational connections among members of the Left in Los Angeles. That a distinctly baby boomer couple had sought the participation of a Cold War–era critic of the Red Scare confirmed the relationship and respect between these two generations of activists.

Furthermore, the fact that Alexander chose to enter into a marriage at the young age of twenty reflects her conventional attitude toward such gender-specific institutions. The decision certainly seems to fit with that made by her predecessor, who had chosen to marry within the Party at an even younger age. Even from this early age, Alexander followed in the antifeminist footsteps of her predecessors, particularly Dorothy Healey. Unlike them, however, within a decade Alexander would be forced to confront and reconcile her class-based understanding of the world with a gender-based one because of the pressing arguments asserted by second-wave feminists. Still, just as Healey had done three decades earlier, Alexander bridged her personal and political life through her marriage. Continuing her forebears' reluctance to personally question the historically unequal arrangements of marriage in the United States, in 1966 Alexander's lifestyle choices mirrored those of the earlier generations of American radicals.

After their wedding Alexander continued as a student at Cal State–LA for the remainder of the year but became more involved in Los Angeles activism through her participation in multiple civil rights, political, and socialist organizations. After such a turbulent summer in 1965, Los Angeles's civil rights and political landscape began to change early in 1966, as civil rights organizations were becoming more radicalized nationwide. That year internal problems with finances and membership started to weaken CORE's influence and membership.[38] The organization virtually folded in Los Angeles in 1966, and other, less centralized groups absorbed most of its members. By this time many members, including Alexander, had begun to question the effectiveness of these national nonviolent civil rights organizations. Especially in the wake of the uprisings, when new groups tried to move into impoverished neighborhoods and politicize the citizens, the national groups tried to support and empower locally based community interest groups working on the ground. But because they lacked internal organization and leadership, many of these organizations also did not last long.[39] A lack of coherent leadership among most activists groups was one reason the Du Bois Club and ultimately the Communist Party continued to appeal to Alexander.

Through the Communist Party and the Du Bois Club, Alexander worked to organize ghetto residents. Just after the August 1965 Watts uprisings, Alexander became active in the neighborhood's Nickerson Gardens housing project when she ran into two female residents with whom she had grown up. These women introduced Alexander to other residents and ultimately permitted her access to the community. Over the next couple of months she chartered a tenants' union in the neighborhood.[40] According to club records, Alexander worked openly through the Du Bois Club, an admittedly Socialist organization, to coordinate residents to rally for cheaper and more stable rents and better community assistance programs. Fulfilling the Communist Party's mission, she tried to organize the most oppressed residents living in the most impoverished and violent neighborhoods. By early 1966 the Du Bois Club proudly announced that Alexander's activity in the Nickerson Gardens project was a success and should be a model for organizing community members around the city.

Taking its cues from the youthful, determined, and moderately successful Alexanders, the Du Bois Club worked to establish itself as a foremost black Socialist club in California. It consciously tried to recruit young African Americans who perceived their racial oppression as a function of their economic condition. The club's leaders embraced Franklin Alexander's ability to recruit members to the Du Bois Club because of his identity as a black man. Evidently, the Party had no theoretical or practical concerns about recruiting support and unity from non-Socialists. Still, leaders cautioned that this form of recruitment should not end merely in social work in impoverished communities. They seemed keenly aware that they should not become a social service organization because that alone would not restructure society to promote equality across race and class lines: "Our purpose in the community should not be solely to 'help those poor people' but to work with them in changing our society."[41] To further this goal, in Watts the Du Bois Club supported four key issues: campaigning to expunge criminal records of people under age twenty-five; using public schools on nights and weekends to teach auto, printing, and woodworking; teaching residents of ghettos how to pass civil service examinations; and encouraging trade unions to have apprenticeship programs for unemployed youth.[42] Thus, leaders tried to balance revolutionary goals with a more immediate agenda, which included empowering those who had been institutionally oppressed.

The goals and public tactics of these young radicals clearly caught the attention—and triggered the anxiety—of local government officials in 1966. Mayor Sam Yorty called Du Bois Club organizers "left-wing agitators who try to throw gasoline on any disturbance that breaks out." Angered by club leaflets decrying police brutality, Yorty singled out Alexander by name. The mayor alleged that Alexander drove through Watts in a "loudspeaker-equipped car," shouting accusations of police brutality and distributing leaflets. The Alexanders' participation in the leafleting convinced Mayor Yorty of the Communists' infiltration of organizations established with the intention of rebuilding Watts. In particular, the Du Bois Club's criticism of the police department worried Yorty to the point that he argued it could "destroy law enforcement and the law and order spirit." He continued to charge that the Communist Party might also force its way onto the statewide campaign agendas through its influence in the Watts community.[43] Indeed, Alexander had earned a reputation as an established radical activist, and now, in 1966, government officials noticed her ability to move between organizations to agitate communities.

By the summer of 1966 Alexander opted to leave college and dedicate her life to the revolution. Just as radical commitments had convinced Healey to leave school more than three decades earlier, Alexander decided to abandon formal education and throw herself into a thriving radical movement. Also like Healey, Alexander's radical actions drew the attention of authorities. In May of that year the federal government observed that Alexander "was one of four organizing members of the Committee to End Legalized Murder by Cops." Dominated by Communist Party members, this organization intended to work with residents of Watts in the months and years after the uprisings.[44] Also during this time she continued to work for the Du Bois Club.[45]

But in the summer of 1966 Alexander had grown increasingly devoted to the Communist Party for practical and ideological reasons. By 1967 the Du Bois Club found itself in financial turmoil, and the Alexanders focused more of their efforts on the older and more established organization that had sustained itself for nearly fifty years. Alexander's transition to focus more exclusively on the Communist Party fits with the Party's evolving identity: by the late 1960s the Communist Party designated positions in the leadership for African Americans and formed separate black club cells. In the wake of the riots the Party reasoned that "black people suffer a special kind of oppression, thereby requiring a special approach to solving their problems."[46] In adopting a black separatist position, the Party had returned to its roots.

Dating back to the founding of the Party, Communists worldwide had a long history of advocating for black nationhood. This orientation reached back to the Sixth World Congress of the Comintern in 1928. From the 1920s through 1958, when James Jackson drafted "New Features of the Negro Question in the U.S.," the Party supported a policy of black nationhood. According to this statement, in the Black Belt areas of the South, where Jim Crow laws oppressed and humiliated virtually all black residents, the only way for blacks to truly gain self-determination was to separate as their own nation. "To speak of integration without equality, without freedom, is dangerous demagogy," the Party proclaimed. "Without equality and freedom, integration is an impossibility."[47] This policy connected national oppression, working-class oppression, and racism as toxic effects of capitalism, just as other radicals came to advocate decolonization and third-world nationalism as ways to confront the problems internationally.[48]

In 1959, however, the Party adopted Jackson's pro-integrationist position and abandoned the black nationhood stance, which fell more in line with the mainstream civil rights movement and the improving economic status of some northern African Americans, thanks to World War II. Becoming a Party strategist in her own right, Alexander wrote on the topic, "One of the major contributing factors in our change of policy in 1959 from nationhood and the right of self-determination to our present policy of the struggle for full economic, political, social and cultural equality of all Black people within the U.S. was the change in the class composition of Black people themselves."[49] The economic opportunities provided by World War II and the postwar industrial expansion thrust millions of blacks into a new class and offered them the chance to attain a new middle-class status. In other words, the Second Great Migration that drew blacks into northern and western cities employed by nonagricultural industries provided an opportunity for them to make the shift "from a primarily peasant class to an overwhelmingly working-class people."[50] This geographic, demographic, and economic movement of blacks throughout the country, the Party reasoned, meant that they were now being exploited as members of a working class rather than oppressed as citizens of a nation.

But in the late 1960s the Party shifted its stance once again and returned to its original identification of African Americans as a uniquely oppressed class. In part the Party's renewed definition of African Americans as a separate class led the Alexanders and Franklin's sister Charlene Mitchell to form an all-black Che-Lumumba Club in late 1967 in Los Angeles (named after famed Argentinian Che Guevara and Congolese Patrice Lumumba). These three founding members argued that an all-black leadership and racially separate Communist Party cell were necessary to organize in the most poverty-stricken, racially segregated neighborhoods, especially within the particular environment of Southern California. And they did so with Healey's approval.

At first Communist Party members worried that organizing blacks separately to foster a collective black consciousness inside the Che-Lumumba Club would have detrimental effects on whites, who would have no choice but to organize only as whites, and this strategy would once again mean an abandonment of a class-based understanding of inequalities in their world. Consequently, national and state leaders cautioned, "totally separate organized efforts can only add to that wall [between the races]."[51] But ultimately in Southern California a few key longtime black members convinced the Southern California district of the merits of a separate black cell. Charlene Mitchell argued that separate clubs served the interests of some of the most oppressed because "the usual meaning attached to integration will not bring equality to a people who have been systematically disenfranchised from every aspect of the economic, social and political life for hundreds of years."[52] In other words, just as legal integration did not translate into de facto integration at polling stations or universities, simple pronouncements of equality would not necessarily foster it within Party cells. While the national Party did not consistently take such a sensitive approach to the delicacies of racial equality in internal Party and community organizing, the Southern California leaders carefully considered it.

When the Southern California Party returned to this racially separatist approach in the late 1960s, it still had to justify this theoretical position to the broader white membership, who generally subscribed to a class-based understanding of the world. But rather than justify it in theoretical terms, both the Du Bois Club and the Che-Lumumba Club argued to the national Communist Party that black separatism was necessary for recruiting success: "The role of the white organizers in the negro community has been, for years, that of the social workers, the 'do-gooder.' This, together with the rise of nationalist tendencies in the negro ghetto, serves to make it virtually impossible for the white organizers to be greeted as other than the stereotype of the social worker."[53] Arguing for pragmatism and efficiency in their attempts to enlist sympathizers in black neighborhoods, Party leaders decided that nonwhite clubs should form and dominate in this area. However, they agreed to this strategy with a caveat: these nonwhite organizers should ultimately introduce ghetto residents to the Party's broader goals by thinking of ways for white members to earn the respect of these potential black members. Whites were told, for example, to be at the forefront of organizing committees to defend blacks who had been victims of police abuse. According to national Party records, "Such a committee organized in the white community could serve to build negro/white unity by instructing white communities on the police harassment in the black ghetto, while serving to give the black community some reason for confidence in white folks."[54]

The Communist Party intended its discussions about separate black cells as a response to the broader radicalization of the civil rights movement, initiated by SNCC's expulsion of its white members when it radicalized in 1966 and bolstered by Stokely Carmichael's coining of the phrase *Black Power*. Some liberal nonviolent civil rights organizations, including CORE, attempted to present a unified front for equality, refusing to expel white members and issuing statements such as "[We] believe that Black Power is entirely consistent with our philosophy and our goals." But even civil rights groups that resisted the call for Black Nationalism found themselves becoming more radical in response to it.[55] Upset over the sluggish pace of improvements in racial relations and issues of economic equality, by 1967 many activists came to believe that pressing for equality "by any means necessary" would be the only way to achieve social change.[56] And the Communist Party, Du Bois Club, and Che-Lumumba Club in particular felt compelled to engage in this dialogue about black separatism in order to maintain their relevance on the civil rights and radical fronts in Los Angeles.

Within the Che-Lumumba Club both Kendra and Franklin Alexander served as Marxist ideological instructors as well as day-to-day organizers. They led meetings on college campuses, in community centers, and among workers' alliances. By late 1966 the Che-Lumumba Club and the broader Party apparatus empowered the Alexanders to raise community awareness and create solidarity against the institutional racism that plagued Southern California.[57] What distinguished their new cell from other racially conscious community organizations, however, was the way its members conceived of community, racial, and class inequalities.

The Che-Lumumba Club, the Communist Party, and even the Du Bois Club's explanations for the multiple uprisings that occurred in 1965 and 1966 collectively centered on the intersection of race and class inequality. "One of the major causes for the Los Angeles explosion is poverty," some of their leaders proclaimed. "The sort of poverty from which there is seemingly no escape. The kind of poverty which isolates the Negro from the mainstream of American life, decrees that he live in substandard housing for most or all of his days, denies to him the quality and quantity of education enjoyed by whites, prevents him from learning a skilled trade, forces him to accept lower pay than whites for the same work, keeps him subject to a much higher rate of unemployment than whites experience, and robs his children of those inalienable rights of liberty, the pursuit of happiness, and even life."[58] In other words, the Che-Lumumba Club connected the institutional discrimination with a perpetual cycle of subordination that occurred in all realms of minorities' lives.

In Los Angeles, club members argued, the police department's and city administration's arrogance and disregard for conditions in the ghettos made these inequalities all the more obvious. They named Los Angeles police chief William H. Parker as the prime culprit in fostering such racist attitudes. And he seemed to do his best to play the role of an ignorant authority figure; in an often-quoted 1965 interview with the local CBS television station, Parker referred to blacks as "monkeys in a zoo" and used phrases such as "By 1970 Los Angeles will be 47% Negro. How are we gonna live with that?"[59] The Communist Party used the police chief's racist attitude toward Watts residents to prove that African Americans needed to be engaged in a colonial struggle within the United States. "Watts is comparable to a colonial area occupied by an invading armed force," the Party argued, "subject to the constant pressures of that alien army."[60] Staking claim to an argument used several years later by Third World Left organizations such as the Black Panther Party, the Communist Party compared the oppression of minorities in the United States with colonized peoples in the Third World.[61] Healey, Charlene Mitchell, and other Southern California leaders pointed to Chief Parker's language about "enemies" and comparisons such as "We're on top, and they're on the bottom" to explain the relationship between police and residents in ghettos.[62] Police oppression amounted to more than a power struggle and violation of civil liberties, according to the Party. Instead, the eruption of violence—and the police and city government response to this violence—signaled a colonial struggle between an oppressed nation and its colonizers.

The Los Angeles city government responded to these allegations by blaming the Communist Party for exacerbating problems in an already racially polarized and poverty-stricken environment. In the aftermath of the Watts uprising, when organizations tried to unite community residents, Los Angeles mayor Sam Yorty attacked the ideal of unity as a Communist scheme. Ironically, he was right. In an interview on CBS's *Face the Nation* Yorty attempted to dismiss the riots and community members' distrust of the police department as "old-time Communist tactics."[63] In this case Yorty was using the decades-old tactic of rationalizing criticism of the government as Communist-inspired plots. But this time Los Angeles residents disregarded Yorty's allegations. In these neighborhoods the Party continued to grow.

In a detailed list of grievances and solutions targeted directly at Watts's economic and social problems, the Los Angeles Du Bois Club branches proposed more than two dozen concrete changes for the community. These proposals, which Alexander helped draft, included requiring police officers to complete two years of liberal arts postsecondary education, providing universal medical and dental coverage, and standardizing food and transportation prices throughout the city to avoid unfair cost inflation for ghetto residents. The club also called for urban renewal and beautification projects, job training programs, the prohibition of derogatory and racist language, and stronger roles for labor unions in the ghettos. Du Bois Club members believed that working for equality in this one corner of the city would lead to a more just society for everyone. As the most oppressed of all working people, African Americans had the capacity and the passion to bring about social revolution throughout the country. "The Negro revolt" that was growing and maturing in Watts, wrote the Du Bois Club, "will eventually do more to bring true democracy to these United States than any other single factor in the life of the nation."[64]

Within this context of social and racial rebellion and intensified organization, the federal government heightened its surveillance of Alexander. Throughout the spring of 1967 the FBI observed both Alexanders as they expanded their activist reach across the nation. According to FBI surveillance records, Kendra Alexander organized "disruptive activities and racial agitation on the campus of the Texas Southern University in Houston, Texas."[65] The Alexanders worked to connect the student movement to what they understood as an ongoing working-class struggle. This pragmatic strategy characterized Alexander's efforts to bridge perceived divides between the Old and New Left. It also reflected Dorothy Healey's efforts to make the Communist Party relevant for the next generation.

To create the New Old Left, the Alexanders worked to build leftist alliances through the New Politics movement in 1967. Coming from the peace movement, the civil rights movement, the Mississippi Freedom Democratic Party, and the student protest movement, New Politics leaders claimed that their "origins lay quite deep ... in the anger and frustration of the un-represented and the alienated." Broadly, the New Politics program sought to connect the oppression caused by U.S. imperialism abroad with poverty and inequality at home. Laying blame loosely on the establishment—represented by two-party politics—and the limits of liberalism, they vowed never to let the "community be dissolved by the shadowy deals and promises of the 'Old Politics.'"[66] The New Politics coalition hosted a series of conferences in California throughout 1966 that consistently drew crowds over two thousand. Speeches about poverty, labor, and racial oppression in Los Angeles dominated the regional agenda. The pinnacle of the movement came, however, when remarkably diverse activists coalesced over their much-anticipated national New Politics Conference held in Chicago over Labor Day weekend in 1967, the summer before the legendary protests at the Democratic National

Convention. Alexander attended the conference as a delegate for two black radical organizations, the Black Caucus and Black Resistance to Wars of Oppression.

In the months leading up to the New Politics Conference and anticipating the cross-organization political alignments that might emerge, the Du Bois Club changed its emphasis from local Los Angeles organizing to promote a third-party national ticket in the 1968 election, a position that had already been promoted by the Communist Party for several years. Beginning in the mid-1960s, the Party sought "a coalition of popular movements" that emphasized "the interconnection between peace and all other progressive goals."[67] As part of Southern California's New Politics coalition, members ran as candidates in state and local elections. Campaigning in 1967 for the state board of education, for instance, a teacher, an ACLU secretary, an SDS organizer, and a professor represented the New Politics platform of "end[ing] military intervention in our schools." They proposed to establish student-run "peace panels" and to abolish the ROTC in high schools. And they advocated supplying free breakfasts and lunches, providing libraries and remedial reading help, and reducing salaries of administrators to match those of teachers. Alexander supported this new local group's platform as it built national momentum.[68]

In spite of such expansive goals, the national New Politics Convention failed to unite the alliance of leftists that it had originally envisioned. The convention itself only amplified ideological, organizational, and personal differences among the various New Left, Old Left, Black Power, and civil rights representatives. At the Chicago sessions activists disagreed about how to prioritize their goals and strategize for social justice.[69] Indeed, whereas Alexander bridged these organizational divides with some success in California, the Chicago convention did not connect diverse activists even of the same generation. Her role in Chicago highlights the exceptional nature of Alexander's Communist leadership style. Like Whitney and Healey, Alexander proved to be exceptional in her ability to move within and between radical organizations, but there were limits.

Outside California, in fact beyond Southern California, this grass-roots radicalism could not unite even sympathetic radicals in 1967.

Although the New Politics convention proved divisive for activists across the country, the following year's turbulence temporarily reunified the New Old Left. April 4, 1968, stood out for most young socially aware baby boomers. Rev. Martin Luther King Jr.'s assassination on that day in Memphis, Tennessee, occurred during his visit to participate in a march to promote the cause of striking sanitation workers. News of his assassination sparked outrage and riots in cities across the country. That evening Alexander, her friend Marian Gordon, and another young black Communist woman were traveling from Brooklyn to Manhattan to attend a Marxist study group at the national Party headquarters. When they arrived at the Party school, the famous theoretician Herbert Aptheker told the three women of the assassination and of the unrest that was unfolding across the nation. They promptly cancelled the study group and returned to Brooklyn to coordinate their Party's response. On the subway ride back to Brooklyn, a shocked and on-edge Alexander confronted a white police officer. According to Gordon, Alexander perceived an insult from an officer on the train, to which she angrily responded by verbally confronting him. No arrest occurred, but Gordon remembered how King's assassination proved to be an emotionally charged event that stunned Alexander and virtually all activists. In the wake of his death, Alexander and other radical activists realized that while critical of King's goals and tactics, they relied on him as the popular leader of the civil rights movement. His death not only personally drove Alexander to an emotional outburst on the subway, but it shook the broader movement's sense of identity.[70]

In the post-King era of polarization, Alexander continued building her radical career in the New Old Left. Attending a Communist convention on the "dynamic left" in New York in the summer of 1968, Alexander first encountered the national leadership's struggle to determine its relationship with the New Left. On several occasions Gus Hall, the Party's longtime leader, notoriously labeled New Leftists as "reactionary, anti-working class, and petit bourgeois radicals."[71] Healey opposed Hall on the issue, as she and many of the younger members sought to build bridges to the New Left. Of the three hundred delegates in attendance at the national convention, Carl Bloice, a close friend and associate of Alexander's, estimated that 25 to 30 percent were youths who may have been skeptical of Hall's condemnation. When questioned about the relationship between the Old Left and the New, Bloice told a reporter: "There's no generation gap in the Communist party.... We youth are proud of the principled position the party has consistently taken on public issues."[72] Alexander and her cohort of baby boomer Communists agreed in 1968 that tactically the Left should unite. And because they offered a potential new source of support among the broader Left, Alexander's generation began to gain power within the Party.[73]

The Party seemed to make an effort to bridge the generational divide when it chose a presidential candidate. In the summer of 1968 it nominated Alexander's sister-in-law, Charlene Mitchell, as its presidential candidate. Then thirty-eight, Mitchell had earned the nomination because of her long-standing membership in the Party and specifically because of her leadership in the realm of "black liberation." In fact, days before her nomination she chaired an influential panel on the topic at the special convention in July. Mitchell's candidacy marked the first time that the Party had run a presidential candidate in twenty-eight years, and it was the first time that a black woman had ever run for president. Her running mate, Michael Zagarell, a twenty-three-year-old white man from the South Bronx who directed the Party's youth program, was selected despite his age, which constitutionally prohibited him from actually serving as U.S. vice president.

At the nominating convention members "chose Mrs. Mitchell, who was described as a great-granddaughter of a slave, and Zagarell because the party considered 'black liberation' and the alienation of youth as two central issues facing the country and the party felt the candidates would appeal to members of these groups."[74] Clearly, the New Left did influence Communist leadership despite what Hall had said. Moreover, beyond the presidential nominees, virtually the entire platform in 1968 also appeared to be in sync with other New Leftists. Like many New Leftists and antiwar protesters in 1968, Mitchell pledged to "halt the war in Vietnam and divert military spending into needed domestic programs, especially in the cities."[75] Although they only received slightly over 1,000 votes in the national election (third-party voters generally devoted their ballots to the Peace and Freedom Party, which received over 130,000 votes), the Party did for the first time in many years attempt to publicly unite Old Left with New Left programs.[76]

The same summer of 1968, after Mitchell's nomination, both Alexanders traveled to Bulgaria to attend a World Youth Festival and then went on to tour the Soviet Union for the first time.[77] Alexander had now become fully committed to the international Communist community. Holding membership in the CPUSA in 1968 meant pledging allegiance to the Party's internal democratic centralist structures, which had managed to keep it afloat for decades. Whereas before 1968 Alexander affiliated primarily with regional or local Communists, the international Communist tour signaled her commitment to the Party's broader directives of worldwide revolution, and in 1968 it still meant devotion to Soviet-style communism. The August 1968 Soviet invasion of Czechoslovakia proved to be a turning point for Healey and her tacit support for Soviet leadership; Alexander left no personal reflection about the Soviets crushing reformist impulses within Czechoslovakia, but even if the violence did make her reticent, she clearly continued to see the merits of belonging to the worldwide Soviet-led Communist movement. While antidemocratic by definition and unappealing in governing style to many activists of her era, the Party for Alexander presented an opportunity to relate to an international world of leftists. She spent the next year developing her identity within this far-reaching Communist and radical network.

But even as a Party-line Communist, Alexander continued to reach out to other groups and individuals with whom the Party might ally on specific priorities. In July 1969 she attended an Oakland conference that attempted to unite Black Power, Communist, free speech, and New Left interests. Angela Davis, a close friend and recent recruit to the Party, accompanied her. Davis had met Franklin and Kendra in 1967, when she was a philosophy graduate student studying under Herbert Marcuse at the University of California–San Diego. Davis first became attracted to the Southern California Party when she watched Franklin chair a workshop on "Black Politics and Economics." She remembered: "His presentation was clear and incisive: power relationships which placed Black people at the bottom stemmed from the use of racism as a tool of the economically ascendant class—the capitalists. Racism meant more profits and, insofar as white workers are concerned, division and confusion."[78] Although she did not officially join the Communist Party until July 1968, Davis quickly developed close personal and political relationships with the Alexanders and their cohort of radical activists in Los Angeles. As an activist, Davis helped to forge a coalition with the Black Panther Political Party (not to be confused with the Black Panther Party for Self-Defense, or BPP), a group of black intellectuals devoted to analyzing various black movements and inserting a Marxist analysis into the struggle for black liberation.[79]

Like Alexander, Davis joined the Party because its leaders convinced her that its long-standing theoretical sophistication balanced with its practical organization would help it prevail in the face of less-experienced radical groups.[80] She chose to join the Che-Lumumba branch because its "primary responsibility would be to carry Marxist-Leninist ideas to the Black Liberation struggle in L.A. and to provide leadership for the larger Party."[81] As leaders and representatives of the Che-Lumumba Club, Davis and Alexander traveled to Oakland in July 1969 to participate in "A United Front against Fascism," a conference named and convened by the Black Panther Party to liken fascism to racism in the United States. As Davis explained in her autobiography, the conference was "one of the most important political events of the season. It established the basis for breaking out of the narrow nationalism so prevalent in the Black Liberation Movement and pointed the way for alliances between people of color and white people."[82] Just as Alexander planned to construct coalitions with non-Communist radicals, Davis hoped for the same multi-issue alliances.

Despite the enthusiasm of activists such as Davis and Alexander, seeking and maintaining alliances with Black Nationalist organizations, particularly with the Black Panther Party, proved challenging even for black members of the CPUSA. While specific conferences, conventions, and events united leftists and radicals across the nation, the organizational links did not typically last beyond a few years. The BPP operated most dominantly and extensively in Northern California, whereas most leading black members in the California Communist Party lived in Southern California. And while the Panthers adopted Marxist rhetoric, they did not see themselves as natural allies of the CPUSA because they distrusted the Party's ties to the Soviet Union. Nevertheless, Che-Lumumba Club members certainly aligned with and supported the BPP in Southern California as part of a broad community of radical black activists attempting to address problems in black neighborhoods.[83]

As soon as the Oakland conference concluded, Davis and Alexander departed for Cuba by way of Mexico City. According to the official Party account, the women traveled there "to work in the heroic 10 million ton sugar cane harvest on that Caribbean island of socialism."[84] In 1969 Cuba established a nationwide campaign to process more sugar than the island had ever produced. Up-and-coming revolutionaries in their own right, Alexander, Davis, and many other young American radicals wanted to join in the celebration. On their journey, however, Davis learned that "romanticizing the plight of oppressed people is dangerous and misleading." Working and living alongside people who toiled daily in the fields gave the women a new view of the struggling Socialist nation. Nevertheless, the two black women felt embraced by the welcoming people and warm culture, which deeply affected their impressions and memories of the country, especially its regard for racial minorities. They became convinced on the trip "that only under socialism could this fight against racism have been so successfully executed," which they witnessed by meeting black leaders of Cuba's economy, government, and school system.[85]

At the end of the intense and busy summer of 1969, Alexander and Davis returned home to Los Angeles only to find themselves thrust into the middle of an entirely different sort of controversy, Davis's own academic career. In the fall of 1969 Davis had plans to start a job as an assistant professor of philosophy at UCLA. Upon her return from Cuba, she discovered a series of newspaper articles planted by the FBI attacking the department for hiring her—a member of the Communist Party, a Maoist, a member of SDS, and a participant in the Black Panther Party. Under the very public direction of Governor Ronald Reagan, the chancellor of UCLA instructed the philosophy department to formally ask Davis whether she held membership in the CPUSA, a membership that had been prohibited for all UC employees since 1949. While the philosophy department condemned the regents' insistence that Davis be interrogated about her political affiliations, her "comrades in the Che-Lumumba Club immediately committed themselves to building a campaign within the Black community in Los Angeles around [her] right to teach at UCLA."[86] While the investigation was under way, a court order restored Davis's one-year contract to teach courses in the 1969-70 school year, which brought her under intense scrutiny by students, faculty, and government officials alike. Moreover, when Davis ultimately affirmed her membership in the Party, she experienced even more severe public criticism and violent threats, which required round-the-clock accompaniment of her by at least one male security guard from the Che-Lumumba Club.[87]

Alexander led the Party's efforts to defend Davis's right to teach at UCLA.[88] She helped to ensure Davis's personal safety and coordinated her public statements. But after a yearlong struggle, the regents decided that Davis's political speeches were "unbefitting a university professor." And at the end of the exhaustive public debate, the administration declined to reinstate Davis to teach courses in future years.[89]

Although no longer a professor, Davis had attracted considerable attention to the Communist Party in Southern California. The publicized war between state officials and Davis's radical black and intellectual supporters also helped to build bridges between Black Nationalists and Communists in Los Angeles. Throughout 1970 Alexander continued to work within the Che-Lumumba Club and coordinate radical activism in Los Angeles. This position often brought this Party cell into alliances with the Black Panther Party and the Black Student Alliance.

Both blacks and leftists shared a common interest in securing a united resistance to police harassment and brutality in the community. This alliance showed its power during a showdown between police and black and leftist activists on December 8, 1969. When police tried to break into Black Panther Party headquarters, the armed nationalists refused to open the door and barricaded themselves inside. Police cordoned off the area outside the building. Alexander, Franklin, and several other Che-Lumumba members came to watch the developing confrontation and to plan a strategy. When an officer discovered Communist literature on Franklin, he took him away and kept him in a patrol car for several hours. The standoff between the BPP and the Special Weapons and Tactical Squad of the LAPD lasted nearly all day. At one point in the afternoon shots rang out from both sides, leaving several Panthers injured.[90] With Jefferson High School only a few blocks away, students inside grew angrier throughout the day because the community was in a state of virtual lockdown. When the police finally released Franklin, he went inside Jefferson High School to help plan a rally in the gym to protest the police raid on the Panther office. Although the Panthers ultimately left the building and acceded to the arrest, Davis and Franklin addressed an angry crowd and called for a general strike in the black community for two days later. Davis's interpretation of this daylong incident was that "the police had crept into the community . . . and launched a murderous attack on the community. . . . But with the support of the people outside, the Panthers had emerged victorious."[91] In other words, she and her cohort of black Communists viewed this intense day as just one more example of police harassment and attempted colonization of a black neighborhood, though this time the community succeeded in protecting itself from oppression by the colonizers.

As a measure of the coalition's success, on the day of the called strike an estimated eight to ten thousand people turned out for a protest at city hall. Attendees carried signs and banners "demanding an end to police repression, demanding a halt to the offensive against the Panthers, demanding immediate release of the captured Panthers."[92] With allegations of aggression, racism, and genocide, activists' speeches aimed to unite African Americans in Los Angeles against the police department and for the rights of the Panthers. Davis and the Alexanders felt triumphant after this successful protest, which temporarily quelled reports of police violence in the area.[93] Still, in the months surrounding these moments of protest, police and the FBI raided the Alexanders' Los Angeles homes at least three times. Accused of robbery, possessing illegal weapons, laundering money, and other illegal political activity, both Alexanders were keenly aware of the government's surveillance of them, in much the same way Healey was well aware of the officials who trailed her.[94]

Alexander and the Che-Lumumba Club were also deeply involved in the trials of radical black activists, some of whom had been key leaders in the Black Panther Party. The Che-Lumumba Club first adopted this issue when it formed a committee to defend three prisoners at the Soledad Prison. When a grand jury determined that prison guards had been justified in their killing of three inmates during a riot at the Soledad Prison in the Central Valley, the prisoners murdered a guard in retaliation on January 16, 1970. After eight days of interrogating the 146 inmates of the wing where the murder occurred, prison officials accused John Wesley Clutchette, Fleeta Drumgo, and George Jackson (men who were all serving time for burglary or robbery) of having perpetrated the murder. Alexander had been friends with Clutchette in high school, which only piqued her interest in the case. In addition, George Jackson corresponded with Davis who, along with Alexander, worked to bring national attention to the case.[95] Supporters of these men established the Soledad Brothers Defense Committee, which attracted sponsorship from diverse figures, including Noam Chomsky, Jane Fonda, Allen Ginsberg, Benjamin Spock, and a slew of prominent ministers, professors, and governing officials. College campuses, black communities, and leftist circles united by distributing "Free the Soledad Brothers" buttons and by publicizing the accusations brought against the three men. Arguing on several points about the legality of charging the three prisoners with the murder, the defense committee members hinged a large part of their argument on what they determined to be a paradox of the criminal justice system: "Three black prisoners are dead at Soledad. This is called justifiable homicide. One white guard is dead. This is called murder."[96]

In the midst of the campaign to raise funds for the defense, Davis developed a close personal relationship with one of the accused, George Jackson. She and Alexander, among other devoted radicals, traveled regularly to Northern California to attend Jackson's trial. They also devoted a great deal of time to speaking in the men's defense at public rallies. In June 1970 Davis appeared at a rally for the Soledad Brothers in front of the State Building in Los Angeles. Standing as a bodyguard on one side of Davis was George Jackson's seventeen-year-old brother, Jonathan Jackson. He proudly situated himself as a protector for the brilliant and beautiful supporter of his brother. Davis had become such a close friend of the Jackson family by this point that she had temporarily moved into the family's home in Pasadena. The following month she and Jonathan traveled to Northern California to visit George.[97]

On that fated visit north, on August 7, 1970, Davis became the centerpiece of a murder case, a nationwide manhunt, and a massively publicized trial. During the trip Jonathan Jackson took several weapons into the San Rafael, California, courtroom where James McClain, a friend of George Jackson, was to be tried for a prison stabbing at San Quentin. Jackson hoped to free his brother by taking hostages in the courtroom. He ended up taking hostages and killing three people, including the judge and two inmates. Police killed Jackson in the shootout that ensued. Three of the guns used in the shootout

had been legally purchased and registered to Angela Davis. By August
11 this piece of evidence led the police to seek Davis's arrest for aiding in the murder. They accused her of having bought three of the
guns and conspiring to use them in the shootout. In response Davis
fled Los Angeles, was placed on the FBI's Ten Most Wanted List, and
hid in multiple cities throughout the country for two months while
she evaded arrest. When the FBI found her in New York on October 13, 1970, and extradited her to California, they charged her with
murder, conspiracy to commit murder, and kidnapping because of
her indirect involvement in the courtroom shootout.[98]

Both before and after her arrest, Davis's closest connection was
to the Communist Party, an organization that by this point was no
stranger to high-profile court cases. Kendra Alexander, the closest
personal, political, and professional friend of the fugitive, found herself in the FBI's sights. From the moment Davis fled Los Angeles, the
FBI watched and trailed Alexander, anticipating Davis would seek
her close friend's support. Following her eventual arrest and temporary imprisonment in New York, both Franklin and Kendra Alexander visited her while providing legal support from the CPUSA.[99]

Davis's imprisonment and trial in Northern California dominated the Party's agenda for nearly two years. Kendra and Franklin
proceeded to coordinate Davis's legal team and devised a worldwide
campaign to free Davis and clear her of all charges. To live closer to
her friend and to coordinate her legal defense on a daily basis, in
1971 Alexander moved to Oakland to serve as Davis's legal investiga-
tor and to coordinate the political defense campaign.[100] Most notably and publicly, the Alexanders coordinated the National United
Committee to Free Angela Davis (NUCFAD), which drew national
and international attention.

Across the country the NUCFAD organized protests, marches, and
speeches in prominent public areas to attract as much attention as
possible to Davis's case. Seeking to broaden the interest of Davis's
supporters to larger issues of race, class, and imprisonment, the Party's rallies attempted to promote "the direct link between racism
and repression, between racism and arrests, and between racism and

the prison conditions which create prison rebellions." Party officials argued that all prisoners were victims of the capitalist system of class exploitation. Furthermore, nonwhites faced the double burden of class exploitation and racism. Interestingly, Communist leaders did not situate gender in this paradigm as a third level of oppression.[101] Instead, they used these race- and class-based connections to build bridges around Davis's trial. While closely working with the CPUSA throughout this campaign, Alexander and most other Party members gladly accepted support from other organizations but maintained full authority over running the campaign.[102] They permitted unions to circulate petitions to their members to urge the court to grant Davis bail. Some media companies and publishers also chose to support the committee in order to gain interview access to Davis's team.[103] The SCLC and Black Caucus backed the NUCFAD because they believed Davis to be innocent of her charges. Even student organizations such as supporters from the University of Wisconsin held rallies and published pamphlets asserting "she is being prosecuted because she challenged the social order."[104] And most famously, the BPP became intimately connected with the trial because of its connection to the Soledad Brothers and its experience with the prison system. Thus, throughout 1971 and 1972 liberal as well as radical organizations pledged their allegiance to Davis's innocence. The Communist Party in California once again leveraged its position as a leader of radicals and established a broad coalition around her trial that succeeded in crossing civil rights, Black Power, radical, progressive, and liberal boundaries. Just as Whitney's and Healey's rights to free speech had drawn important liberal support for their trials much earlier in the century, Davis's trial once again appeared to follow similar patterns.

But in the radical climate of 1971 the Communist Party stood at the forefront of the case, deliberately seeking a renewed public interest and expanded membership base. The Party played a prominent role not only in the public relations of the case but also in the legal strategizing. Davis, Alexander, Mitchell, Davis's lawyers, and other leaders tried to determine the best legal and public strategies to win the most support. In a February 7, 1972, letter to Davis responding to a television interview she had done with journalist Cecil Williams, for example, the legal team informed her she must "deny any knowledge that Jonathan or anyone else for that matter was planning to bring off August 7th."[105] She agreed to comply with this strategy but insisted on declaring her understanding of Jackson's frustrations, which had led him to commit the courtroom murders. While her lawyers worried that this tactic could force the trial into a struggle over the defense of the Communist Party, they agreed to defend Davis as a Communist. Her lawyers feared that popular support, particularly among blacks, would diminish if they saw the trial centering on the Communist Party. One lawyer argued that Davis "must explain that she could not have participated in August 7th, because her *total* experience teaches her that August 7th could not have worked and was an improper means of struggle, and not the type in which she herself had become involved."[106] In this sense Davis, her lawyers, and the NUCFAD consciously agreed to abandon some of the most radical criticism of the prison system and racial and class oppression, in favor of presenting a united coalition to free Davis. Here, as in trials past, Party leaders agreed to tone down some of their revolutionary rhetoric in hopes that it would lead to stronger broad-based support for this black female Communist.

But Davis did not want the Communist Party to fade into the background of her trial. In fact, following her wishes to position the CPUSA at the forefront of her case, Party members in California devoted enormous amounts of time and planning to catapult the Party into public prominence. Their meetings and subcommittees on the case occupied more than half of the broader Party agenda throughout Northern California branches. For her part Alexander worked on the bail campaign, which incorporated petitions, resolutions, and hundreds of volunteers throughout the country. She also fielded letters to Davis. By March 1971, five months after her arrest, she had accumulated eighty bags of unopened mail. In the most controversial of her roles Alexander also coordinated the internal legal struggle to earn Davis the right to serve as her own counsel.[107]

Publicly, Alexander hosted numerous cocktail parties and meetings for prominent donors who supported Davis. The NUCFAD even established regional bulletins containing poetry and rally information to put Davis supporters in touch with each other. Singer Bill Conway wrote a song, "From Joan [of Arc] to Angela: A Bitter Ballad of Oppression and Martyrs," in her honor. With its resounding lyrics, "Angela's done no wrong. And we've got to set her free for if we don't it won't be long till they come for you and me," such efforts by her supporters utilized nearly every realm of media in trying to capture attention for her case.[108] Hoping to publicize the cases of all political prisoners through her situation, Davis and Ruchell Magee, her codefendant, coauthored from prison *If They Come in the Morning: Voices of Resistance* in 1971. They argued that most people detained in prisons or other reformatories should be considered political prisoners or "victims of political oppression." They also attempted to emphasize the poverty of those who were imprisoned. People "who had been framed or had received disproportionately long sentences for the sole reason that they were Black or Brown" must also be considered political prisoners, according to Davis and Magee.[109]

For a time in 1971 and 1972 the Davis trial helped the Communist Party to earn even more media attention than it had when Anita Whitney and Dorothy Healey stood trial for their accused crimes. In part due to the attention surrounding Davis's trial, one author wrote: "Communism in America hasn't been as active as it is today for the past forty years. On campuses, on street corners in major cities, and during mass demonstrations, speakers are constantly proclaiming their determination to overthrow the capitalist system." Fourteen leading Russian scientists sent a letter to President Nixon pleading for Davis's release. In response, Nixon promptly extended an invitation to the scientists to personally attend and observe the trial "to see justice in action," which they accepted.[110] Davis's trial took on many of the same dimensions as those of Whitney and Healey, although this time the Party and her Communist identity were not the main focus. Instead, despite the fact that the number of Communists certainly was smaller than in decades past, in a sense the Party's radical politics were not the most controversial element of the trial and campaign. This time the charges centered on personal criminal behavior.

Imprisoned for sixteen months awaiting trial, Davis finally went before a jury of eleven whites and one Mexican American in late February 1972. Four months later, on June 4, 1972, after deliberating only thirteen hours, the jury acquitted Davis of all charges.[111] Standing ready to take her friend home, Alexander even brought a pair of pants for Davis to put on when she left the courthouse. The entire team had been preparing for this day for nearly two years. After announcing their verdict, a number of jurors publicly announced their support for her. One juror even came out to celebrate with Davis on the evening of her release. Another wrote a book chronicling the ordeal of serving on such a publicized trial of an acclaimed woman.[112]

Maintaining the momentum started by Party members during the trial, Davis and Alexander continued speaking and giving interviews reflecting on Davis's time in prison and, more important to them, attacking the chronic problems of the prison system. In an interview with a Black Panther newspaper, Davis told of repeated injustices that she heard about and became involved in as a prisoner.[113] She and the Party took full advantage of the presence of spectators who lingered after the trial and tried to bring these baby boomer radicals into the Party. Even as early as 1971, an observer noted: "The tired old party realized it couldn't survive with much of an influence unless it jumped into the stream of the younger forces of the so-called 'new left.' That's why they gobble up someone like Angela as a youthful martyr with delight."[114] A three-week tour to raise funds for Davis's $250,000 legal expenses, ending in a massive rally at Madison Square Garden, brought this black Communist woman into the spotlight of the Party. From there the team traveled to several foreign countries, including the Soviet Union, though Davis's official Communist Party status was still as a rank-and-filer. Upon arriving in Moscow, Davis "was accorded a heroine's welcome."[115] If only temporarily, Davis's case brought widespread attention to the Party, which leaders could only hope would carry over into campaigns to help other political prisoners who had been victimized by the capitalist system.

If for no other reason than the impressive leading role she had played coordinating Davis's trial and campaign, Alexander found herself invited by the national leadership of the Communist Party into its ranks. The Party first selected Alexander to serve on its Central Committee in 1972, then as organizational secretary of the Northern California District in 1973, the position that Healey had held for decades in Southern California.[116] She continued in the Party's national leadership for nearly twenty years. Party representatives to the national convention reelected her in 1975, 1979, 1983, and 1987. According to friends, the Central Committee also chose her because of her effective combination of personal charisma, theoretical sophistication, and practical organizational skills, characteristics that summoned memories of Healey more than Whitney. They respected her not only as an organizer who recruited members with her open and seemingly informal leadership style but also as a leader who provoked bold confrontations and maintained high expectations.[117] In fact, Alexander reported that two hundred new members joined the Northern California Party branches between 1977 and 1987, certainly not an astronomically high number but relatively impressive given that during that decade most Party branches lost so many members that they nearly disbanded.[118]

More than her personal achievement of leading the Northern California Party, Alexander's transition to the Party's national level signaled a change in guard for the Communist Party overall. Her generation had finally come of age; more than looking like the public face of a Party grasping for a youthful identity, Alexander's generation had become policy makers in their own right. By extension, when Alexander came to the Central Committee of the Communist Party, she did more than confirm her allegiance to a life of radicalism. She pledged devotion to the philosophy that had sustained the Party for nearly fifty years–namely, democratic centralism. This had real significance for Alexander's radical identity, as several of her friends certainly noticed a shift in her political mind-set. Marian Gordon remembered that before taking on national posts, Alexander sided more often with Healey and her frequent criticism of the democratic centralist system and its boss, Gus Hall. By the mid- to late 1970s Alexander changed her fervent tone and quickly fell into Party line without as much discussion or criticism of policies.[119]

For the first several years of Alexander's leadership, the Party's priorities in Northern California remained centered on the inequalities publicized during Davis's trial. Led by Alexander, for example, Northern California members highlighted the plight of political prisoners by chartering the Coordinating Council of Prisoner Organizations (CCPO). It was "a council of prisoner, ex-prisoner, self-help, and other community groups working with prisoners and ex-prisoners to exchange information on existing services and to unite our common efforts in dealing with the serious deficiencies in the total system of criminal justice." Conveying its multifaceted message through its newsletter, *Peace*, the CCPO sought simultaneously to improve sanitation and medical conditions inside prisons and to promote the abolition of the entire prison system.[120] This dual emphasis on reform and revolution became a hallmark of the Communist Party by the late 1970s. It fit into Alexander's pragmatic leadership style of coalition building around specific issues but also of maintaining the Party's separate revolutionary identity.

In addition to pursuing projects that exposed prison injustices, Northern California Party branches continued with their more traditional goals of organizing workers. Furthermore, throughout the mid- and late 1970s, Party members supported labor, peace, and anti-apartheid movements as well as backing broad-based local electoral politics. They also supported people engaged in revolutionary activities in third world countries.[121] As Northern California chair in 1974, Alexander established an anti-inflation campaign, which aimed to bring awareness to "trade unions, consumer groups and the Black and Chicano communities." Just as mainstream political parties and the country struggled to confront stagflation and the effects of losing the war in Vietnam, in the mid-1970s American Communists tried to adapt their Cold War arguments to a significantly different political and economic landscape. Still committed to advocating for American workers and to publicize the Party's continued relevance, Alexander attended a hearing devoted to inflation held by U.S. senator Alan Cranston, coordinated a press conference at a meeting between the Ford Motor Company and labor leaders, and called for a Bay Area people's economic summit conference.[122]

To maintain a public face in the broader Bay Area community, Alexander frequently participated in community forums and lectures. She made one notable speech in celebration of Black History Week at a public library in San Francisco. In 1975, speaking to a diverse crowd of about seventy, the ever-professional Alexander was one of three black women invited to share her perspective on women and Black History Week. She argued that black men and women faced the same oppression and suffering because of their race. "Alexander pointed out," reported a newspaper, "that while high unemployment rates are used as weapons against blacks and often cause stresses on black men and women, 'black women are black men's natural allies.'"[123] Embracing race and downplaying gender fit with the Party's long-standing ideology and agenda, but the stance took on new significance given the context of the growing women's liberation movement.

Initially, when the women's liberation movement emerged out of civil rights and anti–Vietnam War student organizations, Alexander's Communist Party had voiced deep suspicion and criticism. The leaders in these feminist organizations were predominantly young, educated, and middle class.[124] American Communists felt the need to expose what they observed to be the deeply contradictory messages of the feminist movement. Party members, including Alexander, insisted: "Women are neither a class nor an oppressed nation ... the splitting off of men and women from each other—their specific definition as different kinds of beings—serves to divide the oppressed. It mires them down in petty domestic concerns and restricts their outlook drastically."[125] Instead, the Party argued, focusing on the central contradiction of class rather than gender would elevate Americans as a whole. This fifty-five-year-old position remained remarkably stagnant despite changes in ideology in the world of social justice.

Although their class-based criticism of women's liberationists remained central to the Communist Party's analysis of gender-specific activism, by 1975, with Alexander at the forefront of the California Party, some leaders came to admit that second-wave feminists offered a few important insights. Party leaders had begun to recognize that women did in fact face a unique kind of oppression; unsurprisingly, however, Communists still privileged class over gender when describing the path to American equality. In a "special letter on the equality of women" Gus Hall reiterated the traditional Communist position: "The liberation of women is furthermore dependent on the elimination of the exploitation of the working class by the capitalist class." As proof of this claim, Hall insisted that Soviet women lived with equal legal status and social conditions because only in a true Communist state could such equality be realized. While the lived experience of Soviet women was of course much more complicated than Hall's explanation, his testimony reflects that Communist Party members did not look at gender with the same critical eye that they used when analyzing race or class hierarchies. Yet in the 1970s Communists felt compelled to address the issue of gender oppression because of the popularity of women's liberationists. In attempting to appease this potential group of Communists or Party sympathizers, Hall conceded that the Party had made past mistakes by neglecting women's equality within or alongside working-class struggles.[126]

Similarly, in terms of recognizing or accommodating the situations of its own female leaders, the Party still did not visibly confront their struggles to balance private and professional lives as Communists. Alexander had one son, Jordon, in 1976. As a working mother, Alexander managed Party and home responsibilities, although Franklin took on many domestic duties (in particular food preparation because she was a terrible cook, a close friend recalled). But particularly challenging for Alexander were trips that her leadership role required of her. Again, Franklin stayed home with Jordon, and when they traveled to Eastern Europe together, Alexander's mother stayed with Jordon. Additionally, the Alexanders' close friends in the Party and their families created a strong and supportive community for the families of Communists and especially their children to rely upon.[127] The Communist culture that Healey had cultivated and celebrated still supported Alexander. While the Party did not publicly address special conditions of its women leaders, the informal community networks they established tempered the stress of Party, work, and family obligations. In other words, Alexander worked hard to keep her personal life separate from her official Party duties; thus, while the phrase *personal politics* had started to resound with women's liberationists, Alexander did not make the connection. Personally aware of working mothers' sacrifices, Alexander nevertheless chose to privilege her class-based interests through her continued dedication to communism. Opening herself to professional leadership roles, she was very much a part of a workingwomen's collective consciousness.

By the mid-1970s, however, the challenge from the women's liberation movement had forced the official Communist Party structure to change its policies on gender—at least up to a point. Party leaders saw a new opportunity to appeal to the countless women who had entered the workforce that decade. So the Party set up two organizations to recruit more women to its ranks. Hall hoped that the creation of the Coalition of Labor Union Women (CLUW) and Women for Racial and Economic Equality (WREE) would provide the foundation for organizing new workingwomen and introducing them to Communist principles. Seeking to organize trade union women, the CLUW, chartered nationally in 1974, aimed to unite women workers who could collectively call attention to workplace problems such as the need for day care, maternity leave, and full employment.[128] Meanwhile, WREE, which started publishing newsletters and pamphlets in 1976, was intended to be a haven for women who sympathized with the arguments of second-wave feminists but not with their organizations. According to Hall, "WREE can become a place where women develop both their leadership skills and analysis and become more effective in their unions, PTA's, housing groups, etc."[129] Together, the Communist Party believed that these organizations could best understand and improve the lives of working-class women and respond to the changing economic and demographic environment of the decade.

These class- and gender-specific ideas promoted by Party policy statements and resolutions reached the pages of the *People's World* in 1972, when it published a series of articles outlining the hardships placed on working mothers. Titled "When Mothers Need to Work," the newspaper articles sought to expose not only the plight of poor workingwomen but also the extreme burdens placed on nonwhite women workers.[130] Through articles such as these, by the 1970s the Party appeared to adopt the limited goal of using women to influence a changing working class. Because women made up a growing sector of the industrial working class, Party leaders reasoned that gender-specific organizations (though only among workers) would still focus attention on the broader struggle of workers. Thus, as in decades past, leaders wrestled with questions of how to recruit female members by addressing their unique workplace concerns without actually privileging gender above class.

By the 1970s America's Communist Party had adjusted its overall strategies and goals in other ways as well. The Party's path to socialism had changed substantially from its early years. First, it was no longer the most radical organization in the United States; it was not as far Left as other Maoist revolutionary groups that espoused immediate revolution. Second, by the mid-1970s Gus Hall had conceded that his grandchildren most likely would not live under communism. Instead, he and the national Party leadership came to embrace a gradual replacement of capitalism by socialism through the democratic process. Communists in the 1970s even declared "that U.S. socialism will clearly be marked 'made in the USA.'"[131] Communist publications heralded the prediction that while "the future of humanity is socialism," the majority of Americans would have to decide democratically to pursue this end to monopoly capitalism.

This revision of goals and strategies went even further in the coming decade. By the early 1980s the Communist Party had fully come to support a Left-Center alliance, although it continued to run candidates in national elections. Through her activity in the 1984 Vote Peace movement at the Democratic Party convention and through her coalition building with issue-specific organizations, Alexander continued to help to keep the Party relevant on a broader political level, despite its muted rhetoric.[132]

Living in Oakland in the early 1980s, the Alexanders firmly established themselves as the Communist component of a broader progressive coalition of political activists. Despite national fractures that led to the emergence of new Communist organizations such as the Communist Party (Marxism-Leninism) (CPML), based in Chicago, and the Revolutionary Communist Party (RCP), California, Alexander led the way in maintaining a strong network of support for the enduring CPUSA. Regional newspapers even continued to document the strength of the organization and to remark that the "committed cadre of minority members has become more active in recent years." Due in part to its strong internal organization but also to its willingness to participate in the democratic process, Alexander's California Party stayed relevant in the 1980s.[133] The Communist Party continued to run candidates in the 1980 and 1984 elections, with Gus Hall running for president and Angela Davis running as vice president. In California, Alexander coordinated a petition campaign that collected 135,000 signatures to put the Hall-Davis ticket on the 1984 California ballot.[134]

Moreover, in carrying forward the Party's pursuit of racial equality, Franklin chaired the Party's Black Liberation Commission in Northern California. This experience introduced him to non-Communist leftists curious about the Party's racial ideas and eager to exchange views and establish networks. The Line of March Editorial Board, for example, a local civil rights group, talked with Franklin and deferred to the Party's theories and publications on black liberation to strengthen their own understandings of the connections between race and class. Embracing the Party's Left-Center commitment, Franklin eagerly responded: "We welcome and seek out dialogue, discussion and exchange with others on the left, especially those who want to work together and actively struggle for equality, for Black Liberation and against national and racial oppression. In this period the first and last point on our agenda is how with others in our community and workplace do we help develop a mass upsurge and militant and effective fightback against a crises-ridden state monopoly capitalism and its attendant racist oppression."[135] Franklin appeared to live the Left-Center alliance through his work in the 1980s.

Alexander and her cadre of leaders in Northern California also continued to promote economic initiatives into the 1980s that would serve the most oppressed. The Party committed itself to the Coalition to Fight the High Cost of Living and Unemployment, a San Francisco group that tried to resolve economic struggles facing the working class. One of its most popular issues was rallying support for the Hawkins Equal Opportunity and Full Employment Bill (HR 50). Backed by labor, civil rights, and women's organizations alike, the Hawkins Bill "makes the Federal Government guarantee that everyone willing and able to work has a right to a job at decent wages." When it was signed into law in 1975, it also increased funding for housing, education, and other social services.[136] Working to strengthen—if not preserve—specific components of a safety net in the welfare state occupied much of the Party's meeting agendas in these increasingly conservative years of the late 1970s and 1980s.

Likewise, responding to President Reagan's sweeping welfare cuts, in addition to longer-term structural changes in the industrial economy, radicals and progressives in California united to form Unemployed Committees and Networks similar to those that existed at the time of the Party's inception. In the 1980s, as in the 1930s, Unemployed Councils gave laid-off employees ID cards with the slogan printed on the back "A Job Is a Human Right." These councils tried to lobby the federal government for aid with unemployment, evictions, and medical coverage. They also attempted to provide access to medical care, legal counseling, and emergency food. Franklin was actively involved with the councils.[137] By 1983 he became the official Unemployed Council field organizer in Los Angeles, and he claimed that more than one hundred people had joined together and pledged membership in this organization.[138] By the 1980s, however, the manufacturing economy was changing so dramatically that the Party's attempts to organize workers were often futile. Communists found the most success in making alliances with individuals and small groups over single-issue campaigns.

This coalition strategy proved relatively successful on the foreign policy front. In the early 1980s Kendra Alexander led Northern California Communists and radicals in protesting South Africa's apartheid policies. She organized support for Bay Area dockworkers who refused to handle South African cargo in November 1984. The Bay Area Free South Africa Movement, coordinated by Alameda County supervisor John George, welcomed Alexander as one of many radicals and progressives united to protest international injustices.[139] Building coalitions continued to be a hallmark of her Party, which was relatively easier in the leftist political climate of the Bay Area than in other areas of the state and country.

Alexander also galvanized a core group of committed revolutionary activists who urged the Party to respond to the changing problems of the country and specifically her region. A leader in the consistently liberal climate of the Bay Area, Alexander supported programs that focused on labor, peace, antiracism, and local electoral politics.[140] In San Francisco the local Party branch focused its activism on homelessness, while in Oakland it devoted its attention to manufacturing plant closings. The Party also operated Bread and Roses, a bookstore in San Jose, where Party members and sympathizers gathered to discuss local and national issues. Regardless of the Party's national and internal political battles, Alexander took the Northern California Party's priorities in a local and public direction in the 1980s. This open strategy allowed Party members' involvement to be more in line with contemporary politics and more legitimate in the public realm. Furthermore, Alexander's acceptance of diverse programs, coupled with the Bay Area community's acceptance of her as a Communist and a progressive social activist, allowed her to thrive as a leader, just as Dorothy Healey had stayed relevant throughout the doldrums of the Cold War.

During the 1980s Alexander made several trips to Eastern Europe and was treated as something of a dignitary, touring hospitals, fields, and factories.[141] But the Party suffered from intense divisiveness when the Soviet Union began to crumble. A key breaking point for some arose over Mikhail Gorbachev's visit to California in 1990. Upset over the capitalist-leaning tendencies of his new policies as well as his scheduled meetings with wealthy California business-men, many longtime devoted Party members opposed and boycot-ted the planned visit. But Alexander, who at the time was serving as the chair of the CPUSA's Northern California district, reluctantly supported the USSR's leader.[142]

While some leftists in the United States expressed anxiety about Gorbachev's burgeoning relationship with the capitalist world, the Communist Party, including Alexander, greeted these changes with an uncritical and characteristically supportive attitude. In the spring of 1989 author, activist, and cultural critic Michael Parenti penned a letter to the editor in which he spoke for the national Party lead-ership: "[We] welcome perestroika and glasnost . . . [and] believe present changes in the Soviet Union dramatically refute the image, so long fed to the American people, of an incorrigible, immutable totalitarian Soviet system . . . the Soviet Union is a dynamic, chang-ing society, capable of achieving new stages of development."[143] Not anticipating that these changes could hasten the demise of the Soviet Union, in the midst of this reformulated international world order, in 1989 Gus Hall proclaimed a renewed relevance for the Party. Invited to appear on television on *The Phil Donahue Show* and to speak at Harvard and Yale, Hall announced, "There is defi-nitely a decline in anti-Soviet feeling that makes it easier for us to reach wide audiences." Although he still insisted that he wanted to overthrow the capitalist system, that year Hall explained that revo-lution should now come through education and propaganda rather than violence. As the California face of the Party, Alexander agreed to take positions that would have been difficult to justify even in the Popular Front years.[144]

When the Soviet Union did officially disintegrate in 1991, the CPUSA wholeheartedly supported democratization yet simultaneously voiced concern for the treatment of the fifteen million Communists in the country. The editor of the *People's World*, Carl Bloice, wrote: "They are honest, hardworking, dedicated men and women who have the same interests and lofty goals—and faith in the higher aspirations of humanity—as progressive people all over the world. They have done nothing wrong. They do not deserve to be reviled by the Johnny-come-lately democrats and pseudo-democrats holding sway in Moscow."[145] Expressing sympathy for the victims of potential unemployment and inflation, the Party slowly became more critical of the changing guard in the Soviet Union. In particular, when reports surfaced of Communists in the Soviet Union being persecuted and their political activities banned, Hall likened their treatment to Communists who had suffered under McCarthyism in the United States. Hall even declared a new ally when in 1991 he voiced strong support for the Stalinist government in North Korea. As the Soviet Union abandoned communism, the CPUSA reacted by distancing itself from the crumbled state and by presenting American communism as an indigenous political movement, continuing its decades-long effort to frame the Party, its members, and ideas as homegrown.[146]

Throughout the 1980s and into the 1990s the Party forged ahead in Northern California, despite its flailing national membership. Nationwide, in 1990, the Party had between four thousand and fifteen thousand members; California accounted for one quarter of this base.[147] These members kept busy under the leadership of Alexander, who continued to participate in local and global anti-apartheid movements as well as to reaching out to labor unions.[148] Coinciding with international political changes and realignments, however, rifts inside the Party in the late 1980s caused a group of Northern California leaders to push the national Party to reform its authoritarian ways.

Alexander was a late and reluctant convert to this reformist impulse among California Communists. While her California friends and associates became frustrated with the Party's rigid structure in the 1980s, Alexander remained personally committed to the CPUSA's hierarchy and programs much longer than others.[149] Her devotion to the Party convinced her to maintain her regional and national leadership roles and to work within democratic centralism to enact changes. Proclaiming her steadfast commitment to the Communist Party and her certainty of its ability to adapt to the post–Cold War world, Alexander did not waiver in her faith in the Party. She cited the need for far-reaching coalitions of people, including Communists, to support health care, fight poverty, improve race relations, and save the environment. She continued to hope that the Communist Party's Left-Center alliance would be the best organization to push for these far-reaching reforms that other leftists also embraced.[150]

Despite this more introspective and critical perspective, in a 1990 interview she admitted: "I think we've had a narrow attitude toward other political forces in this country.... There's been an ideological block in this country about anti-communism.... That's going to recede with the end of the Cold War and create a situation where people will open their minds more." Even in 1991, Alexander continued to justify her leadership of the beleaguered political organization. She spoke of the need to democratize Eastern Europe in order to create a more humanitarian socialist environment. "The roots of socialism," she asserted, "have got to be the democratic participation of the people." And the Party's direction in the United States must be to "work for change with other political forces that are not communist. That means you make compromises."[151] Illustrating her decades-long commitment to coalition building, Alexander continued to hope that the Party could survive nationally the way it had in Northern California. Within Central Committee meetings and throughout the Northern California branch meetings, however, members had grown dissatisfied with the policies of Gus Hall, which they believed to be overly repressive.[152]

Although Alexander did not create this renegade sect, her friends did, and after several months of trying, they succeeded in convincing her of their frustrations and of the Party's limitations in its current form. In an attempt to reform it from within, Alexander and her generation of members began to criticize the Party's lack of democracy publicly. Charlene Mitchell and Danny Rubin, both National Board members, announced at a December 1991 national Party conference in Cleveland, Ohio: "We believe that a majority of the Party will agree that substantial alterations from past practice must be made in our method of election of leadership to make it more democratic.... We are convinced that for the membership to have a full voice in policy-making, it needs and has a right to know of major alternatives and differences." Calling for a considerably different democratic structure within the Communist Party, reformers demanded to have direct input to the Central Committee.[153]

Naturally, staunch supporters of Hall and the Party's traditional democratic centralist structure felt betrayed. Jarvis Tyler, speaking on behalf of the Presiding Committee at the December 1991 conference, denounced eleven members by name, including Alexander, who he claimed were plotting a Party secession in the hospitality room of the conference hotel.

For six months leading up to the conference, these eleven members had indeed been formulating their criticisms of the Party's current democratic centralist structure and policies. In "A Message to the National Committee" they condemned the Party for straying away from its 1980 goal of attacking the ultra-Right and instead adopting what they believed to be a more ambitious and divisive goal of creating an antimonopoly alliance. They feared that this broader agenda, advocated by Hall, might alienate labor alliances and African Americans. The message went on to criticize the Party for failing to give adequate attention to promote disarmament. Furthermore, they charged that Hall refused to allow the Party to focus on organizing service industry workers and rejected calls to place women's oppression high on the agenda. Using the democratic centralist structure of the Party to push it in these unpopular directions,

Hall ultimately forced many prominent members, such as Alexander, Davis, and Mitchell, to join the reformist group.[154] Most alarming to Hall, the reformers called upon the Party, and Socialist and Communist Parties around the world, to turn inward; they insisted that the Party look realistically at the collapse of the Socialist world and rely on self-criticism as a path to understand and adapt to the changing global economy. Just as Dorothy Healey had insisted in the 1970s, when she departed, the Party needed to become more open and democratic. Alexander and the other separatists decreed, "The existence in our ranks, including in the leadership, of diverse opinions should not be considered harmful or exceptional."[155] But their opinions did not convince Hall to change the Party's ways.

At the national Party convention in December 1991, Hall and other devoted leaders immediately dismissed from their leadership roles all people associated with the reform movement, including Alexander.[156] After spending nearly thirty years of her life in the Party, Alexander left it in March 1992. She did so in the company of nearly all Northern California Party members; the branch voted openly and overwhelmingly to leave the CPUSA.[157] The policies and tactics of the Central Committee, particularly of Gus Hall, frustrated her and most other members in the Bay Area to the point of no reconciliation. Those who ultimately decided to leave had a very hard time making the break, but they determined that they could enact the social and economic changes they wanted through a more democratic leftist organization. Ironically, after having criticized Healey for leaving the Party for similar reasons nearly two decades earlier, Alexander departed much the same way.

Upon officially resigning from the Party, Alexander moved quickly to establish the Committees of Correspondence (COC), which claimed one thousand members upon its inception—80 percent of them former Northern California CPUSA members. Created in California in the spring of 1992 and extended nationally the following year, the COC allowed itself a greater degree of internal democracy. It claimed as its goal "to create a broad front against reaction and militarism, for expanded democracy, equality, jobs, economic security, peace and solidarity, and radical social reforms."[158] A national conference on "Perspectives for Democracy and Socialism in [the] 90s" held at University of California–Berkeley in July 1992 formally founded the Committees of Correspondence as a national left activist organization. Attendees of the conference elected Alexander as one of five cochairs and selected her to head the Northern California body of the national COC.[159] In taking this new post, she committed to "see to it that all opinions were heard and reflected on leadership bodies and in assignments to activist work."[160] Their goals paralleled the goals of the local CPUSA, but they could pursue them without accountability to and interference from the Central Committee. Support for the peace movement, fighting racism and sexism (a topic surprisingly near the top of their agenda), and combating a declining standard of living for working people were their foremost goals.[161] Working in a more open and democratic organization also led Alexander to a job as an aide to Berkeley city council member Maudelle Shirek. In this capacity Alexander demonstrated her enduring desires to blend a socialistic agenda with American-style democracy. She began to consider applying to law schools and pursuing an entirely new career path.

During her brief time working for Shirek, Alexander had the opportunity to contribute her uniquely radical perspective to more mainstream political programs. On May 1, 1993, for example, while attending a National Strategy Session to Stop Police Crimes during the Twentieth Anniversary Conference of the National Alliance against Racist and Political Repression, Alexander spoke on the situation of children—specifically her seventeen-year-old son, Jordon. "Our babies are in crisis," she announced. "We need to do something about it. We've got to rebuild the movement that is going to bring them out of the crisis that they are in, into solving the crisis."[162] Clinging to her lifelong commitment to bring attention to the plight of impoverished urban residents, Alexander's radical agenda had withstood and transcended her nearly thirty years in the Party.

On May 23, 1993, after less than a year after leaving the Party, Alexander's life ended suddenly and tragically in a fire that swept through her home. It started accidentally and spread while she napped on the second floor. Franklin and their son, Jordon, escaped to safety, while Alexander could not get out. Radical communities all around the country and the world felt a deep loss of a friend and a leader. Letters of condolence from Communist Parties in Cuba, the German Democratic Republic, South Africa, Australia, and New Zealand; even the American Socialist Party flooded coc office headquarters. A German Socialist wrote: "We knew her as a leading comrade of the Communist Party of the USA, a highly respected fighter in the labor, peace, anti-racist and civil rights movements of the other America.... Mourning with you this heavy loss we wish you courage and strength to continue striving to the goals Kendra Alexander was so committed to."[163] They all reflected memories of the unwavering spirit that Alexander exhibited in her determination to effect progressive and radical change.[164] The end of Alexander's life signaled the end of an era in which California Communists maintained a delicate balance between liberalism and radicalism.

At a press conference a week before her death, she remarked: "My reasons for leaving the CPUSA are complex. But my political convictions remain much the same as they always have been. I do not regret that I belonged to the Communist Party nor do I regret that I left it. The struggle to make our country a better place to live will always remain my life's work."[165]

She lived in and led one of the most tumultuous generations of activists. Her career demonstrates the far-reaching relationships that she as a Party leader established and sustained with broader-based social justice programs. In fact, her activism counters common assumptions about the Party's exclusivity and exclusion from other realms of activism. It shows that in the years after McCarthyism cooled, the worlds of civil rights activists and radicals existed in conjunction with each other, if only for the purpose of coalition building. Furthermore, a black woman's rise within the Party demonstrates how it changed the face of its leadership, its membership, and its agendas in the closing decades of the twentieth century. Finally, Alexander's importance lies in the direction in which she took the

California Party branches and the CPUSA. While remaining a steadfast devotee of the CPUSA's hierarchy for decades, her cohort's eventual criticism and abandonment of the Stalinist structures led the Party to fracture permanently. Although in the end she exited the Party in a similarly dramatic and controversial way as her immediate predecessor, Alexander's pragmatic tactics of coalition building allowed Communists in California to survive and not be isolated from mainstream politics throughout the early 1990s. She and her generation of radicals maintained yet adapted the revolutionary spirit of the Party's original intent and reshaped American communism in the last decades of the twentieth century.

5 American Communism after Three Generations

As the lives of these three women show, radicalism in America continually reinvented itself. Radicals' grievances, agendas, goals, and strategies regularly shifted to respond to their changing worlds and constituencies. Whitney, Healey, and Alexander's collective experiences offer insight into why they and others like them became drawn to the Party, what they found once they did become members, how the Party changed over time because of them, and why California played a central role in creating their radical worlds.

Whitney, Healey, and Alexander all saw the American Communist Party as the most attractive option for attaining their goals. Although the women joined under very different circumstances, their shared interest in grassroots political activism prompted their initial interest and subsequent decision to join the Communist Party. They were not drawn to the Party for theoretical or philosophical reasons. Neither Marxism or the abstract study of class-based inequalities played a strong role in attracting any of the women to the Party. Instead, it was the California Communist Party's on-the-ground activism and concrete stances on local events that spurred their interest. For Whitney the Party represented the best way to protect workers' constitutional rights—namely, free speech and assembly. In Healey's case she joined not simply because of her leftist family and radical social background but also because she respected the Party's labor organizing and protests. Alexander came to the Party because of its strong and increasingly radical stance on civil rights—an issue about which she already cared deeply. Indeed, through this radical political organization each woman discovered practical avenues for tackling the economic, racial, and—at least occasionally—gender inequalities around her. The three women were drawn to the Communist Party initially for its actions and then later, in varying degrees, became interested in its theoretical underpinnings. Over time they combined their concern for specific issues with a deeper explanation of why abolishing capitalism offered the most comprehensive solution to problems in their worlds.

Whitney, Healey, and Alexander also enjoyed the camaraderie of the Party. Because the Communist Party demanded many sacrifices of its members, it created a self-selected group of stable, serious, and strong-willed radicals. Not only did they enjoy meeting people who cared about the same political causes they did, but they also found a social environment that was in many ways akin to a religious community. They all found friendships within the Party that lasted throughout their lifetimes. These friends supported each other through illness, childcare demands, and times of financial need. Healey met all three of her husbands through these networks, while all three women regularly participated in a Party culture of rituals and celebrations. This dynamic Communist culture allowed the women to live as feminists but not embrace feminism.

The democratic centralist structure of the Party gave these women a methodical way to go about waging their struggles as professional revolutionaries. The women ascended through the ranks of the Party to create and sustain a long-lasting radical movement. When the national leaders invited each woman to serve on the Party's Central Committee, Whitney, Healey, and Alexander professionally benefited from the committee's desire to appoint a few women to the highest ranks. Wearing as a badge of honor her Party leadership title, Whitney ran for public office, Healey took a state job promoting the rights of workers, and Alexander traveled the world to learn about international communism. Sometimes, however, the Central Committee failed to address topics of prime concern to California members or directed them to take stances that were unpopular with their West Coast comrades. These positions fractured the Party's internal cohesion and created coalitions of unlikely bedfellows in California. Such was the case in the 1970s, when Alexander's Party aligned with the Black Panthers and other nationalist movements against the wishes of Gus Hall's Central Committee. But ultimately, the rigid structure helped the national Party stay unified and press forward as an organization, one that stuck together much longer than any other radical group in the twentieth century. Despite the contentious nature of the Party hierarchy, this structure offered the base of support for the radical struggles that were so important to Whitney, Healey, and Alexander.

Indeed, this structure was so effective that the three women decided to stomach many of the indiscretions and even atrocities committed by their national and international Party. Whitney, Healey, and Alexander all tolerated—if not excused—many of the lies of the Party's leadership. Whitney refused to engage in any open discussion about brutalities inflicted against Soviet citizens; Healey excused the Nazi-Soviet Pact and by extension consented to genocide; and Alexander brushed aside claims about deteriorating conditions within Communist nations. Thus, they willfully accepted a deceitful—and at times malevolent—leadership in pursuit of their higher belief in communism. This acceptance signals not simply the deep devotion they felt toward the Party, but it also shows how they distanced themselves and their local Party branches from international scandals. In some ways American Communists lived in a bubble. The deep-rooted anticommunism that characterized most of the twentieth century in the United States, which spiked after World War I and with the Cold War, convinced American radicals that the press, mainstream political parties, and the government would never accurately portray events and trends occurring in Communist countries.

These three women's experiences also demonstrate how the American Communist Party defined itself through its specific agendas and policies over time. Although the overarching concerns of protecting and promoting the rights of labor and the oppressed remained at the top of the agenda, each generation shifted the ways in which the Party pursued these ideals. Whitney personified the Party at a moment when it needed to stake a claim to a distinguished American national identity. Her reputation, earned through her early charity and reform work inside mainstream and elite circles, enabled the Party to highlight its reformist impulses. Beginning in the late 1910s, when the Party had just emerged as a political organization, to the 1920s, during its underground years and its burgeoning but seriously stigmatized labor activism, the Party stood to benefit through its association from Whitney.

Yet as the decades progressed and as the Party's identity morphed, so too did the qualities of its female leaders. Although it still clung to Whitney in an official public capacity because of her ability to draw votes and recognition in the 1930s, Healey suited the Party's new character. Eager to locate herself in the trenches of the labor movement, Healey fought for the Party to play a role in a labor movement that was entering into its heyday. Belonging to a strong, growing, and relatively stable Communist Party in the 1930s and 1940s, Healey's heritage was American communism. Her Communist activism and leadership came from within California's comparatively thriving radical community.

By the 1970s, as the Party's standing changed because of the Cold War and as it became mired in internal struggles, Alexander's generation came to the fore and once again reshaped the organization. Alexander did not come from Whitney's elite class, nor did she share Healey's working-class focus in her early politicization. Rather, she initially came to the revolutionary organization through her dedication to racial equality and social justice. This orientation served the purposes of the California Party because it appealed to other like-minded radicals. Thus, Alexander's defense of longtime Party positions on social justice in America, coupled with her ability to forge coalitions over many of these issues, stretched the Party's lifetime and legacy through the last decade of the twentieth century. These alliances kept communism in America afloat as it protested global racism and apartheid, fought for better pay for migrant farmworkers, and brought attention to the disproportionate numbers of minorities serving jail time, among other efforts.

While each woman effectively changed the face of the Party, she did so because the national leadership determined that she should. In other words, the Party consciously used—and at times manipulated—each woman for its own purposes to showcase itself at different points in the twentieth century. National male Party leaders positioned Whitney, Healey, and Alexander as the public faces of American communism, which served an explicit goal of making the Party appear more in line with mainstream images. It promoted Whitney because she had an American story to which it could stake a claim, Healey because she toiled with all sorts of workers across the state, and Alexander because of her racial and radical identity. Above all, each woman—and her ascent to the leadership circle—served the Party's public commitment to gender equality. Nevertheless, they were not passive about the Party's use of them; they tolerated their roles as the poster girls for the Party because they continued to see the merits of working within the Party to push for radical change throughout the state.

Furthermore, all three strove to build coalitions beyond the Party. Whitney, Healey, and Alexander embraced political and legal alliances for the sake of stretching the Party's popularity and influence outside the limited bounds of its card-carrying membership. In particular, the Party sought to create alliances over free speech cases. Whitney's criminal syndicalism trial, Healey's Cold War era arrests, and Alexander's support for Angela Davis's case all fostered coalitions that focused on a fundamental right to free speech.

The fluid political and social environment of California played a key role in making these coalitions possible. In general organizational and personal alliances came relatively easy to California Communists. Non-Communists in California tended to support their Communist counterparts because both sides appeared to be more independent minded than their national or eastern counterparts. This greater flexibility applied to the Communist Party at several important moments in the mid-twentieth century, such as when Healey denounced the 1968 Soviet invasion of Czechoslovakia. Sometimes Californians proved to be far more tolerant of Communists than their colleagues in national organizations. In the 1930s and 1940s, for example, when the Southern California ACLU supported California Communists, the local ACLU deviated from its increasingly conservative national counterparts. And coalitions began even earlier, in the 1910s, for instance, when Whitney's western suffragists had no problem adopting positions that lent support to working-class feminist Socialists, which went against the grain of their national counterparts. These positions—specific to California—enabled Whitney, Healey, and Alexander to build strong bases of support. And though they varied over time in source, these California coalitions outlasted each woman individually.

While California's diverse population contributed to the Party's enduring influence, the state's politics did change, and these shifts reveal how organizational alliances fluctuated throughout the century. Whitney's free speech alliances came from her elite liberal circle of supporters, while Healey's free speech supporters came from the ACLU and other political progressives in California. And Alexander's circle of non-Communist supporters held their primary allegiances to Black Nationalist and New Left groups. Although the coalitions were created around struggles for similar rights, the groups that came to the aid of Communists varied greatly over time. This variability resulted not only from the personal identity of the leaders at any specific time but also from the dramatically shifting identities of radical sympathizers throughout the twentieth century. Those active on the Left varied from laborers to minorities to students. Thus, while free speech was reliably a transcendent cause that united a multitude of activists, the particular groups of allies did not necessarily endure in their support for Communists.

Struggles for racial justice and equality also regularly united California Communists with their neighbors. Particularly in California, where few mainstream groups protected the rights of minorities before the century's midpoint, the Party did rightfully earn a reputation for demanding equal treatment. And though the organizational alliances shifted as civil rights struggles changed, the Party's consistently antiracist—and often racially separatist—positions earned these three women notable support. Whitney's early public criticism of Jim Crow laws, Healey's protest of housing discrimination laws, and Alexander's alliances with Black Panthers against police brutality demonstrate the Party's century-long commitment to confronting explicit and implicit racism throughout California. Race drove the Party's agenda, and this commitment helped to keep Communists at the forefront of many local civil rights cases.

While the Party's unfailing commitment to racial equality brought it recognition and new members, its stances on gender inequalities were not as consistently egalitarian or popular. The Party's positions about gender—which applied to women who belonged to the Party and those it sought to attract—remained muddled. Lenin insisted that real gender equality would only emerge with the abolition of a class-based society, but the national Party believed it prudent to appoint these three women to its highest ranks even though it operated in the context of a capitalist society. Likewise, American Communists proudly celebrated International Women's Day well into the 1980s yet opposed the Equal Rights Amendment. Consequently, many women did find it liberating to belong to a Party that supported gender equality alongside its broader worker-centered campaigns, but they ultimately agreed to give a lower priority to their gender. Whitney, Healey, and Alexander recognized the importance of women's rights but also believed there should be limits in pushing for gender equity alone. Even in their own professional revolutionary lives, the three women sidestepped gender-specific concerns and preferred to focus on campaigns for workers or minorities.

Moreover, on a personal level each woman acted in accordance with the mainstream gender norms of her era. Although she never married, Whitney surrounded herself with well-to-do society women and emphasized her skills in the domestic arts. Healey—perhaps the most conventional of the three in terms of her gender expression—married young, bore a son, and underwent plastic surgery to change her appearance. Alexander also married and embraced motherhood. Their radical communities embraced traditional American gender norms. At the same time, however, their Party also appointed these women to its highest posts and gave them opportunities for leadership that were hard to find within mainstream organizations. Ultimately, their experiences show how California became a space in which members could subscribe to American notions of womanhood and become leading Communists.

Finally, the life stories of these women underline the importance of local studies in understanding the role of radicalism in U.S. history. For these three women communism often had as much or more to do with the lives they led as Californians, women, activists, and local leaders as it did with centralized, structured, secretive commandments that came from Moscow. These three leaders were all grassroots activists, and the Party they helped build was a significant component of California's local political culture. Campaigns supporting Imperial Valley migrant workers, protesting police brutality in Los Angeles, and denouncing Bay Area discriminatory housing ordinances became centerpieces of their struggles. Their careers as female Communist leaders must be framed through their local experiences.

Nevertheless, these romances with California communism did not always end happily. Healey and Alexander ultimately decided that the Party inhibited real revolution. Indeed, the workers' party that Communists sought never materialized, nor did class become a decisive factor in American politics. Still, Whitney, Healey, and Alexander's California Communist Party was much more than a political party and should be redefined as such. Scholars of American communism need to frame their studies around local struggles to gain new insights into political, social, and cultural movements in the twentieth century. By allying with mainstream reformers, by fighting consistently for free speech and racial equality, by organizing the state's most dispossessed workers, these three women helped to define California's radical heritage.

Notes

1. THREE GENERATIONS

1. For theoretical background on women and communism, see Engels, *Origin of the Family*; Engels, *Women and Communism*; Zetkin, *Lenin on the Woman Question*.
2. Kathryn Johnson and Peggy Somers, "A Socialist/Feminist View of the Capitalist Organization of Production," June 1972, Dorothy Healey Collection, California State University–Long Beach Library (hereafter cited as CSULBL).
3. Engels, *Origin of the Family*.
4. Dixler, "Woman Question"; Roach, "Women in the American Communist Party"; Baxandall, "Question Seldom Asked"; Schaffer, "Women and the Communist Party, USA."
5. Weigand, *Red Feminism*, 20; see also Weigand, "Red Menace." Other historians who have written about women in the CPUSA include Dixler, "Woman Question"; Schaffer, "Women and the Communist Party, USA"; Gosse, "'To Organize in Every Neighborhood'"; Baxandall, "Question Seldom Asked"; and Ware, "Women on the Left."

6. Schaffer, "Women and the Communist Party, USA."

7. Olmsted, *Red Spy Queen*.

8. Dorothy Healey, *A Communist Talks to Students*, folder Healey's Speeches at Colleges, Dorothy Healey Collection, CSULBL.

9. Gardner, *Tradition's Chains Have Bound Us*, 1415. Works that highlight women's concerns within radical leftist organizations include Inman, *In Woman's Defense*; Jones, "End to the Neglect"; Sherwood, *Claudia Jones*, 20–34; Washington, "Alice Childress, Lorraine Hansberry, and Claudia Jones"; Schaffer, "Women and the Communist Party, USA"; Cobble, *Other Women's Movement*, 50–68, 145–79.

10. Weigand, *Red Feminism*, 28–45, 67–96.

11. Cook, *Eleanor Roosevelt*, vols. 1–2; Downey, *Woman behind the New Deal*.

12. Weigand, *Red Feminism*, xii.

13. Kelley, "Life of the Party," 82.

14. Multiple organizations came to align with the California branches of the Communist Party over specific issues throughout the twentieth century. The ACLU in the 1930s and 1940s, e.g., aided the Communist Party and the Congress of Industrial Organizations in securing equal access to public space (see chapter 3). Civil rights groups, free speech organizations, and labor unions above all found common ground with California Communists in each generation.

15. Casteldine, *Cold War Progressives*.

16. Cohen, *Making a New Deal*; Freeman, *In Transit*; Keeran, *Communist Party and the Auto Workers Union*; Klehr, *Heyday of American Communism*; Ruiz, *Cannery Women, Cannery Lives*; Storch, *Red Chicago*.

17. Kelley, *Hammer and Hoe*; Sides, *L.A. City Limits*, 134, 141–46; Hutchinson, *Blacks and Reds*; Gilmore, *Defying Dixie*; McDuffie, *Sojourning for Freedom*.

18. For similar analyses of coalition building as a strategy of activists especially in California, see Cherny, Irwin, and Wilson, *California Women and Politics*; Deverell and Sitton, *California Progressivism Revisited*.

19. Stegner, "California Rising," 8. See also McWilliams, *California*, 3; McWilliams, *Southern California Country*; Eisen and Fine, *Unknown California*; Murdock, "California Communists."

20. For background on California political history, see Cherny, Irwin, and Wilson, *California Women and Politics*; Starr, *California*; Cornford, *Working People of California*.

21. Draper, *Roots of American Communism*; Howe and Coser, *American Communist Party*; Starobin, *American Communism in Crisis*; Kraditor, *"Jimmy Higgins"*; Klehr, *Heyday of American Communism*; Klehr and Haynes, *American Communist Movement*; Klehr, Haynes, and Firsov, *Secret World of American Communism*.

22. Isserman, *Which Side Were You On*; Kelley, *Hammer and Hoe*; Kelley, *Race Rebels*; Naison, *Communists in Harlem*; Cherny, "Prelude to the Popular Front."

23. See, e.g., Haynes, *Early Cold War Spies*; Haynes, *In Denial*; Haynes and Klehr, *Venona*; Olmsted, *Red Spy Queen*.

24. Barrett, *William Z. Foster*; Ryan, *Earl Browder*; Palmer, *James P. Cannon*; Aptheker, *Intimate Politics*; Mitford, *Fine Old Conflict*; Dennis, *Autobiography of an American Communist*; Flynn, *Rebel Girl*; Gorn, *Mother Jones*; MacKinnon, *Agnes Smedley*; Davis, *Great Day Coming*; Price, *Lives of Agnes Smedley*.

25. Weigand, *Red Feminism*; Storch, *Red Chicago*; Kelley, *Hammer and Hoe*; Kelley, *Race Rebels*; Naison, *Communists in Harlem*; Solomon, *Cry Was Unity*; McDuffie, "Long Journeys."

26. For a loose model of generational scholarship, see García, *Mexican Americans*; and Isserman, *If I Had a Hammer*.

2. PARLOR PINK TURNED SOAPBOX RED

1. "Women's Christian Temperance Union Asks Freedom for Miss Whitney: Organization Hits State Law under Whitney Social Worker Is Condemned to San Quentin," *Oakland Examiner*, October 24, 1925, 4.

2. For similar analyses, see Naison, *Communists in Harlem*; Buhle, *Women and Socialism*.

3. Katz, "Socialist Women and Progressive Reform"; Kerber and De Hart–Matthews, *Women's America*; Blumberg, *Florence Kelley*; O'Connor, *Revolution in Seattle*; Kipnis, *American Socialist Movement*.

4. Richmond, *Native Daughter*; Flynn, *Rebel Girl*.

5. Collins and Skover, "Curious Concurrence"; Blasi, "First Amendment."

6. Davis, *California Women*, 181; Richmond, *Native Daughter*, 25.

7. Flynn, *Daughters of America*, 6.

8. "Courses Taken at Wellesley College by Charlotte Anita Whitney, Class of 1889," 1–2, Wellesley College Archives (hereafter cited as WCA).

9. Richmond, *Native Daughter*, 27.

10. "Class Letters, '89 Wellesley College," January 1894, WCA. See also Wellesley College Alumnae Association, "1942 Biographical Record," October 22, 1941, 2; Davis, *California Women*, 181. When Whitney graduated from Wellesley in 1889, she traveled throughout Europe for six months, visiting the Paris Exposition, England, Belgium, Holland, Denmark, and St. Petersburg. Following her travels, Whitney returned home to Oakland, where she served on the Wellesley Alumnae Association committees, which brought her to the position of the director of the California Branch of the Association of Collegiate Alumnae from 1890 to 1891. She continued in several other administrative positions on the board until 1900.

11. Lagemann, *Generation of Women*.

12. Flynn, *Daughters of America*, 7. For Roosevelt's experience in this settlement house, see Cook, *Eleanor Roosevelt*, 1:135, 137–38.

13. "Class Letters, '89 Wellesley College," January 1893, 46, WCA.

14. Flynn, *Rebel Girl*, 196.

15. Richmond, *Native Daughter*, 32–33.

16. Davis, *California Women*, 181.

17. State Board of Charities and Corrections of the State of California, *Eighth Biennial Report*; Binheim, "Biographies," 95.

18. Richmond, *Native Daughter*, 36.

19. "Appointed Probation Officer for the Oakland Juvenile Court," *San Francisco Chronicle*, May 28, 1903, 7.

20. "Class Letters, '89 Wellesley College," January 1905, 36, WCA.

21. "Class Letters, '89 Wellesley College," January 1909, 40, WCA.

22. Anna Garlin Spencer, "Fitness of Women to Become Citizens from the Standpoint of Moral Development," 1898 NAWSA Convention.

23. Gullett, *Becoming Citizens*; Blair, *Clubwoman as Feminist*; Miller, "Within the Bounds of Propriety"; Dorr, *Woman of Fifty*; Lagemann, *Generation of Women*.

24. "Class Letters, '89 Wellesley College," January 1911, 33, WCA.

25. Sonia Baltron Kaross, interview by Lucy Kendall, November 3, 1977, Labor Archives and Research Center.

26. "Clergymen, Actors, Teachers, Businessmen and Politicians Champion Amendment," *San Francisco Call*, April 16, 1911, 67.

27. Harriot Blatch, "An Open Letter to Mrs. Stanton," *Woman's Journal*, December 22, 1894, 402; DuBois, *Harriot Stanton Blatch*, chaps. 3–4; DuBois, "Woman Suffrage and the Left."

28. DuBois, "Woman Suffrage and the Left," 253.

29. Englander, *Class Conflict and Class Coalition*; Katz, "Politics of Coalition."
30. "Class Letters, '89 Wellesley College," January 1912, 27, WCA.
31. "Class Letters, '89 Wellesley College," January 1912, 27, WCA.
32. "Class Letters, '89 Wellesley College," January 1912, 27, WCA.
33. "Class Letters, '89 Wellesley College," January 1913, 33, WCA.
34. Kaross, interview by Kendall.
35. Kaross, interview by Kendall.
36. Kaross, interview by Kendall.
37. Kaross, interview by Kendall.
38. "Resigns from Congressional Union," *Oakland Examiner*, September 26, 1915, 4. Whitney continued to speak at NWP meetings and events well into the 1920s.
39. For an overview of post-suffrage women's activism, see Cott, *Grounding of Modern Feminism*.
40. "Miss Whitney Attacks Bar to Mixing Races," *Los Angeles Times*, February 17, 1926, 7.
41. Mason, "Neither Friends nor Foes"; Hall, *Harvest Wobblies*; Daniel, *Bitter Harvest*; White, "Crime of Economic Radicalism," 649.
42. Parker, "California Casual and His Revolt," 114; Mason, "Neither Friends nor Foes," 57–72.
43. Buhle, *Women and American Socialism*, chap. 2.
44. Flynn, *Daughters of America*, 9.
45. Flynn, *Rebel Girl*, 196–97.
46. "Throws Bomb among Women: Clergyman Asserts Fair Sex Dress Indecently," *Los Angeles Times*, November 12, 1913, 119.
47. Draper, *Roots of American Communism*, 39–42.
48. Constance Carruthers, "Suffragists Are Awed by Steam Roller's Toot," *San Francisco Call*, November 26, 1912, 3.
49. Whitney, "President's Foreword," 13.
50. *Socialist Woman*, June 1907.
51. *Socialist Woman*, June 1907.
52. Buhle, *Women and American Socialism*, 216.
53. Buhle, *Women and American Socialism*, chap. 6; Englander, *Class Coalition and Class Conflict*.
54. Buhle, *Women and American Socialism*, 120.
55. Weinstein, *Decline of Socialism in America*, 50–62; Kipnis, *American Socialist Movement*.
56. Richmond, *Native Daughter*, 72.

57. "Class Letters, '89 Wellesley College," March 1915, 44, WCA.

58. Kessler-Harris, "Where Are the Organized Women Workers," 244.

59. Cook, "Female Support Networks and Political Activism," 287.

60. Davis, *California Women*, 182.

61. "Whitney, Charlotte Anita," *American National Biography*.

62. "Class Letters, '89 Wellesley College," February 1917, 40, WCA.

63. Degen, *History of the Woman's Peace Party*, 26. See also Early, *World without War*; Klejment, "Radical Origins of Catholic Pacifism," an important account of an alternative religiously inspired pacifism in which "Catholic pacifism invokes the protection of the Christian law of love on everyone" (24).

64. "Anita Whitney Answers," file Miscellaneous, Charlotte Anita Whitney, B68, 103/4, Franklin Hichborn Papers, UCLA Special Collections.

65. "Miss Charlotte Anita Whitney," file Miscellaneous, Charlotte Anita Whitney, B68, 103/4, Franklin Hichborn Papers, UCLA Special Collections; letter, September 9, 1919, Office of the President, 1919–21, file no. 1, IIB 83w Miscellaneous, Aurelia Reinhardt Collection, Mills College Special Collections.

66. Klehr and Haynes, *American Communist Movement*, 22.

67. Richmond, *Native Daughter*, 77.

68. Franklin Hichborn, "The Case of Charlotte Anita Whitney," 1920, 4, file Miscellaneous, Charlotte Anita Whitney, B68, 103/4, Franklin Hichborn Papers, UCLA Special Collections; Richmond, *Native Daughter*, 77.

69. Bennett, *Party of Fear*, 197. For historiography relating to the causes and implications of the First Red Scare, see Murray, *Red Scare*; Levin, *Political Hysteria in America*; Kovel, *Red Hunting in the Promised Land*; Heale, *American Anticommunism*; Nielsen, *Un-American Womanhood*.

70. California State Legislature, "Appendix A to the Criminal Syndicalism Act of California," October 1919.

71. Blasi, "First Amendment," 649.

72. "Miss Whitney Gave Reds Aid, League Avers: Protest Lodged against Her Appearing as Speaker in Oakland Today," *San Francisco Chronicle*, November 28, 1919, 6.

73. John D. Barry, "Ways of the World: The Case of Miss Whitney: Some of the Circumstances Associated with the Arrest of a Woman Highly Esteemed for Her Public Activities," December 6, [no year], file Miscellaneous, Charlotte Anita Whitney, B68, 103/4, Franklin Hichborn Papers, UCLA Special Collections.

74. "Rich Woman Must Serve Prison Term: Miss Charlotte Whitney Convicted of Criminal Syndicalism Loses Appeal," *Los Angeles Times*, April 26, 1922, 11. In response to the question "Have you ever belonged to the iww?" Whitney insisted, "No, I have not." "Anita Whitney Answers," file Miscellaneous, Charlotte Anita Whitney, B68, 103/4, Franklin Hichborn Papers, UCLA Special Collections.

75. Barry, "Ways of the World"; "Anita Whitney Home Raided: Incriminating Literature and Correspondence Seized, Is Police Report," *Oakland Examiner*, January 22, 1920, 13.

76. "Anita Whitney on Bail Bond," *Oakland Examiner*, January 15, 1920, 11; "Anita Whitney on Reed's Bond: Clubwoman Convicted of Syndicalism Helps Communist to Freedom," *Oakland Examiner*, March 11, 1920, 8.

77. "Pardoning Power Exists for Such Cases as This," *Oakland Examiner*, November 9, 1925, 24.

78. "Red Flag Plant Story Barred in Whitney Trial," *San Francisco Chronicle*, January 30, 1920, 6.

79. *The People of the State of CA, Plaintiff, v. Charlotte A. Whitney, Defendant*, Superior Court of California, Oakland CA, no. 7456, January 29, 1920, 2:61.

80. *The People of the State of CA, Plaintiff, v. Charlotte A. Whitney, Defendant*, 2:61–63; "Memo for Franklin Hichborn," March 1, 1920, file Miscellaneous, Charlotte Anita Whitney, B68, 103/4, Franklin Hichborn Papers, UCLA Special Collections.

81. *In the Superior Court of the State of California, In and For the County of Alameda*, "The People of the State of California vs. Charlotte Anita Whitney, No. 7456," Statement of the District Attorney and Judge Concerning the Above-Named Defendant.

82. "Anita Whitney Denies Intent to Break Laws," *San Francisco Chronicle*, February 20, 1920, 6.

83. *The People of the State of CA, Plaintiff, v. Charlotte A. Whitney, Defendant*, 2:111.

84. Hichborn, "Case of Charlotte Anita Whitney."

85. Barry, "Ways of the World." See also Issel, "Liberalism and Urban Policy," 438.

86. "iww Record Introduced in Whitney Trial," *San Francisco Chronicle*, February 11, 1920, 8; "Anita Whitney Confers with iww Leaders," *San Francisco Chronicle*, February 14, 1920, 6; "Trial Woman: Alleged Radical, Three Years: Federal and State Agents Shadowed Anita Whitney, Now on Trial," *Los Angeles Times*, February 5, 1920, 13.

87. *Application for Pardon Charlotte Anita Whitney*, file 556E4017, "Trial Testimony," January 30, 1920, 177.

88. *Charlotte Anita Whitney against the People of the State of California in Error to the District Court of Appeal, First Appellate District, Division 1, State of California*, U.S. Supreme Court, no. 10, October 1925.

89. *Whitney v. California*, 274 UW, 71 L. Ed. 1095, 47 S. Ct. 641 (1927, 57 Cal. App. 449).

90. "Miss Whitney Gets One to Fourteen Year Term: Sympathizers Weep in Court as Judge Pronounces Sentence in the Oakland Syndicalist Case," *Oakland Examiner*, February 25, 1920, 17.

91. "Anita Whitney Falsely Pictured as Martyr to a Holy Cause," n.d., file Miscellaneous, Charlotte Anita Whitney, B68, 103/4, Franklin Hichborn Papers, UCLA Special Collections.

92. "Women Storm Jail to See Miss Whitney: Fifty Club Members and Other Friends Foiled Plans to Shower Her with Flowers," *Oakland Examiner*, February 27, 1920, 16.

93. G. E. O. Fitzgerald, E. G. Carter, and M. J. McDonough, "Finish Fight: Building Trades Council Notes," *Alameda County Union Labor Record*, March 5, 1920, 1.

94. C. E. Kunze, "Anita Whitney Sentence Severe as That Given Dangerous Criminals," *San Francisco Call*, November 28, 1925.

95. "L.A. Halts Miss Whitney's Talk," *Oakland Examiner*.

96. "Class Letters, '89 Wellesley College," June 1920, 20–21, WCA.

97. "State Drive on to Free Miss Whitney: Miss Alicia Mosgrove Chosen Secretary of Citizens Committee to Make Pardon Appeal," *Oakland Examiner*, October 28, 1925, 12.

98. Kaross, interview by Kendall.

99. "Class Letters, '89 Wellesley College," January 1923, 39, WCA. For background on the public perception leading up to her trial, see Alma Reed, "Case against Anita Whitney for 'Syndicalism' Up to Supreme Court," *New York Times*, September 17, 1922, 94.

100. *Whitney v. California* (1926), CA 274 U.S. 357, 371.

101. *Whitney v. California*, 274 U.S. 357.

102. Introduction to the Court Opinion on the *Whitney v. California Case*, http://usa.usembassy.de/etexts/democrac/44.htm.

103. Blasi, "First Amendment," 653.

104. Kaross, interview by Kendall; "Class Letters, '89 Wellesley College," January 1926, 22, WCA.

105. "Class Letters, '89 Wellesley College," January 1926, 22, WCA.

106. "State Women Ask Clemency of Governor," *San Francisco Chronicle*, October 22, 1925, 1; "State Drive on to Free Miss Whitney," 12.
107. "State Drive on to Free Miss Whitney."
108. "Whitney Trial Is Denounced, Mills College Professor Flays Gov. Richardson," *San Francisco Daily News*, November 18, 1925, 1.
109. Letter from Governor Wm. Richardson to Aurelia Reinhardt about Charlotte Anita Whitney's case, November 24, 1925, Office of the President, 1924–26, file no. 2, R Misc 2 IID 137, Aurelia Reinhardt Collection, Mills College Special Collections.
110. Statement on Anita Whitney, October 26, 1925, file no. 6, Writings of Aurelia Reinhardt, 1924–25, v5, Aurelia Reinhardt Collection, Mills College Special Collections.
111. "William J. Locke, Attorney and Counselor at Law, June 7, 1927," Letters to Governor Young Petitioning for the Pardon of Charlotte Anita Whitney, Governor Young Collections, California State Archives.
112. "William Kehoe, Attorney at Law, June 9, 1927," Letters to Governor Young.
113. "Upton Sinclair, November 9, 1925," Letters to Governor Young.
114. "About Anita Whitney: Mary Van Kleeck Discusses Famous Oakland Case in Its Relation to Americanism of Today and Yesterday," *Oakland Post*, October 6, 1922.
115. "State Drive on to Free Miss Whitney," 12.
116. "Daughters of the American Revolution, Santa Ysabel Chapter, May 30, 1926," Letters to Governor Young.
117. Henry Carr, "The Lancer," *Los Angeles Times*, May 19, 1927, A1; "Raymond Benjamin, Attorney at Law, May 25, 1927," Letters to Governor Young.
118. "William J. Locke, Attorney and Counselor at Law, June 7, 1927," Letters to Governor Young.
119. "Syndicalism Act Raked in New Whitney Pardon Plea," *San Francisco Chronicle*, June 13, 1927.
120. "Pardon Her," *Oakland Examiner*, October 28, 1925, 30.
121. John Francis Neylan, *Petition for Pardon of Charlotte Anita Whitney and Brief in Support Thereof*, San Francisco, June 3, 1927, 15.
122. "Anita Whitney Pardoned as Young Capitulates," *Los Angeles Times*, June 21, 1927, 1.
123. "The Pardon of Miss Whitney," *Los Angeles Times*, June 22, 1927, A4.
124. "*The Locomotive Engineers Journal*, July 1927," 503, Letters to Governor Young.

125. "Class Letters, '89 Wellesley College," January 1928, 27, WCA.

126. "Arrested as a Soviet Propagandist," *San Francisco Chronicle*, December 20, 1930, 1.

127. Kaross, interview by Kendall.

128. Richmond, *Native Daughter*, 151–63.

129. "Class Letters, '89 Wellesley College," December 1931, 31, WCA.

130. "Governor Refuses to Comment," *San Francisco Chronicle*, August 1, 1929, 3; "Tso Jan Wang's Comment on Demonstration," *San Francisco Chronicle*, July 30, 1929, 3.

131. "San Francisco Red Cases Are Postponed," *San Francisco Chronicle*, August 6, 1929, 13.

132. Chester Rowell, "Rowell's Comment on Pardon," *San Francisco Chronicle*, August 14, 1929, 15.

133. Strom, "Challenging 'Women's Place,'" 156.

134. Weigand, *Red Feminism*.

135. Kaross, interview by Kendall.

136. "Trying to Be Martyr: Nephew Saves Anita Whitney from Jail Cell," *San Francisco Chronicle*, December 11, 1935, 9; "Red Lady," *Time*, December 9, 1935.

137. "Into Jail and Out Again: Anita Whitney Plan to Go to Jail Balked by Nephew," *Los Angeles Times*, December 11, 1935, 3.

138. Kaross, interview by Kendall.

139. "Class Letters, '89 Wellesley College," December 1934, 25, WCA.

140. Richmond, *Native Daughter*, chap. 9.

141. Kaross, interview by Kendall.

142. Letter, Sunday, October 21, 1934, folder s1, b1, fl. Reports of Undercover Informant "A.X.," 1937 series, California Surveillance Collection, Labor Archives and Research Center; Richmond, *Native Daughter*, 162–70.

143. "Anita Whitney Vote Retains Party on Ballot: Communist Vote in San Francisco Alone Will Exceed 2,500 in Controller Race," *Western Worker: Western Organ of the Communist Party San Francisco*, November 8, 1934, 1.

144. Flynn, *Daughters of America*, 12; Richmond, *Native Daughter*, 190; U.S. Department of Justice, "Background Information on Charlotte Anita Whitney, alias Cora Reed," Washington DC.

145. "Class Letters, '89 Wellesley College," December 1937, 30, WCA.

146. Richmond, *Native Daughter*, 169–71.

147. Kaross, interview by Kendall.

148. U.S. Department of Justice, "Anonymous Report on Charlotte Anita Whitney, alias Cora Reed," March 29, 1941, San Francisco.

149. "Letter on Appellate Court's Freeing on Sacramento Communists," *San Francisco Chronicle*, October 4, 1937, 8.

150. W. R. Patton, "No Appeal from Firing Squad," *San Francisco Chronicle*, October 5, 1937, 10.

151. Richmond, *Native Daughter*. At several points throughout the biography Richmond highlights her (and other early members') surprising ignorance of Communist ideology in the early 1910s and then showcases how she came to embrace a sophisticated theoretical understanding of Marxism in her later years.

152. Folder s1, b1, fl. Reports of Undercover Informant "Tommy," 1938 series, California Surveillance Collection, Labor Archives and Research Center.

153. "Candidate for Communist Party Nomination for U.S. Senator," *San Francisco Chronicle*, May 6, 1940.

154. Richmond, *Native Daughter*, 173–83; Yellin, *Our Mothers' War*, chap. 7.

155. "Long-Time Radical Anita Whitney Dead," *San Francisco Examiner*, February 5, 1955, 1.

156. See files about 1920s organizing, file 515, reel 1, box 3345, Communist International (Comintern) Archive Project, Library of Congress.

157. U.S. Department of Justice, "Background on Charlotte Anita Whitney, alias Cora Reed," file no. 61-221, 3-29-41, San Francisco.

158. U.S. Department of Justice, "Memorandum for Mr. L. M. C. Smith, Chief, Special Defense Unit from John Edgar Hoover, Director," December 1, 1941, Washington DC.

159. Flynn, *Daughters of America*, 12.

160. Kaross, interview by Kendall.

161. "Candidacy for State Controller Rejected," *San Francisco Chronicle*, June 18, 1942, 24; "Nomination Papers Accepted," *San Francisco Chronicle*, June 20, 1942, 4.

162. "Petition to Have Name Placed on Ballot as Candidate of Communist Party for Secretary of State," *San Francisco Chronicle*, April 18, 1942, 6.

163. "Class Letters, '89 Wellesley College," December 1947, n.p., WCA.

164. Kaross, interview by Kendall.

165. "Long-Time Radical Anita Whitney Dead," 1.

166. "Anita Whitney, Socialite Red, Dead," *San Francisco Chronicle*, February 5, 1955, 1.

1. For historiography relating solely to Healey herself, see Healey and Isserman, *Dorothy Healey Remembers*; Gardner, *Tradition's Chains*; Reichert and Klein, *Seeing Red*.

2. For a survey of the historiography of women in the American Communist Party, see Weigand, *Red Feminism*; Weigand, "Red Menace," 70–94; Dixler, "Woman Question"; Schaffer, "Women and the Communist Party, USA," 73–118; Gosse, "'To Organize in Every Neighborhood,'" 109–41; and Baxandall, "Question Seldom Asked."

3. Barbara Nestor, interview by Sherna Berger Gluck, October 11, 1974, interview 01a segment 1 (0:00–2:00), Segkey: a1481, June 19, 2007, www.csulb.edu/voaha, Women's History: Reformers and Radicals, Virtual Oral/Aural History Archive, CSULBL; Maurice Isserman, interview with Carol Jean Newman, July 29, 1986, 9, CSULBL.

4. Healey and Isserman, *Dorothy Healey Remembers*, 23.

5. Isserman, interview with Newman, 2.

6. Gardner, *Tradition's Chains*, 40.

7. Gardner, *Tradition's Chains*, 47.

8. Gardner, *Tradition's Chains*, 47–48.

9. Gardner, *Tradition's Chains*, 51.

10. Dorothy Healey to Joseph Rosenblum, n.d., F31/B142, Dorothy Healey Collection, CSULBL.

11. Georg Ewart, "Interviews on the Organization of the Cannery and Agricultural Workers' Industrial Union in the 1930s," Dorothy Healey interview, reel 4, Bancroft Library.

12. Malca Chall, "Activist in the Radical Movement, 1930–1960, the International Labor Defense, the Communist Party," interview with LaRue McCormick, 1976, 20, Women in Politics Oral History Project, Regional Oral History Office, Bancroft Library; *You Can't Scare Me . . . Labor Heroines, 1930s–1980s, A Union Wage Pamphlet* (San Francisco: Union Women's Alliance to Gain Equality, 1981), Union Women's Alliance to Gain Equality Collection, University of California–Davis Special Collections.

13. Ewart, "Interviews on the Organization." For other sources on the strike, see "FBI—copies of released information, 1941," F7/B1, 1245, Dorothy Ray Healey Papers, UCLA Special Collections; Healey and Isserman, *Dorothy Healey Remembers*, 36–37; Gardner, *Tradition's Chains*, 57–65.

14. Isserman, interview with Newman, 6.
15. Healey and Isserman, *Dorothy Healey Remembers*, 38.
16. Healey and Isserman, *Dorothy Healey Remembers*, 38.
17. Beulah Learned, International Labor Defense League, "Equal Justice Yearbook of the Fight for Democratic Rights, 1938," 62, FII/BI2A, Dorothy Healey Collection, CSULBL.
18. Malca Chall, "Activist in the Radical Movement," 17–19.
19. Gardner, *Tradition's Chains*, 80–82.
20. John A. Beardsley, attorney-at-law, "Freedom of Speech in Los Angeles," address given over KNX, July 10, 1932, F38/BIOA, Dorothy Healey Collection, CSULBL.
21. Ewart, "Interviews on the Organization." See also Gardner, *Tradition's Chains*, 70–76; Healey and Isserman, *Dorothy Healey Remembers*, 41–57.
22. FBI report, "Dorothy Ray, with aliases Dorothy Raye, Dorothy Ross, #78954," July 29, 1941, FBI FOIA Records, F7/BI, 1245, Dorothy Ray Healey Papers, UCLA Special Collections.
23. Ewart, "Interviews on the Organization."
24. Ewart, "Interviews on the Organization."
25. On the Imperial Valley strike, see Daniel, *Bitter Harvest*, 222–57; McWilliams, *Factories in the Fields*, 224–26; Jamieson, *Labor Unionism in American Agriculture*, 107–10; Irving Bernstein, *Turbulent Years*, 160–68; Starr, *Endangered Dreams*, 157–60; González, "Company Unions"; González, *Mexican Consuls and Labor Organizing*, 159–96.
26. Pettis Perry, Organizer of District 14 of International Labor Defense, "Letter on the Safety of Dorothy Ray and Stanley Hancock," October 7, 1934, F54/B38B, Dorothy Healey Collection, CSULBL.
27. Marston represented the network of wealthy radical activists that sustained the Party and aided in financially supporting the strike from urban centers. Healey and Isserman, *Dorothy Healey Remembers*, 40–55.
28. Ewart, "Interviews on the Organization."
29. Healey and Isserman, *Dorothy Healey Remembers*, 54.
30. Gardner, *Tradition's Chains*, 142.
31. Perry, "Letter on the Safety of Dorothy Ray and Stanley Hancock."
32. Healey and Isserman, *Dorothy Healey Remembers*, 59.
33. Murdock, "California Communists," 478–87.
34. Referencing the launch of the *Daily People's World*. Murdock, "California Communists," 484.

35. Harry Bridges, Tom Mann, Upton Sinclair, Ellis Patterson, Sam Yorty, Paul Richie, Jack Tenney, and Henry Schmidt, "Greetings to the People's World," *People's World*, January 1, 1938, 4.

36. National Election Committee of the Communist Party, *Working Women and the Elections* (New York: Workers Library Publishers, October 1932), 11, Union Women's Alliance to Gain Equality Collection, University of California–Davis Special Collections.

37. "Platform of the Communist Party in the California Elections," *Western Worker*, May 21, 1934, 6.

38. Her new role came about during this divisive time, when the CIO recruited unskilled industrial workers in opposition to the AFL's craft union method.

39. Healey and Isserman, *Dorothy Healey Remembers*, 66.

40. "Who Is Who in Our Union, Dorothy Ray Outstanding Leader," UCA-PAWA *News*, October 1939, Philadelphia PA, F103/B38C, Dorothy Healey Collection, CSULBL.

41. Maurice Isserman, interview with Elizabeth Eudey, July 30, 1986, CSULBL.

42. Ruiz, *Cannery Women, Cannery Lives*, 75.

43. Ruiz, *Cannery Women, Cannery Lives*, 77.

44. Regular postings in the *People's World* advertised such social gatherings. See "What's Doing in California," *Western Worker*, January 11, 1937, 6; "Pageant Planned for LA Picnic," *People's World*, May 7, 1938, 3.

45. Malca Chall, "Activist in the Radical Movement," 19.

46. C. A. Hathaway, "Who Are the Friends of the Negro People?" (New York: Workers Library, 1932), 5–6, F54/B68A, Dorothy Healey Collection, CSULBL.

47. Doxey A. Wilkerson, "Why Negroes Are Joining the Communist Party" (New York: CPUSA New Century Publishers, 1946), F23/B67A, Dorothy Healey Collection, CSULBL.

48. James W. Ford and James S. Allen, *The Negroes in a Soviet America* (New York: Workers Library Publishers, 1935), 38, F34/B67A, Dorothy Healey Collection, CSULBL.

49. Beulah Learned, International Labor Defense, "Equal Justice, Yearbook of the Fight for Democratic Rights, 1938," 49, F11/B12A, Dorothy Healey Collection, CSULBL.

50. Gardner, *Tradition's Chains*, 64–65. See also "Fight Grows to Rescue Innocent Scottsboro Boys," *Western Worker*, April 15, 1932, 1; "Fight

to Have Scottsboro Case in Birmingham," *Western Worker*, March 27, 1933, 1.

51. Beulah Learned, International Labor Defense, "Equal Justice, Yearbook of the Fight for Democratic Rights, 1938," 21, FII/BI2A, Dorothy Healey Collection, CSULBL.

52. American Civil Liberties Union, Local Civil Liberties Committees Reports, 1937–38, New York, June 1938, 36, F25/BI0A, Dorothy Healey Collection, CSULBL.

53. Kutulas, *American Civil Liberties Union*, 43.

54. Kutulas, *American Civil Liberties Union*, chap. 2. See also Walker, *In Defense of American Liberties*.

55. Kutulas, *American Civil Liberties Union*, 76.

56. Sub-Committee on Subversive Activities of the Crime Prevention Committee, "The Communist Situation in California," Seventeenth Annual Convention of the Peace Officers' Association, State of California, Oakland, September 16–18, 1937, 1, CSULBL.

57. Sub-Committee, "Communist Situation," 18.

58. Gardner, *Tradition's Chains*, 170.

59. Gardner, *Tradition's Chains*, 170. See also Healey and Isserman, *Dorothy Healey Remembers*, 70–72.

60. Young Democratic Clubs of California, "Platform of the Young Democratic Clubs of California," adopted at the Third Biennial State Convention, Santa Barbara, May 21–23, 1937, F95/B5B, Dorothy Healey Collection, CSULBL.

61. General Committee, Communist Party, USA, "The La Follette Third Party: Will It Unite or Split the Progressive Forces?" (New York: Workers Library Publishers, 1938), 22, F25/B30A, Dorothy Healey Collection, CSULBL.

62. "Criticizes Olson for Changed Attitude for the Communist Party," *San Francisco Chronicle*, October 12, 1940, 4.

63. Healey and Isserman, *Dorothy Healey Remembers*, 77.

64. Healey and Isserman, *Dorothy Healey Remembers*, 84.

65. Healey and Isserman, *Dorothy Healey Remembers*, 84.

66. Healey and Isserman, *Dorothy Healey Remembers*, 82.

67. The American Party legally dissolved in 1944 and reconvened into a Communist Political Association. The Comintern had dissolved one year earlier to serve the Soviet Union's wartime alliances. See Gardner, *Tradition's Chains*, 247–48.

68. Eva Lapin, *Mothers in Overalls* (New York: Workers Library Publishers, 1943), F17/B125A, Dorothy Healey Collection, CSULBL.

69. Healey and Isserman, *Dorothy Healey Remembers*, 87.

70. Marx, Engels, Lenin, and Stalin, *Woman Question*, 18.

71. Zetkin, *Lenin on the Woman Question*, 74.

72. Zetkin, *Lenin on the Woman Question*, 11–12.

73. Healey and Isserman, *Dorothy Healey Remembers*, 89.

74. Dennis, *Autobiography of an American Communist*, 42 and chaps. 3–4.

75. Earl Browder, "Teheran and America," New York, 1944. Quote taken from Howe and Coser, *American Communist Party*, 427.

76. Maurice Isserman, interview with Elenore Hitelman, July 26, 1986, 8, CSULBL.

77. Dorothy Healey, Organizational Secretary, Communist Party of Los Angeles, "Convention Bulletin: Excerpts from Major Reports Delivered to Los Angeles County Convention," July 10–11, 1948, F11/B21A, Dorothy Healey Collection, CSULBL.

78. Healey, "Convention Bulletin"; Healey and Isserman, *Dorothy Healey Remembers*, 102–13.

79. Maurice Isserman, interview with Ben Margolis, July 25, 1986, 3, CSULBL.

80. Healey and Isserman, *Dorothy Healey Remembers*, 120.

81. Isserman, interview with Margolis, 2.

82. Isserman, interview with Margolis, 4–5; Healey and Isserman, *Dorothy Healey Remembers*, 121.

83. *United States of America v. Max Appelman, Alvin Abram, Averbuck, Elvador G. Greenfield, Dorothy Ray Healey, and Horace Morton Newman, Jr.* (Reporter's Transcript, June 28, 1949; DH is defendant no. 20746, 287–88).

84. Healey and Isserman, *Dorothy Healey Remembers*, 125.

85. Discrepancy: Healey's FBI record reports that her arrest occurred on July 31, 1951, while her autobiography says that it occurred on July 26, 1951.

86. Healey and Isserman, *Dorothy Healey Remembers*, 114. See also Auerbach, *Unequal Justice*; Belknap, *Cold War Political Justice*; Eastland, *Freedom of Expression in the Supreme Court*; Martelle, *Fear Within*; Rabban, *Free Speech in Its Forgotten Years*; Schrecker, *Many Are the Crimes*; Starobin, *American Communism in Crisis*.

87. Healey and Isserman, *Dorothy Healey Remembers*, 140.

88. Dorothy Healey to Richard Healey, July–August 1951, F31/B142, Dorothy Healey Collection, CSULBL.

89. Slim Connelly to Richard Healey, July–August 1951, F31/B142, Dorothy Healey Collection, CSULBL.

90. Healey and Isserman, *Dorothy Healey Remembers*, 139.

91. Healey and Isserman, *Dorothy Healey Remembers*, 148.

92. Healey and Isserman, *Dorothy Healey Remembers*, 146.

93. Joy Horowitz, "A Change of Coasts for the 'Red Queen,'" *Los Angeles Times*, June 6, 1983, View sec., 7; Reichert and Klein, *Seeing Red*.

94. Weigand, *Red Feminism*, 31–71; Schaffer, "Women and the Communist Party, USA," 73–118. For primary sources that document the struggle, see Betty Feldman, "Some Housewives May Protest," *The Worker*, June 7, 1953, 12.

95. See, e.g., "Tips on Beauty," *Daily Worker*, November 17 and 14, 1936, 4.

96. "Leg Art," *Daily Worker*, March 24, 1949, 11; "Irish Mermaid," *Daily Worker*, March 18, 1949, 11.

97. Healey and Isserman, *Dorothy Healey Remembers*, 67.

98. "International Women's Day," *Daily People's World Magazine*, March 6, 1953, 3.

99. Grace Hutchins, Labor Research Association, *Women Who Work* (New York: International Publishers, 1952), 35–36, F16/B125A, Dorothy Healey Collection, CSULBL.

100. Healey and Isserman, *Dorothy Healey Remembers*, 152.

101. Healey and Isserman, *Dorothy Healey Remembers*, 153.

102. Dorothy Healey, May Day Address, Los Angeles, May 1, 1956, F27–5/B38A, Dorothy Healey Collection, CSULBL.

103. Healey and Isserman, *Dorothy Healey Remembers*, 161.

104. Ben Dobbs, "Abridged Report on Organization to the District Council," November 1, 1957, F1/B21A, Dorothy Healey Collection, CSULBL; Healey and Isserman, *Dorothy Healey Remembers*, 150, 164. Healey reported that nationally in 1949 the Party membership stood at fifty thousand, and by the end of 1955 it had fallen to less than twenty thousand.

105. Communist Party of Southern California, Los Angeles, "The Cold War Stand," n.d., F115/B21B, Dorothy Healey Collection, CSULBL.

106. Nemmy Sparks, Southern California District Council, "Report of the District Board on the Results of the Elections," November 23, 1958, F93/B21B, Dorothy Healey Collection, CSULBL.

107. Dorothy Ray Healey, "The American Road to Socialism," October 1956, speech in the Embassy Auditorium, Los Angeles, F1/B38A, Dorothy Healey Collection, CSULBL.

108. Ben Davis, speech to National Committee of the CPUSA, 1958, F96/B21, Dorothy Healey Collection, CSULBL.

109. Healey and Isserman, *Dorothy Healey Remembers*, 171.

110. "Two Nations—White and Black," *Monthly Review*, New York, n.d., F26/B27, Dorothy Healey Collection, CSULBL.

111. Morton Deutch and Mary Evans Collins, Research Center for Human Relations, "Interracial Housing—Three Articles on a Study Financed by the Marshall Field Foundation on Racial Relations in Public Housing," New York, January–April 1950, F28/B27, Dorothy Healey Collection, CSULBL.

112. Fair Employment Practice Commission, State of California, "Answers to Questions about the California Fair Housing Law," 1963, F2/B27, Dorothy Healey Collection, CSULBL; By-Laws of FAIR (Fellowship for Advancing Intergroup Relations), 1963, F11/B27, Dorothy Healey Collection, CSULBL.

113. League for Decency in Real Estate, East Bay Center, "An Appeal to East Bay Home Sellers, Buyers, and Renters," Berkeley CA, n.d., F39/B27, Dorothy Healey Collection, CSULBL.

114. American Friends Service Committee, Summary of "Property Values and Race," Pasadena CA, n.d., F50/B27, Dorothy Healey Collection, CSULBL.

115. For recent scholarship on the political shifts and polarization of postwar California, see Self, *American Babylon*; McGirr, *Suburban Warriors*; Nickerson, *Mothers of Conservatism*.

116. Healey and Isserman, *Dorothy Healey Remembers*, 170.

117. U.S. Department of Justice, FBI, "Background on Dorothy Ray Healey," 1969, Washington DC.

118. Healey and Isserman, *Dorothy Healey Remembers*, 185.

119. Dorothy Healey, "A Communist Talks to Students," March 1964, 5, F7/B38A, Dorothy Healey Collection, CSULBL.

120. Dorothy Healey, "Communist Commentary," KPFK radio broadcast, April 22, 1964, F4-2/B38A, Dorothy Healey Collection, CSULBL.

121. Healey and Isserman, *Dorothy Healey Remembers*, 195.

122. Dorothy Healey, Report of District Board, Southern California District Convention, file Dorothy Healey, Niebyl-Proctor Center for Marxist Research.

123. Healey and Isserman, *Dorothy Healey Remembers*, 231.

124. Healey and Isserman, *Dorothy Healey Remembers*, 243.

125. Communist Party USA, "For Immediate Release, Statement on Expulsion of Richmond and Healey," December 21, 1973, New York, F97/B38B, Dorothy Healey Collection, CSULBL.

126. Isserman, interview with Hitelman.

127. Dorothy Healey to Gil Green, January 1, 1973, Los Angeles, BI/FI7, Healey, D., 1967–87, Gil Green Papers, Tamiment Library, New York University.

128. See, e.g., Dennis McLellan, "Obituaries, Dorothy Healey, 91," *Los Angeles Times*, August 8, 2006, BIO.

4. THE NEW OLD LEFT

1. Healey and Isserman, *Dorothy Healey Remembers*, 243.

2. Marian Gordon, interview by author, Los Angeles, February 7, 2006; Patrice Sewell, interview by author, Los Angeles, July 10, 2006.

3. Sewell, interview by author.

4. "Violence in the City—an End or a Beginning?" Report by the Governor's Commission on the Los Angeles Riots, December 2, 1965. For a survey of early civil rights activism in Los Angeles, see Sides, *L.A. City Limits*; Flamming, *Bound for Freedom*; Aimin, *Origins of the African American Civil Rights Movement*.

5. Congress of Racial Equality (CORE), *This Is CORE*, New York, n.d., folder 4, box 14, CORE, 1959–64, Twentieth Century Organizational Files, Southern California Library for Social Studies and Research (hereafter cited as SoCalLib).

6. Los Angeles CORE, Calendar, March–May 1964, Los Angeles, folder 4, box 14, CORE, 1959–64, Twentieth Century Organizational Files, SoCalLib.

7. Los Angeles CORE, chapter bulletin DU 9 444, Los Angeles, 1964, folder 4, box 14, CORE, 1959–64, Twentieth Century Organizational Files, SoCalLib.

8. "L.A. CORE: A Tract Bias Buster," *Community Reporter*, April 1963, folder 18, box 25, CORE of California, Twentieth Century Organizational Files, SoCalLib.

9. "City Council Denounces Actions of Selma Police: CORE Picketing at Federal Building, Will Continue Demonstration for Three Days," *Los Angeles Times*, March 9, 1965, 7.

10. "Civil Rights and Wrong Protests," *Los Angeles Times*, March 12, 1965, A4; Robert Jackson, "All-Night Prayer Vigil Defies 8 L.A. Judges:

Police Make No Arrests Because Doorways of Federal Buildings Are Not Blocked," *Los Angeles Times*, March 13, 1965, 12.

11. Paul Weeks, "Tactics Used Here Dismay Rights Leaders," *Los Angeles Times*, March 12, 1965, 3, 35.

12. Gordon, interview by author.

13. Gordon, interview by author.

14. Gordon, interview by author.

15. Los Angeles CORE, "CORE Rules for Action Projects," n.d., folder 4, box 14, CORE, 1959–64, Twentieth Century Organizational Files, SoCalLib.

16. Kendra Alexander, "The Impact of the Communist Party's Theory and Practice on the Freedom Cause of Black People," 1979, 19–20, folder Kendra Alexander, Franklin and Kendra Alexander Collection, SoCalLib.

17. Kelley, *Hammer and Hoe*, esp. pts. 1–2, epilogue. For another perspective on the Party's history with civil rights, see Gilmore, *Defying Dixie*; Naison, *Communists in Harlem*.

18. Garrow, *FBI and Martin Luther King, Jr.*, see chaps. 1–3; Woods, *Black Struggle, Red Scare*, 143–68.

19. Woods, *Black Struggle, Red Scare*, 70; see also Fosl, *Subversive Southerner*, 245–312.

20. Alexander, "Impact of the Communist Party's Theory and Practice," 18–19.

21. His obituary states: "He became one of the first of his generation to join the Communist Party, helping to rebuild it after the ravages of the anti-Communist crusades of the 1950s. . . . Bob's political life had the consistent theme of anti-racism." Obituary for Robert Paul Kaufman, 1938–79, folder Angela Davis, Franklin and Kendra Alexander Collection, SoCalLib.

22. Alexander, "Impact of the Communist Party's Theory and Practice," 18–19.

23. For the evolution of New Left activists, see "Part IV: From Civil Rights to Black Power: African American Women and Nationalism," "Part V: Law, Feminism, and Politics," in Collier-Thomas and Franklin, *Sisters in the Struggle*; Isserman and Kazin, *America Divided*; Anderson, *Movement and the Sixties*; Gitlin, *Sixties*; Matusow, *Unraveling of America*; Rorabaugh, *Berkeley at War*; Heineman, *Put Your Bodies upon the Wheels*.

24. Hutchinson, *Blacks and Reds*, 2.

25. Sides, *L.A. City Limits*, 134, 141–46.
26. "Violence in the City."
27. "Violence in the City."
28. "Violence in the City," 3–9.
29. Ridenour, Leslie, and Oliver, *Fire This Time*; Horne, *Fire This Time*.
30. Mike Myerson, "Report to the National Coordinating Committee of the W. E. B. Du Bois Clubs," Philadelphia, November 20–December 2, 1966, folder 3, box 2, 1120, W. E. B. Du Bois Clubs, Los Angeles and National, Robert Duggan Collection, UCLA Special Collections.
31. Myerson, "Report."
32. National Executive Committee of W. E. B. Du Bois Clubs of America, memo to Du Bois Clubs and Key Contacts, San Francisco, November 11, 1965, folder 3, box 2, 1120, W. E. B. Du Bois Clubs, Los Angeles and National, Robert Duggan Collection, UCLA Special Collections.
33. Anna Louise Strong, letter to Venice Du Bois Club, April 19, 1966, Peking, China, folder 2, box 3, 1120, W. E. B. Du Bois Club, Los Angeles, Robert Duggan Collection, UCLA Special Collections.
34. Cesar Chavez, national director, United Farm Workers of California, in the AFL-CIO, letter to Venice Du Bois Club, n.d., folder 2, box 2, 1120, W. E. B. Du Bois Club, Los Angeles, Robert Duggan Collection, UCLA Special Collections.
35. They fostered these mutual interests and forged new alliances at conferences held throughout the state in the late 1960s. The Du Bois Club, e.g., hosted a Statewide Conference on Power and Politics in which chapter representatives and students from high schools and colleges throughout the state gathered to share ideas, tactics, and goals. These meetings produced relationships whereby students would invite representatives from the Du Bois Club, e.g., to speak on their home campuses. Student Open Forum, Grossmont College, letter to Bob Duggan, El Cajon CA, n.d., folder 2, box 2, W. E. B. Du Bois Club, Los Angeles, UCLA Special Collections.
36. Gordon, interview by author.
37. "Red Inquiry and the Clergy," *Los Angeles Times*, September 24, 1951, A4; "Hearings in Red Inquiry Start Here Tomorrow: House Group Will Delve into Southland Communist Efforts Involving Security," *Los Angeles Times*, December 5, 1956, 30; Dan L. Thrapp, "Controversial Pastor Dr. Fritchman Retires after 22 Years at First Unitarian," *Los Angeles Times*, December 22, 1969, SF7.

38. Gordon, interview by author.

39. For background about the shifts within regional and local civil rights groups, see Flamming, *Bound for Freedom*; Pulido, *Black, Brown, Yellow, and Left*; Sides, *L.A. City Limits*; Stevens, *Radical L.A.*

40. Los Angeles Community Organizing Committee, Position Paper, 1966–67, folder 3, box 2, 1120, W. E. B. Du Bois Clubs, Los Angeles and National, Robert Duggan Collection, UCLA Special Collections; Paul Houston, "Two Slain in New Watts Riot: 25 Hurt as Negro Mobs Roam Streets," *Los Angeles Times*, March 16, 1966, 1. The *Los Angeles Times* reports the spelling of the name of the housing project as *Nickerson*, while Du Bois Club records refer to it as *Knickerson*.

41. Los Angeles Community Organizing Committee, Position Paper, 1966–67.

42. Los Angeles Community Organizing Committee, Position Paper, 1966–67.

43. Richard Bergholz, "Yorty Cites Watts Violence as Proof Reds Are Election Issue," *Los Angeles Times*, May 19, 1966, 3, 30.

44. House Un-American Activities Committee (HUAC), *Subversive Involvement of Disruption of 1968 Democratic Party National Convention*, 90th Cong., 2nd sess., October 1, 3, and 4, 1968 (SuDoc No. Y4.Un1/2:D39/pt.1).

45. HUAC, *Subversive Involvement*.

46. Los Angeles Community Organizing Committee, Position Paper, 1966–67.

47. Gus Hall, "Marxism and Negro Liberation," speech made in celebration of Negro History Week, 1951, file Kendra Alexander, Franklin and Kendra Alexander Collection, SoCalLib.

48. Kelley, *Hammer and Hoe*, xiii–13.

49. Alexander, "Impact of the Communist Party's Theory and Practice," 11.

50. Alexander, "Impact of the Communist Party's Theory and Practice," 12.

51. They also wrote, "How will the white worker acquire the knowledge, which comes thru joint activity, of the common human identity of black and white?" Dorothy Healey, Southern California District Policy, Los Angeles, 1966, 5, folder Kendra Alexander, Franklin and Kendra Alexander Collection, SoCalLib.

52. Healey, Southern California District Policy, Los Angeles, 1966, 5.

53. Los Angeles Community Organizing Committee, Position Paper, 1966–67.

54. Los Angeles Community Organizing Committee, Position Paper, 1966–67.

55. Los Angeles CORE, *Here We Stand*, n.d., folder 4, box 14, CORE, 1959–64, Twentieth Century Organizational Files, SoCalLib.

56. Carmichael, *Toward Black Liberation*; Van Deburg, *New Day in Babylon*; Dittmer, *Local People*; Isserman and Kazin, *America Divided*; Heineman, *Put Your Bodies upon the Wheels*, 106–35.

57. Sides, *L.A. City Limits*; Hartman, *Double Exposure*; Marable, *Beyond Black and White*; Kelley, *Race Rebels*; Yamamoto, *Interracial Justice*.

58. Ron Ridenour, Anne Leslie, and Victor Oliver, *The Fire This Time*, Los Angeles, November 1965, 2, folder 3, box 2, 1120, W. E. B. Du Bois Clubs, Los Angeles and National, Robert Duggan Collection, UCLA Special Collections.

59. Ridenour, Leslie, and Oliver, *Fire This Time*, 4.

60. Healey, Southern California District Policy, CPUSA Convention, Los Angeles, 1966, 5.

61. This is unique because third-world leftist organizations were often anti-Soviet Maoist Marxists, which of course countered CPUSA positions. See Pulido, *Black, Brown, Yellow and Left*, chap. 4.

62. Healey, Southern California District Policy, Los Angeles, 1966, 5.

63. Ridenour, Leslie, and Oliver, *Fire This Time*.

64. Ridenour, Leslie, and Oliver, *Fire This Time*, 9–12, 14.

65. HUAC, *Subversive Involvement*.

66. California Coordinating Committee for New Politics, "New Politics: A Report of the Conference," newsletter 1, San Francisco, November 2, 1966, folder 22, box 39, Southern Californians for New Politics, Twentieth Century Organizational File, SoCalLib.

67. In particular the Party sought to unite labor with other progressive organizations. Hall, *New Program of the Communist Party USA*, 44. For a survey of the Party's support of and criticism of third-party tickets throughout the 1960s and 1970s, see Hall, *Lame Duck in Turbulent Waters*. The Northern California 1967 Draft Resolution declared that the Party "has made significant advances in . . . its relationship to mass movements; the resumption of recruiting, particularly among youth, flowing from the development of an active youth policy." Main Political Resolutions and Motions on Resolutions Adopted at the District Convention, April 1967, folder Northern California District 1960s, Niebyl-Proctor Center for Marxist Research.

68. Southern Californians for New Politics, "Who Are the Peace Candidates in This Election?" campaign poster, folder 22, box 39, Southern Californians for New Politics, Twentieth Century Organizational File, SoCalLib.

69. Gordon, interview by author.

70. Gordon, interview by author.

71. "Communism Hailed by Young Delegates," *New York Times*, July 7, 1968, 52.

72. "Communism Hailed by Young Delegates," 52.

73. Healey wrote of the debate: "I was startled to find in a youth club that they understood our concern for security to mean that they could not recruit a new member because he insisted he could join only if he could say to others that he was a Communist. . . . When our youth recruit, it is because they handle it in an organized manner, listing names of people to be invited to sessions with whom they have worked in peace or civil rights activities." Dorothy Healey, excerpts from Report to the District Convention, *Draft Resolution on Party Organization, Southern California District Convention*, June 1966.

74. "U.S. Reds Nominate Negro for Presidency," *Los Angeles Times*, July 8, 1968, 20.

75. Dorothy Townsend, "Woman Seeks Presidency: Communist Counts on Disgruntled Vote," *Los Angeles Times*, July 18, 1968, B3.

76. "U.S. Presidential Elections: Leftists Votes," Marxists Internet Archive, www.marxists.org/history/usa/government/elections/president/time line.htm, April 25, 2006.

77. *Daily World*, September 3, 1968.

78. Davis, *Angela Davis*, 160.

79. Davis also partook in the Los Angeles Black Congress, "a broad coalition of community groups in the area." This broad collective did not last long; factionalism and violence similar to the discord of the New Politics convention split the alignments of these multiple organizations. See Davis, *Angela Davis*, 159–76.

80. Davis, *Angela Davis*, 159–76.

81. Davis, *Angela Davis*, 188–89.

82. Davis, *Angela Davis*, 199.

83. Davis, *Angela Davis*, 197–204. For a survey of Black Panther activism, see Ogbar, *Black Power*; Brown, *Taste of Power*; Cleaver and Katsificas, *Liberation, Imagination and the Black Panther Party*; Foner, *Black Panthers Speak*.

84. "Kendra Alexander, Bay Area Activist," *Committees of Corresponder Newsletter* (May–June 1993): 4.

85. Davis, *Angela Davis*, 210.

86. Davis, *Angela Davis*, 217.

87. For Davis's hate mail and other letters of criticism and support, see folders 1–3, box 1, Angela Davis Correspondence; and Angela Davis UCLA Case Hate Mail, August–October 1969, Angela Davis Collection, SoCalLib.

88. "Kendra Alexander, Bay Area Activist," 4.

89. Davis, *Angela Davis*, 273; Angela Yvonne Davis (1944–), folders 1–3, box 1, Records: UCLA Academic Freedom Case, 1969–71, and Angela Davis Defense Committee, 1969–75, Angela Davis Collection, SoCalLib.

90. Dial Torgerson, "Police Seize Panther Fortress in 4-Hour Gun Fight, Arrest 13," *Los Angeles Times*, December 9, 1969, 1.

91. Davis, *Angela Davis*, 231, 223–30.

92. Davis, *Angela Davis*, 238.

93. Art Berman and Roy Haynes, "Negro Leaders Call for City Hall Mass Rally; Police Clash with Panthers Inspires Plans for Protest: Negroes Plan March on City Hall," *Los Angeles Times*, December 11, 1969, 3; Art Berman, "Thousands Protest Panther Raid in Rally at City Hall: Thousands Rally at City Hall to Protest Raid on Panthers," *Los Angeles Times*, December 12, 1969, 1.

94. Kendra Alexander's FBI records report surveillance, though not explicitly "break-ins," over the months and years surrounding these protests. Davis, *Angela Davis*, 231–40.

95. Davis, *Angela Davis*, 256–60; folder Soledad Brothers Defense Committee, Franklin and Kendra Alexander Collection, SoCalLib.

96. Angela Yvonne Davis (1944–), folders 1–3, box 1, Records: UCLA Academic Freedom Case, 1969–71, and Angela Davis Defense Committee, 1969–75, Angela Davis Collection, SoCalLib; Soledad Brothers, and Soledad Brothers Legal Committee, letters of support, folder Soledad Brothers, Franklin and Kendra Alexander Collection, SoCalLib.

97. Professor, *Angela*, 27–45.

98. Professor, *Angela*; Olden, *Angela Davis*; Davis, *Angela Davis*; Mitchell, *Fight to Free Angela Davis*.

99. Davis, *Angela Davis*, 16–73.

100. "Kendra Alexander, Bay Area Activist," 4.

101. Mitchell, *Fight to Free Angela Davis*, 6; unauthored speech, 1970, folder Angela Davis, Niebyl-Proctor Center for Marxist Research. See also

"Angela Rally: Massive March Monday," *Sacramento Observer*, February 10, 1972, A1; "Free Angela Office in Fillmore," *Sun-Reporter* (San Francisco), February 6, 1971, xxvii, 52, 9; for general clippings folders from *People's World*, policy statements, speeches, and letters, see folders 1–3, box 2, Angela Davis Collection; and Franklin and Kendra Alexander Collection, SoCalLib.

102. The CPUSA took immediate control of her defense. See Communist Party of the United States of America, "For Immediate Release, Press Release," October 14, 1970, folder Angela Davis, Niebyl Proctor Center for Marxist Research.

103. The American Dream Machine, e.g., part of Quest Productions, solicited the NUCFAD seeking to make short documentaries about Davis. Letter, October 13, 1971, folder 9, box 2, Publicity Press Releases, Angela Davis Collection, SoCalLib.

104. Pat Nelson, chairperson of Committee on Angela Davis and International Longshoremen's & Warehousemen's Union, "Organized Labor Demands Bail of Angela Y. Davis," unions proclaiming "that the California Democratic Council through its committee on Angela Davis be empowered to collect funds on her behalf," March 15, 1972, file 8, box 2, Angela Davis Collection, SoCalLib; letters from 1971–72, file Angela Davis, Franklin and Kendra Alexander Collection, SoCalLib.

105. Letter to Angela Davis, February 7, 1972, file Angela Davis, Franklin and Kendra Alexander Collection, SoCalLib.

106. Leo Branton Jr., reply to November 1971 memo on Legal Strategy, January 17, 1972, file Angela Davis, Franklin and Kendra Alexander Collection, SoCalLib.

107. ML, Minutes, National Sub-Committee, San Francisco, April 24, 1971; and Charlene Mitchell, Report on the Angela Davis Case, Berkeley, March 1971, both in file Angela Davis, Niebyl-Proctor Center for Marxist Research.

108. Conway, *From Joan to Angela*, refrain and music, file 5, box 2, Angela Davis Defense Committee Publicity, Angela Davis Collection, SoCalLib; Mitchell, Report on the Angela Davis Case; Kendra Alexander, Minutes of National Sub-Committee, San Francisco CPUSA, April 24, 1971, Angela Davis Collection, Niebyl-Proctor Center for Marxist Research.

109. Davis, *Angela Davis*, 306; Davis, Magee, Soledad Brothers, and other political prisoners, *If They Come in the Morning*.

110. Professor, *Angela*, 154–55, 164–65.

111. Earl Caldwell, "Angela Davis Acquitted on All Charges," *New York Times*, June 5, 1972; Angela Yvonne Davis (1944–), files 1–3, box 1, Records: UCLA Academic Freedom Case, 1969–71; and Angela Davis Defense Committee, 1969–75, Angela Davis Collection, SoCalLib.

112. Timothy, *Jury Woman*; Davis, *Angela Davis*, 336–38.

113. Elaine Brown, "Welcome Home, Angela Davis," *Black Panther Intercommunal News Service*, March 4, 1972.

114. Professor, *Angela*, 154.

115. Angela Yvonne Davis (1944–), files 1–3, box 1, Records: UCLA Academic Freedom Case, 1969–71; and Angela Davis Defense Committee, 1969–75, Angela Davis Collection, SoCalLib.

116. "Kendra Alexander, Bay Area Activist," 4.

117. Giuliana Milanese, interview by author, San Francisco, September 24, 2005. See discussion of Healey's decision to leave the Party in chapter 3. In addition, further rifts between Marxists and the CPUSA continued as the Party stayed devoted to the Soviet Union and its foreign policies in Czechoslovakia and Afghanistan, while others criticized what they perceived to be an imperialist policy.

118. Dennis Rockstroh, "Communist Leader Capitalizes on 'Regular People' Image," *San Jose Mercury News*, November 10, 1987, 1C.

119. Gordon, interview by author.

120. Legislative Affairs Committee of the Coordinating Council of Prisoner Organizations, "Statement of Purpose," 1971, Franklin and Kendra Alexander Collection, SoCalLib.

121. "Kendra Alexander, Bay Area Activist," 4.

122. Kendra Alexander, letter to Arnold, Oakland, August 28, 1974, file Kendra Alexander, Franklin and Kendra Alexander Collection, SoCalLib.

123. "Black Women on Black Women," *Sun-Reporter* (San Francisco), February 22, 1975, 19.

124. For a survey of the emergence of second-wave feminism, see Evans, *Personal Politics*; Duchess Harris, "From the Kennedy Commission to the Combahee Collective: Black Feminist Organizing, 1960–80," in Collier-Thomas and Franklin, *Sisters in the Struggle*, 280–305; Gitlin, *Sixties*, see chap. 16, "Women: Revolution in the Revolution," 362–75; Echols, *Daring to Be Bad*; Rosen, *World Split Open*.

125. Northern California District Convention, "Resolution of Women," April 1969, file Women, Niebyl-Proctor Center for Marxist Research.

126. Gus Hall, special letter, "Equality of Women," 1975, file Kendra Alexander, Franklin and Kendra Alexander Collection, SoCalLib.

127. Milanese, interview by author. Milanese and Alexander reared their children together. Milanese had two sons who were similar ages with Jordon. The families spent nights, weekends, and vacations in Clear Lake, California, together.

128. For a discussion of women in unions, see Gabin, *Feminism in the Labor Movement*; Dollinger, *Not Automatic*; Balser, *Sisterhood and Solidarity*; Fonow, *Union Women*.

129. Hall, special letter, "Equality of Women"; "Policy Statement on Women's Equality: Coalition of Labor Union Women," n.d., file Kendra Alexander, Franklin and Kendra Alexander Collection, SoCalLib; Angela Davis, "Racism and Male Supremacy: A Discussion Paper Submitted to the Women's Commission of the Northern California District of the Communist Party," 1977, file Kendra Alexander, Franklin and Kendra Alexander Collection, SoCalLib.

130. Juan Lopez, "When Mothers Need to Work," *People's World*, January 22, 1972, 3.

131. Professor, *Angela*, 156.

132. "Kendra Alexander, Bay Area Activist," 4.

133. Roger Smith, "Communists—It's Hard to See Red These Days," *Los Angeles Times*, July 17, 1980, 1, 24–25. The national fracturing leading to the emergence of these two organizations stemmed back to student movements of the 1970s. Major differences stemmed from disagreements over the Soviet Union's aggressive foreign policy.

134. "Communist Ticket Nears Qualification," *Sacramento Bee*, August 8, 1984, Metro A.

135. Franklin Alexander, chairman of Black Liberation Commission, CPUSA–Northern California, letter to Linda Burnham, Line of March Editorial Board, February 1, 1982, Oakland CA.

136. The Coalition to Fight the High Cost of Living and Unemployment, Bill Campaign Meeting, San Francisco; "Petition to the Congress of the United States" for the Hawkins Equal Opportunity and Full Employment Bill, HR 50, file Kendra Alexander, Franklin and Kendra Alexander Collection, SoCalLib.

137. Andy Furillo, "Jobs: 'Council' of Jobless Formed to Beat the Unemployment Blues," *Los Angeles Herald Examiner*, December 23, 1982 C4; South-Side Unemployed Council, "Membership Card," Los Angeles; Westside Unemployed Council, "A Job Is a Human Right . . . Unite the Unemployed," Venice CA; Anthony Smith, SCLC Youth Awareness and Action, Melvin Washington, NAACP Youth and College Division,

James Johnson, CES Unemployed Center, letter to promote a June 4, 1983, march, May 10, 1983, Los Angeles, file Unemployment, Franklin and Kendra Alexander Collection, SoCalLib. For Northern California unemployment councils, see Oakland Citizens' Committee for Urban Renewal, 1982, file OURS/EDCO, Franklin and Kendra Alexander Collection, SoCalLib. OURS was a group of people, nonprofit community groups, and churches in Oakland that met to discuss, monitor, and promote redevelopment in Oakland with special attention paid to unemployed and black residents.

138. Franklin Alexander, field organizer for Unemployed Council, Coalition for Economic Survival of Southside Unemployed Center, memo, April 6, 1983, Los Angeles, file Los Angeles Unemployment, Franklin and Kendra Alexander Collection, SoCalLib.

139. "Kendra Alexander, Bay Area Activist," 4; Perry Lang, "A Year of Anti-Apartheid Action Dock Workers Launched a Crusade," *San Francisco Chronicle*, November 25, 1985, 18; Clarence Johnson, "Bay Ship Line Ending Service to South Africa," *San Francisco Chronicle*, April 16, 1987, 14.

140. Rockstroh, "Communist Leader Capitalizes on 'Regular People' Image," 1C.

141. Milanese, interview by author September 24, 2005.

142. Lonn Johnston, "Leftists Scoff at 'Bourgeois' Itinerary: Gorbachev Neglecting Working People, Bay Area Marxists Say," *San Francisco Chronicle*, June 2, 1990, A8.

143. Michael Parenti, "In Spirit of Glasnost, a Half-Toast to Perestroika," *New York Times*, June 16, 1989, A26; see also Alexander Amerisov, "Confused Puppies," *New York Times*, May 27, 1989, 23.

144. Michael T. Kaufman, "For Gus Hall, the Fight Is Good, if Not the Fortune," *New York Times*, January 24, 1989, A11.

145. Carl Bloice, "Preconvention Discussion: Extended Remarks of Carl Bloice to the National Committee," September 8, 1991, folder CPUSA December 1991, CPUSA Convention Dissent Papers, SoCalLib.

146. Alessandra Stanley, "A Lament by America's Top Communist," *New York Times*, August 31, 1991, 10.

147. The lower estimate was referenced by Richard Starr, editor of the *Yearbook on International Communist Affairs*, while the higher number was supplied by the CPUSA. Carrick Leavitt, "Aghast U.S. Communists Make Lonely Bid to Evolve toward More Democratic Goals," *Deseret News*, October 22, 1990, A8.

148. Milanese, interview by author. She talked about labor activism in 1980s. She also described how committed Alexander was to the Free South Africa Movement.

149. Milanese, interview by author. Milanese and several other members had become outspoken about their frustration with the Party and Hall by the late 1980s, while she remembers that Alexander retained her leadership and commitment until late 1990 or early 1991.

150. "Is the Party Over? Local Communists See Silver Lining in Capitalist Cloud," *Sacramento Bee*, March 14, 1990, FI.

151. Larry Slonaker, "Communists Divided on Crisis Impact," *San Jose Mercury News*, August 25, 1991, 1B.

152. Milanese, interview by author. She spoke with intense emotion and frustration about the leadership style of Gus Hall.

153. Charlene Mitchell and Danny Rubin, National Board Members, *Democratic Leadership Elections: A Critical Question*, September 1991, folder CPUSA December 1991, CPUSA Convention Dissent Papers Collection, SoCalLib; Record of motions acted on, National Committee Meeting, CPUSA, September 8, 1991, folder CPUSA December 1991, CPUSA Convention Dissent Papers, SoCalLib.

154. Charlene Mitchell, interview by author, New York, September 20, 2005; Milanese, interview by author.

155. Most tellingly, the group wrote: "We uncritically defended practices which have proven themselves historically outmoded, at best. Of course, we do not need to apologize for our defense of socialism, but we do need to acknowledge that in defending it, we also voluntarily put on blinders about its weaknesses." Kendra Alexander et al., *Message to the National Committee*, May 18, 1991, 3, 14, folder CPUSA December 1991, CPUSA Convention Dissent Papers, SoCalLib. See also Charlene Mitchell, "Remarks of Charlene Mitchell to National Committee / National Council," August 5, 1990; Kendra Alexander et al., letter to "Comrades," October 21, 1991, folder CPUSA December 1991, CPUSA Convention Dissent Papers, SoCalLib; Gus Hall, national chairman, CPUSA, *The Crisis in Our Party: Report to the National Committee, November 16–17, 1991*, folder CPUSA December 1991, CPUSA Convention Dissent Papers, SoCalLib.

156. "Kendra Alexander, Bay Area Activist," 4.

157. "Kendra Alexander, Bay Area Activist," 4.

158. Committees of Correspondence, "Press Release for Immediate Release," New York, December 23, 1991.

159. "Kendra Alexander, Bay Area Activist," 4.

160. Barry Sheppard, "U.S. Socialist Kendra Alexander Dies," *Green Left Weekly Online Edition*, June 9, 1993; Milanese, interview by author.

161. Dennis Rockstroh, "Communist Leader Capitalizes on 'Regular People' Image," *San Jose Mercury News*, November 10, 1987, 1C.

162. Kendra Alexander, speech at National Strategy Session to Stop Police Crimes, Twentieth Anniversary Conference of the National Alliance against Racist and Political Repression, Detroit, May 1, 1993, folder Committees of Correspondence, Franklin and Kendra Alexander Collection, SoCalLib.

163. Lothar Bisky, chairman of Partie des Demodratischen Sozialismus, correspondence with Committees of Correspondence, Berlin, May 27, 1993, file Kendra Alexander, Committees of Correspondence Collection, Tamiment Library, New York University.

164. The COC headquarters collected numerous memorials written by her comrades and close friends. Mitchell, interview by author; Milanese, interview by author. Both referenced speeches by Angela Davis.

165. "Kendra Alexander, Bay Area Activist," 4.

Notes to pages 188–189   231

Bibliography

ARCHIVAL SOURCES

Bancroft Library, University of California–Berkeley
  Georg Ewart, "Interviews on the Organization of the Cannery and
    Agricultural Workers' Industrial Union in the 1930s"
  John Francis Neylan Papers
  Women in Politics Oral History Project, Regional Oral History Office
California State Archives, Sacramento
  Clipping Files on Charlotte Anita Whitney
  Governor Young Collections
California State University–Long Beach Library
  Al Richmond Papers
  Dorothy Healey Collection
  Maurice Isserman Interviews
  Virtual Oral/Aural History Archive
Federal Bureau of Investigation, U.S. Department of Justice,
  Washington DC
  Angela Davis Papers

Charlotte Anita Whitney Papers

Dorothy Ray Healey Papers

Kendra Claire Harris Alexander Papers

Labor Archives and Research Center, San Francisco

California Surveillance Collection

Sonia B. Kaross, interview by Lucy Kendell, November 3, 1977

Library of Congress, Washington DC

Communist International (Comintern) Archive Project

Mills College Special Collections, Oakland CA

Aurelia Reinhardt Collection

Niebyl-Proctor Center for Marxist Research, Oakland CA

Angela Davis Papers

Bay Area Communist Party Pamphlets and Records

Charlotte Anita Whitney Files

Dorothy Ray Healey Papers

Women's Commission

Oakland Public Library, Oakland CA

California History Collections

Clipping Files on Charlotte Anita Whitney

Southern California Library for Social Studies and Research, South Central Los Angeles

Angela Davis Collection

Celeste Strack Kaplan Papers, 1931–66

Che-Lumumba Club Collection

Civil Rights Council Papers

CPUSA Convention Dissent Papers

Dorothy Ray Healey Papers

Franklin and Kendra Alexander Collection

Twentieth Century Organizational Files

W. E. B. Du Bois Club Papers

Tamiment Library, New York University, New York

Betty Gannett Papers

Committees of Correspondence Collection

Dorothy Ray Healey Letters and Papers

Gil Green Papers

Kendra Alexander Papers

Oral History of the American Left (interviews)

University of California–Davis Special Collections

Union Women's Alliance to Gain Equality Collection

University of California–Los Angeles Special Collections
    Dorothy Ray Healey Papers
    Franklin Hichborn Papers
    Robert Duggan Collection
    W. E. B. Du Bois Club Papers
Wellesley College Archives
    Charlotte Anita Whitney Records
    Class of 1889 Letters

PUBLISHED SOURCES

Aimin, Zhang. *The Origins of the African American Civil Rights Movement, 1865–1956.* New York: Routledge, 2002.

Anderson, Mary. *Woman at Work.* Minneapolis: University of Minnesota Press, 1951.

Anderson, Terry. *The Movement and the Sixties.* New York: Oxford University Press, 1995.

Aptheker, Bettina. *Intimate Politics: How I Grew Up Red, Fought for Free Speech, and Became a Feminist Rebel.* Emeryville CA: Seal Press, 2006.

———. "Red Feminism: A Personal and Historical Reflection." *Science and Society* 66 (Winter 2002–3): 519–26.

Auerbach, Jerold S. *Unequal Justice: Lawyers and Social Change in Modern America.* New York: Oxford University Press, 1977.

Balser, Diane. *Sisterhood and Solidarity: Feminism and Labor in Modern Times.* Boston: South End Press, 1987.

Baron, Ava, ed. *Work Engendered: Toward a New History of American Labor.* Ithaca NY: Cornell University Press, 1991.

Barrett, James R. *William Z. Foster and the Tragedy of American Radicalism.* Urbana: University of Illinois Press, 1999.

Baxandall, Rosalyn Fraad. "Precursors and Bridges: Was the CPUSA Unique?" *Science and Society* 66 (Winter 2002–3): 500–506.

———. "The Question Seldom Asked: Women and the CPUSA." In *New Studies in the Politics and Culture of U.S. Communism,* edited by Michael E. Brown et al. New York: Monthly Review Press, 1993.

———. *Words on Fire: The Life and Writing of Elizabeth Gurley Flynn.* New Brunswick: Rutgers University Press, 1987.

Becker, Susan D. *The Origins of the Equal Rights Amendment: American Feminism between the Wars.* Westport CT: Greenwood Press, 1981.

Belknap, Michael R. *Cold War Political Justice: The Smith Act, the Communist Party, and American Civil Liberties.* Westport CT: Greenwood Press, 1978.

Bennett, David H. *The Party of Fear: From Nativist Movements to the New Right in American History*. New York: Vintage Books, 1988.

Binheim, Max, comp. and ed. "Biographies of California Women." *Women of the West: A Series of Biographical Sketches of Living Eminent Women in the Eleven Western States of the United States of America*. Los Angeles: Publishers Press, 1928.

Blair, Karen J. *The Clubwoman as Feminist: True Womanhood Redefined, 1868–1914*. New York: Holmes & Meier, 1980.

Blasi, Vincent. "The First Amendment and the Ideal of Civil Courage: The Brandeis Opinion in *Whitney v. California*." *William and Mary Law Review* 29 (1988): 653–97.

Blumberg, Dorothy Rose. *Florence Kelley: The Making of a Social Pioneer*. New York: Augustus M. Kelley, 1966.

Brown, Elaine. *A Taste of Power: A Black Woman's Story*. New York: Anchor Books, 1994.

Brown, Kathleen. "Ella Reeve Bloor: The Politics of the Personal in the American Communist Party." PhD diss., University of Washington, 1996.

———. "The 'Savagely Fathered and Un-Mothered World' of the Communist Party, USA: Feminism, Maternalism and 'Mother Bloor.'" *Feminist Studies* 25 (1999): 537–70.

Brown, Kathleen, and Elizabeth Faue. "Social Bonds, Sexual Politics, and Political Community on the U.S. Left, 1920s–1940s." *Left History* 7 (Spring 2000): 9–45.

Brown, Michael, Randy Martin, Frank Rosengarten, and George Snedeker, eds. *New Studies in the Politics and Culture of United States Communism*. New York: Monthly Review Press, 1993.

Buhle, Mari Jo. *Women and Socialism, 1870–1920*. Urbana: University of Illinois Press, 1981.

Butler, Judith, and Joan W. Scott, eds. *Feminists Theorize the Political*. New York: Routledge, 1992.

Carmichael, Stokeley. *Toward Black Liberation*. Ithaca NY: Glad Day Press, 1966.

Carter, Dan T. *Scottsboro: A Tragedy of the American South*. Baton Rouge: Louisiana State University Press, 1979.

Castledine, Jacqueline. *Cold War Progressives: Women's Interracial Organizing for Peace and Freedom*. Urbana: University of Illinois Press, 2012.

Ceplair, Larry. *Under the Shadow of War: Fascism, Anti-Fascism, and Marxists, 1918–1939*. New York: Columbia University Press, 1987.

Cherny, Robert W. "Prelude to the Popular Front: The Communist Party in California, 1931–35." *American Communist History* 1, no. 1 (2002): 4–42.

Cherny, Robert W., Mary Ann Irwin, and Ann Marie Wilson, eds. *California Women and Politics: From the Gold Rush to the Great Depression*. Lincoln: University of Nebraska Press, 2011.

Cleaver, Kathleen, and George Katsificas. *Liberation, Imagination and the Black Panther Party: A New Look at the Panthers and Their Legacy*. New York: Routledge Press, 2001.

Cobble, Dorothy Sue. *The Other Women's Movement: Workplace Justice and Social Rights in Modern America*. Princeton: Princeton University Press, 2004.

Cohen, Lizabeth. *A Consumers' Republic: The Politics of Mass Consumption in Postwar America*. New York: Knopf, 2003.

———. *Making a New Deal: Industrial Workers in Chicago, 1919–1939*. Cambridge: Cambridge University Press, 1990.

Coiner, Constance. *Better Red: The Writing and Resistance of Tillie Olsen and Meridel Le Sueur*. New York: Oxford University Press, 1995.

Cole, Peter. *Wobblies on the Waterfront: Interracial Unionism in Progressive-Era Philadelphia*. Urbana: University of Illinois Press, 2013.

Collier-Thomas, Bettye, and V. P. Franklin, eds. *Sisters in the Struggle: African American Women in the Civil Rights–Black Power Movement*. New York: New York University Press, 2001.

Collins, Ronald K. L., and David Skover. "Curious Concurrence: Justice Louis Brandeis and His Opinion in *Whitney v. California*." *Supreme Court Review* (2005): 333–97.

Conway, Bill, with an introduction by Oakley C. Johnson. *From Joan to Angela: A Bitter Ballad of Oppression and Martyrs*. Los Angeles: FAD Publishers, 1971.

Cook, Blanche Wiesen. *Eleanor Roosevelt*. Vol. 1: *1884–1993*. New York: Penguin Books, 1993.

———. *Eleanor Roosevelt*. Vol. 2: *The Defining Years: 1933–1938*. New York: Penguin Books, 2000.

———. "Female Support Networks and Political Activism: Lillian Wald, Crystal Eastman, Emma Goldman, and Jane Addams." In *Women's America: Refocusing the Past*, edited by Linda Kerber and Jane De Hart–Matthews. New York: Oxford University Press, 1987.

Cornford, Daniel, ed. *Working People of California*. Berkeley: University of California Press, 1995.

Coser, Lewis. *The American Communist Party: A Critical History*. New York: Praeger, 1957.

Cott, Nancy. *The Grounding of Modern Feminism*. New Haven: Yale University Press, 1987.

Daniel, Cletus E. *Bitter Harvest: A History of California Farmworkers, 1870–1941*. Berkeley: University of California Press, 1982.

Davis, Angela. *Angela Davis: An Autobiography*. New York: International Publishers, 1974.

Davis, Angela, Ruchell Magee, the Soledad Brothers, and other political prisoners. *If They Come in the Morning: Voices of Resistance*. New York: Third Press, 1971.

Davis, Hope Hale. *Great Day Coming: A Memoir of the 1930s*. South Royalton VT: Steerforth Press, 1994.

Davis, Reda. *California Women: A Guide to Their Politics, 1885–1911*. San Francisco: California Scene Publishers, 1968.

Degen, Marie Louise. *The History of the Woman's Peace Party*. Baltimore: Johns Hopkins Press, 1939.

Denning, Michael. *The Cultural Front: The Laboring of American Culture in the Twentieth Century*. London: Verso, 1996.

Dennis, Peggy. *The Autobiography of an American Communist: A Personal View of a Political Life*. Westport CT: L. Hill, 1977.

———. "A RESPONSE to Ellen Kay Trimberger's Essay, 'Women in the Old and New Left.'" *Feminist Studies* 5, no. 3 (Fall 1979).

Deverell, William, and Tom Sitton, eds. *California Progressivism Revisited*. Berkeley: University of California Press, 1993.

Dittmer, John. *Local People: The Struggle for Civil Rights in Mississippi*. Urbana: University of Illinois Press, 1994.

Dixler, Elsa Jane. "The Woman Question: Women and the American Communist Party, 1929–1941." PhD diss., Yale University, 1974.

Dollinger, Sol. *Not Automatic: Women and the Left in the Forging of the Auto Workers' Union*. New York: Monthly Review Press, 2000.

Dorr, Rheta Childe. *A Woman of Fifty*. New York: Funk & Wagnalls, 1924.

Downey, Kirstin. *The Woman behind the New Deal: The Life and Legacy of Frances Perkins, FDR's Secretary of Labor and His Moral Conscience*. New York: Doubleday, 2009.

Draper, Theodore. *The Roots of American Communism: Communism in American Life Series*. New York: Viking, 1957.

DuBois, Ellen Carol. *Harriot Stanton Blatch and the Winning of Woman Suffrage*. New Haven: Yale University Press, 1997.

————. "Woman Suffrage and the Left: An International Socialist-Feminist Perspective." *Woman Suffrage and Women's Rights*, 252–82. New York: New York University Press, 1998.

DuBois, Ellen Carol, and Vicki L. Ruiz, eds. *Unequal Sisters: A Multicultural Reader in U.S. Women's History*. New York: Routledge, 2000.

Early, Frances H. *A World without War: How U.S. Feminists and Pacifists Resisted World War I*. Syracuse NY: Syracuse University Press, 1997.

Eastland, Terry. *Freedom of Expression in the Supreme Court: The Defining Cases*. New York: Rowman & Littlefield, 2000.

Echols, Alice. *Daring to Be Bad: Radical Feminism in America, 1967–1975*. Minneapolis: University of Minnesota Press, 1989.

Eisen, Jonathan, and David Fine, with Kim Eisen, eds. *Unknown California*. New York: Macmillan, 1985.

Engels, Friedrich. *The Origin of the Family, Private Property, and the State*. New York: International Publishers, 1942.

————. *Women and Communism: Selections from the Writings of Marx, Engels, Lenin, and Stalin*. London: Lawrence & Wishart, 1950.

Englander, Susan. *Class Conflict and Class Coalition in the California Woman Suffrage Movement, 1907–1912: The San Francisco Wage Earners' Suffrage League*. San Francisco: Mellen Research University Press, 1992.

Evans, Sara. *Personal Politics: The Roots of Women's Liberation in the Civil Rights Movement and the New Left*. New York: Knopf, 1979.

Flamming, Douglas. *Bound for Freedom: Black Los Angeles in Jim Crow America*. Berkeley: University of California Press, 2005.

Flynn, Elizabeth Gurley. *Daughters of America: Ella Reeve Bloor, Anita Whitney*. New York: Workers Library Publishers, 1942.

————. *The Rebel Girl: An Autobiography of My First Life (1906–1926)*. New York: International Publishers, 1955.

Foner, Philip, ed. *The Black Panthers Speak*. Philadelphia: Lippincott, 1970.

Fonow, Mary Margaret. *Union Women: Forging Feminism in the United Steelworkers in America*. Minneapolis: University of Minnesota Press, 2003.

Fosl, Catherine. *Subversive Southerner: Anne Braden and the Struggle for Racial Justice in the Cold War South*. New York: Palgrave Macmillan, 2002.

Freeman, Joshua. *In Transit: The Transport Workers Union in New York City, 1933–1966*. New York: Oxford University Press, 1986.

Freeze, Gregory L., ed. *Russia: A History*. Oxford: Oxford University Press, 2002.

Gabin, Nancy F. *Feminism in the Labor Movement: Women and the United Auto Workers, 1935–1975*. Ithaca NY: Cornell University Press, 1990.

García, Mario T. *Mexican Americans: Leadership, Ideology, and Identity, 1930–1960.* New Haven: Yale University Press, 1991.

Gardner, Joel. *Tradition's Chains Have Bound Us.* UCLA Oral History Program, October 10, 1972–March 7, 1974.

Garrow, David. *The FBI and Martin Luther King, Jr.: From "Solo" to Memphis.* New York: Norton, 1981.

Geary, Daniel. "Carey McWilliams and Anti-Fascism, 1934–1943." *Journal of American History* 90 (December 2003): 912–34.

Gilmore, Glenda Elizabeth. *Defying Dixie: The Radical Roots of Civil Rights, 1919–1950.* New York: Norton, 2008.

Gitlin, Todd. *The Sixties: Years of Hope, Days of Rage.* New York: Bantam Books, 1993.

Glazer, Nathan. *The Social Basis of American Communism.* New York: Harcourt, Brace & World, 1961.

González, Gilbert. "Company Unions, the Mexican Consulate, and the Imperial Valley Agricultural Strikes, 1928–1934." *Western Historical Quarterly* 27, no. 1 (Spring 1996): 53–73.

———. *Mexican Consuls and Labor Organizing: Imperial Politics in the American Southwest.* Austin: University of Texas Press, 1999.

Gordon, Max. "The Communist Party of the 1930s and the New Left." *Socialist Revolution* 6 (January–March 1976): 11–66.

Gorn, Elliott J. *Mother Jones: The Most Dangerous Woman in America.* New York: Hill & Wang, 2001.

Gornick, Vivian. *The Romance of American Communism.* New York: Basic Books, 1977.

Gosse, Van. "Red Feminism: A Conversation with Dorothy Healey." *Science and Society* 66 (Winter 2002–3): 511–19.

———. "'To Organize in Every Neighborhood, in Every Home': The Gender Politics of American Communists between the Wars." *Radical History Review* 50 (1991): 109–41.

Gullett, Gayle Ann. *Becoming Citizens: The Emergence and Development of the California Women's Movement, 1880–1911.* Urbana: University of Illinois Press, 2000.

Hall, Greg. *Harvest Wobblies: The Industrial Workers of the World and Agricultural Laborers in the American West, 1905–1930.* Corvallis: Oregon State University Press, 2001.

Hall, Gus. *A Lame Duck in Turbulent Waters: The Next 4 Years of Nixon.* New York: New Outlook Publishers, 1972.

————. *New Program of the Communist Party USA*. New York: Political
Affairs Publishers, 1966.

Hartman, Chester, ed. *Double Exposure: Poverty and Race in America*.
Armonk NY: M. E. Sharpe, 1997.

Haynes, John Earl. *Early Cold War Spies: The Espionage Trials That Shaped
American Politics*. Cambridge: Cambridge University Press, 2006.

————. *In Denial: Historians, Communism, and Espionage*. San Francisco:
Encounter Books, 2003.

Haynes, John Earl, and Harvey Klehr. *Venona: Decoding Soviet Espionage in
America*. New Haven: Yale University Press, 1999.

Heale, M. J. *American Anticommunism: Combating the Enemy Within, 1830–
1970*. Baltimore: Johns Hopkins University Press, 1990.

Healey, Dorothy, and Maurice Isserman. *Dorothy Healey Remembers: A Life
in the Communist Party*. New York: Oxford University Press, 1990.

Heineman, Kenneth. *Put Your Bodies upon the Wheels: Student Revolt of the
1960s*. Chicago: I. R. Dee, 2001.

Hill, Rebecca. "Fosterites and Feminists, or 1950s Ultra-Leftists and the
Invention of Americakkka." *New Left Review* 228 (1998): 67–90.

Horne, Gerald. *Fire This Time: The Watts Uprising and the 1960s*. Charlottes-
ville: University of Virginia Press, 1995.

————. "The Reddening of the Women." *Science and Society* 66 (Winter
2002–3): 506–10.

Horowitz, Daniel. *Betty Friedan and the Making of* The Feminine Mystique: *The American Left, the Cold War, and Modern Feminism*. Amherst:
University of Massachusetts Press, 1998.

————. "Rethinking Betty Friedan and *The Feminine Mystique*: Labor
Union Radicalism and Feminism in Cold War America." *American
Quarterly* 48, no. 1 (1996): 1–42.

Howe, Irving, and Lewis Coser. *The American Communist Party: A Critical
History, 1919–1957*. Boston: Beacon Press, 1957.

Hutchinson, Earl Ofari. *Blacks and Reds: Race and Class Conflict, 1919–
1990*. East Lansing: Michigan State University Press, 1995.

Inman, Mary. *In Woman's Defense*. Los Angeles: Committee to Organize
the Advancement of Women, 1940.

Issel, William. "Liberalism and Urban Policy in San Francisco from the
1930s to the 1960s." *Western Historical Quarterly* 22, no. 4 (November
1991): 431–50.

Isserman, Maurice. *If I Had a Hammer . . . : The Death of the Old Left and
the Birth of the New Left*. New York: Basic Books, 1987.

————. *Which Side Were You On? The American Communist Party during the Second World War*. Middletown CT: Wesleyan University Press, 1982.

Isserman, Maurice, and Michael Kazin. *America Divided: The Civil War of the 1960s*. New York: Oxford University Press, 2000.

Jackson, James E. "New Features of the Negro Question in the U.S." Draft resolution. Communist Party, USA, New York, 1959.

Johanningsmeier, Edward P. *Forging American Communism: The Life of William Z. Foster*. Princeton: Princeton University Press, 1994.

Jones, Claudia. "An End to the Neglect of the Problems of the Negro Woman." *Political Affairs* 28, no. 6 (June 1949): 51–67.

Kaplan, Judy, and Linn Shapiro, eds. *Red Diapers: Growing Up in the Communist Left*. Urbana: University of Illinois Press, 1998.

Katz, Sherry. "A Politics of Coalition: Socialist Women and the California Suffrage Movement, 1900–1911." In *One Woman, One Vote: Rediscovering the Woman Suffrage Movement*, edited by Marjorie Spruill Wheeler, 245–62. Troutdale OR: New Sage Press, 1995.

————. "Socialist Women and Progressive Reform." In *California Progressivism Revisited*, edited by William Deverell and Tom Sitton. Berkeley: University of California Press, 1994.

Keeran, Roger. *The Communist Party and the Auto Workers Union*. Bloomington: Indiana University Press, 1980.

Kelley, Robin D. G. *Hammer and Hoe: Alabama Communists during the Great Depression*. Chapel Hill: University of North Carolina Press, 1990.

————. "A Life of the Party." *Tikkun* 6, no. 4 (July–August 1991): 82.

————. *Race Rebels: Culture, Politics, and the Black Working Class*. New York: Free Press, 1996.

Kennedy, David M. *Freedom from Fear: The American People in Depression and War, 1929–1945*. New York: Oxford University Press, 1999.

Kerber, Linda, and Jane De Hart–Mathews. *Women's America: Refocusing the Past*. New York: Oxford University Press, 1987.

Kerber, Linda, Jane De Hart–Mathews, Alice Kessler-Harris, and Kathryn Kish Sklar, eds. *U.S. History as Women's History: New Feminist Essays*. Chapel Hill: University of North Carolina Press, 1995.

Kessler-Harris, Alice. *In Pursuit of Equity: Women, Men and the Quest for Economic Citizenship in 20th-Century America*. Oxford: Oxford University Press, 2001.

————. "Where Are the Organized Women Workers?" In *Women's America: Refocusing the Past*, edited by Linda K. Kerber and Jane De Hart–Mathews. 2nd ed. New York: Oxford University Press, 1987.

Kipnis, Ira. *The American Socialist Movement, 1897–1912*. New York: Columbia University Press, 1952.

Klehr, Harvey. *Communist Cadre: The Social Background of the American Communist Party Elite*. Stanford: Hoover Institution Press, 1978.

———. "Female Leadership in the Communist Party of the United States of America." *Studies in Comparative Communism* 10, no. 4 (Winter 1977): 394–402.

———. *The Heyday of American Communism: The Depression Decade*. New York: Basic Books, 1984.

Klehr, Harvey, and John Earl Haynes. *The American Communist Movement: Storming Heaven Itself*. New York: Twayne, 1992.

Klehr, Harvey, John Earl Haynes, and Fridrikh Igorevich Firsov. *The Secret World of American Communism*. New Haven: Yale University Press, 1996.

Klejment, Anne. "The Radical Origins of Catholic Pacifism: Dorothy Day and the Lyrical Left during World War I." In *American Catholic Pacifism: The Influence of Dorothy Day and the Catholic Worker Movement*, edited by Anne Klejment and Nancy L. Roberts. Westport CT: Praeger, 1996.

Kovel, Joel. *Red Hunting in the Promised Land: Anticommunism and the Making of America*. New York: Basic Books, 1994.

Kraditor, Aileen S. *"Jimmy Higgins": The Mental World of the American Rank-and-File Communist, 1930–1958*. New York: Greenwood Press, 1988.

Kruks, Sonia, Rayna Rapp, and Marilyn B. Young, eds. *Promissory Notes: Women in the Transition to Socialism*. New York: Monthly Review Press, 1989.

Kutulas, Judy. *The American Civil Liberties Union and the Making of Modern Liberalism, 1930–1960*. Chapel Hill: University of North Carolina Press, 2006.

Lagemann, Ellen Condliffe. *A Generation of Women: Education in the Lives of Progressive Reformers*. Cambridge: Harvard University Press, 1979.

Levin, Murray B. *Political Hysteria in America: The Democratic Capacity for Repression*. New York: Basic Books, 1971.

Lubin, Carol Riegelman, and Anne Winslow. *Social Justice for Women: The International Labor Organization and Women*. Durham: Duke University Press, 1990.

Lynn, Susan. *Progressive Women in Conservative Times: Racial Justice, Peace, and Feminism*. New Brunswick NJ: Rutgers University Press, 1992.

MacKinnon, Janice R. *Agnes Smedley: Life and Times of an American Radical*. Berkeley: University of California Press, 1988.

Mansbridge, Jane J. *Why We Lost the ERA*. Chicago: University of Chicago Press, 1986.

Marable, Manning. *Beyond Black and White: Transforming African American Politics*. New York: Verso Press, 1995.

Martelle, Scott. *The Fear Within: Spies, Commies, and American Democracy on Trial*. Rutgers NJ: Rutgers University Press, 2011.

Marx, Karl, Frederick Engels, V. I. Lenin, and Joseph Stalin. *The Woman Question: Selections from the Writings of Karl Marx, Frederick Engels, V. I. Lenin, and Joseph Stalin*. New York: International Publishers, 1951.

Mason, Mary Ann. "Neither Friends nor Foes: Organized Labor and the California Progressives." In *California Progressivism Revisited*, edited by William Deverell and Tom Sitton, 57–72. Berkeley: University of California Press, 1994.

Matusow, Allen. *The Unraveling of America: A History of Liberalism in the 1960s*. New York: Harper & Row, 1984.

McDuffie, Erik S. "Long Journeys: Four Black Women and the Communist Party, USA, 1930–1956." PhD diss., New York University, 2003.

———. *Sojourning for Freedom: Black Women, American Communism, and the Making of Black Left Feminism*. Durham: Duke University Press, 2011.

McGirr, Lisa. *Suburban Warriors: The Origins of the New American Right*. Princeton: Princeton University Press, 2002.

McWilliams, Carey. *California: The Great Exception*. New York: Current Books, 1949.

———. *Southern California Country: An Island on the Land*. New York: Duell, Sloan, & Pierce, 1946.

Meyerowitz, Joanne, ed. *Not June Cleaver: Women and Gender in the Postwar America, 1945–1960*. Philadelphia: Temple University Press, 1995.

Miller, Dorothy Grace. "Within the Bounds of Propriety: Clara Burdette and the Women's Movement." PhD diss., University of California–Riverside, 1984.

Mitchell, Charlene. *The Fight to Free Angela Davis: Its Importance for the Working Class*. New York: 20th National Convention Communist Party, USA, 1972.

Mitford, Jessica. *A Fine Old Conflict*. New York: Knopf, 1977.

Murdock, Steve. "California Communists—Their Years of Power." *Science and Society* 34, no. 4 (1970): 478–87.

Murray, Robert K. *Red Scare: A Study in National Hysteria, 1919–1920.* Minneapolis: University of Minnesota Press, 1955.

Murray, Sylvie. *The Progressive Housewife: Community Activism in Suburban Queens, 1945-1965.* Philadelphia: University of Pennsylvania Press, 2003.

Naison, Mark. *Communist in Harlem during the Depression.* Urbana: University of Illinois Press, 1983.

Nekola, Charlotte, and Paula Rabinowitz, eds. *Writing Red: An Anthology of American Women Writers, 1930–1940.* New York: The Feminist Press, City University of New York, 1987.

Nickerson, Michelle. *Mothers of Conservatism: Women and the Postwar Right.* Princeton: Princeton University Press, 2012.

Nielsen, Kim E. *Un-American Womanhood: Antiradicalism, Antifeminism, and the First Red Scare.* Columbus: Ohio State University Press, 2001.

North, Joseph. "Communist Women Leaders." *Political Affairs* 1 (March 1971): 29–36.

O'Connor, Harvey. *Revolution in Seattle: A Memoir.* New York: Monthly Review Press, 1964.

Ogbar, Jeffrey Ogbonna Green. *Black Power: Radical Politics and African American Identity.* Baltimore: Johns Hopkins University Press, 2004.

Olden, Marc. *Angela Davis: An Objective Assessment.* New York: Lancer Books, 1973.

Olmsted, Kathryn S. *Red Spy Queen: A Biography of Elizabeth Bentley.* Chapel Hill: University of North Carolina Press, 2002.

Olsen, Tillie. *Yonnondio: From the Thirties.* Lincoln: University of Nebraska Press, 2004.

Orleck, Annelise. *Common Sense and a Little Fire: Women and Working-Class Politics in the United States, 1900-1965.* Chapel Hill: University of North Carolina Press, 1993.

———. "'We Are That Mythical Thing Called the Public': Militant Housewives during the Great Depression." In *Unequal Sisters: A Multicultural Reader in U.S. Women's History,* edited by Ellen Carol DuBois and Vicki L. Ruiz. New York: Routledge, 2000.

Ottanelli, Fraser M. *The Communist Party of the United States: From the Depression to World War II.* New Brunswick: Rutgers University Press, 1991.

Painter, Nell Irvin. *The Narrative of Hosea Hudson: His Life as a Negro Communist in the South.* Cambridge: Harvard University Press, 1979.

Palmer, Bryan D. *James P. Cannon and the Origins of the American Revolutionary Left.* Urbana: University of Illinois Press, 2007.

————. "Rethinking the Historiography of U.S. Communism." *American Communist History* 2 (June 2003): 139–73.

Parker, Carleton H. "The California Casual and His Revolt." *Quarterly Journal of Economics* 30, no. 1 (November 1915): 110–26.

Plummer, Brenda Gayle. *Rising Wind: Black Americans and U.S. Foreign Affairs, 1935–1960.* Chapel Hill: University of North Carolina Press, 1996.

Price, Ruth. *The Lives of Agnes Smedley.* New York: Oxford University Press, 2005.

The Professor [pseud.]. *Angela: A Revealing Close-Up of the Woman and the Trial.* North Hollywood CA: Leisure Books, 1971.

Pulido, Laura. *Black, Brown, Yellow, and Left: Radical Activism in Los Angeles.* Berkeley: University of California Press, 2006.

Rabban, David. *Free Speech in Its Forgotten Years.* Cambridge: Cambridge University Press, 1999.

Rabinowitz, Paula. *Labor and Desire: Women's Revolutionary Fiction in Depression America.* Chapel Hill: University of North Carolina Press, 1991.

Reichert, Julia, and James Klein. *Seeing Red: Stories of American Communists.* Dayton OH: Heartland Productions and New Day Films, 1990.

Richmond, Al. *A Long View from the Left: Memoirs of an American Revolutionary.* Boston: Houghton Mifflin, 1973.

————. *Native Daughter: The Story of Anita Whitney.* San Francisco: Anita Whitney 75th Anniversary Committee, 1942.

Ridenour, Ron, Anne Leslie, and Victor Oliver. *The Fire This Time: The W. E. B. Du Bois Clubs View the Explosion in South Los Angeles.* Los Angeles: W. E. B. Du Bois Clubs of America, 1965.

Roach, Joe H. "Women in the American Communist Party and How Their Party Activities Affected Their Home Lives as Wives and Mothers." PhD diss., New York University, 2000.

Rorabaugh, W. J. *Berkeley at War: The 1960s.* New York: Oxford University Press, 1989.

Rosen, Ruth. *The World Split Open: How the Modern Women's Movement Changed America.* Rev. ed. New York: Penguin, 2006.

Rossinow, Doug. *Visions of Progress: The Left-Liberal Tradition in America.* Philadelphia: University of Pennsylvania Press, 2009.

Rosswurm, Steve, ed. *The CIO's Left-Led Unions.* New Brunswick: Rutgers University Press, 1992.

Ruebens, Lisa. "The Patrician Radical: Charlotte Anita Whitney." *California History* 65, no. 3 (1986): 158–71.

Ruiz, Vicki. *Cannery Women, Cannery Lives: Mexican Women, Unionization, and the California Food Processing Industry, 1930–1950*. Albuquerque: University of New Mexico Press, 1987.

Ryan, James G. *Earl Browder: The Failure of American Communism*. Tuscaloosa: University of Alabama Press, 1997.

Ryder, David Warren. "California: Ashamed and Repentant." *New Republic*, June 1, 1927, 41–44.

Schaffer, Robert. "Women and the Communist Party, USA, 1930–1940." *Socialist Review* 45 (May–June 1979): 73–118.

Scharf, Lois, and Joan M. Jensen, eds. *Decades of Discontent: The Women's Movement, 1920–1940*. Westport CT: Greenwood Press, 1983.

Scholten, Pat Creech. "Militant Women for Economic Justice: The Persuasion of Mary Harris Jones, Ella Reeve Bloor, Rose Pastor Stokes, Rose Schneiderman, and Elizabeth Gurley Flynn." PhD diss., Indiana University, 1978.

Schrecker, Ellen. *Many Are the Crimes: McCarthyism in America*. Boston: Little, Brown, 1998.

Schwartz, Bernard. *A History of the Supreme Court*. Oxford: Oxford University Press, 1993.

Self, Robert O. *American Babylon: Race and the Struggle for Postwar Oakland*. Princeton: Princeton University Press, 2003.

Service, Robert. *A History of Twentieth-Century Russia*. Cambridge: Harvard University Press, 1997.

Shapiro, Linn. "Red Feminism: American Communism and the Women's Rights Tradition." PhD diss., American University, 1996.

Sherwood, Marika. *Claudia Jones: A Life in Exile*. London: Lawrence & Wishart, 1999.

Sibley, Katherine A. S. *Red Spies in America: Stolen Secrets and the Dawn of the Cold War*. Lawrence: University Press of Kansas, 2004.

Sides, Josh. *L.A. City Limits: African American Los Angeles from the Great Depression to the Present*. Berkeley: University of California Press, 2003.

Solomon, Mark. *The Cry Was Unity: Communists and African Americans, 1917–1936*. Jackson: University Press of Mississippi, 1998.

Starobin, Joseph R. *American Communism in Crisis, 1943–1957*. Berkeley: University of California Press, 1972.

Starr, Kevin. *California: A History*. New York: Modern Library, 2007.

State Board of Charities and Corrections of the State of California. *Eighth Biennial Report, July 1, 1916 to June 30, 1918*. Sacramento: California State Printing Office, 1918.

Stegner, Wallace. "California Rising." In *Unknown California*, edited by Jonathan Eisen and David Fine. New York: Macmillan, 1985.

Stevens, Errol Wayne. *Radical L.A.: From Coxey's Army to the Watts Riots, 1894–1965*. Norman: University of Oklahoma Press, 2009.

Storch, Randi. *Red Chicago: American Communism at Its Grassroots, 1928–35*. Urbana: University of Illinois Press, 2009.

Storrs, Landon R. Y. "Red Scare Politics and the Suppression of Popular Front Feminism: The Loyalty Investigation of Mary Dublin Keyserling." *Journal of American History* 90 (September 2003): 491–524.

Strom, Sharon Hartman. "Challenging 'Woman's Place': Feminism, the Left, and Industrial Unionism in the 1930s." *Feminist Studies* 9 (Summer 1983): 359–86.

Swerdlow, Amy. *Women Strike for Peace: Traditional Motherhood and Radical Politics in the 1960s*. Chicago: University of Chicago Press, 1993.

Timothy, Mary. *Jury Woman: The Story of the Trial of Angela Y. Davis*. San Francisco: Glide Publications, 1975.

Tone, Andrea, ed. *Controlling Reproduction: An American History*. Wilmington DE: Scholarly Resources, 1997.

Triece, Mary. *On the Picket Line: Strategies of Working-Class Women during the Great Depression*. Urbana: University of Illinois Press, 2009.

Trimberger, Ellen Kay. "Women in the Old and New Left: The Evolution of a Politics of Personal Life." *Feminist Studies* 5, no. 3 (Fall 1979): 432–49.

Trumbo, Dalton. *Johnny Got His Gun*. New York: Kensington, 1991.

Van Deburg, William. *New Day in Babylon: The Black Power Movement and American Culture, 1965–1975*. Chicago: University of Chicago, 1992.

Vogel, Lisa. "Red Feminism: A Symposium." *Science and Society* 66 (Winter 2002–3): 498–99.

Wald, Alan M. *Writing from the Left: New Essays on Radical Culture and Politics*. London: Verso, 1994.

Walker, Samuel. *In Defense of American Liberties: A History of the ACLU*. New York: Oxford University Press, 1990.

Ware, Susan. *Beyond Suffrage: Women in the New Deal*. Cambridge: Harvard University Press, 1981.

——, ed. *Holding Their Own: American Women in the 1930s*. Boston: Twayne, 1982.

——. "Women on the Left: The Communist Party and Its Allies." In *Holding Their Own: American Women in the 1930s*, edited by in Susan Ware. Boston: Twayne, 1982.

Washington, Mary Helen. "Alice Childress, Lorraine Hansberry, and Claudia Jones: Black Women Write the Popular Front." In *Left of the Color Line: Race, Radicalism and Twentieth-Century Literature of the United States*, edited by Bill V. Mullen and James Smethurst, 183–204. Chapel Hill: University of North Carolina Press, 2003.

Weigand, Kate. *Red Feminism: American Communism and the Making of Women's Liberation*. Baltimore: Johns Hopkins University Press, 2001.

———. "The Red Menace, *The Feminine Mystique*, and the Ohio Un-American Activities Commission: Gender and Anti-Communism in Ohio, 1951–1954." *Journal of Women's History* 3, no. 3 (Winter 1992): 70–94.

———. "A Reply to Critics." *Science and Society* 66 (Winter 2002–3): 506–10.

Weinstein, James. *Ambiguous Legacy: The Left in American Politics*. New York: New Viewpoints, 1975.

———. *The Decline of Socialism in America, 1912–1925*. New York: Monthly Review Press, 1967.

Wheeler, Marjorie Spruill, ed. *One Woman, One Vote: Rediscovering the Woman Suffrage Movement*. Troutdale OR: New Sage Press, 1995.

White, Ahmed A. "The Crime of Economic Radicalism: Criminal Syndicalism Laws and the Industrial Workers of the World, 1917–1927." *Oregon Law Review* 85 (2006): 649–770.

Whitney, Charlotte Anita. "The President's Foreword: Suggestions for Successful Organization." In *Winning Equal Suffrage in California*, by College Equal Suffrage League of Northern California. San Francisco: National College Equal Suffrage League, 1913.

Wilson, Joan Hoff, ed. *Rights of Passage: The Past and Future of the ERA*. Bloomington: Indiana University Press, 1986.

Woods, Jeff. *Black Struggle, Red Scare: Segregation and Anti-Communism in the South, 1948–1968*. Baton Rouge: Louisiana State University Press, 2004.

Yamamoto, Eric. *Interracial Justice: Conflict and Reconciliation in Post–Civil Rights America*. New York: New York University Press, 1999.

Yellin, Emily. *Our Mothers' War: American Women at Home and at the Front during World War II*. New York: Free Press, 2004.

Zahavi, Gerald. "Passionate Commitments: Race, Sex, and Communism at Schenectady General Electric, 1932–1954." *Journal of American History* 83 (September 1996): 514–48.

Zetkin, Clara. *Lenin on the Woman Question*. New York: International Publishers, 1934.

Index

Hawkins Equal Opportunity and
  Full Employment Bill, 181
Harris, Myron, 47–48
Harris, Patrice, 133–34
Harris, Sidney, 133
Harvard University, 183
Haynes, John Earl, 42
Healey, Don, 101–3, 109, 115
Healey, Richard, 103, 107, 110–11, 113, 128
Henry, Whitney, 41, 60
Hichborn, Franklin, 48, 54
Hiss, Alger, 110
Holmes, Oliver Wendell, 52
Hoover, J. Edgar, 67
House Un-American Activities Com-
  mittee (HUAC), 106, 148
Housewives Club of Santa Clara, 56
Hungary, 118
Hutchinson, Earl Ofari, 143
Hynes, William "Red," 81, 94

Industrial Workers of the World
  (IWW), 16, 33–34, 40, 43, 45, 49,
  82–83
Inman, Betty, 11
Intercollegiate Socialist Society, 51
International Labor Defense Com-
  mittee, 59
International Labor Defense League
  (ILD), 65, 79, 86–87, 92, 94–95
International Women's Day, 32, 115,
  197

Jackson, George, 167–68
Jackson, James, 152
Jackson, Jonathan, 168, 171
Jim Crow, 14, 33, 44–45, 72, 92–93,
  143, 197
John Birch Society, 126
Johnson, Lyndon B., 136–37
Jones, Claudia, 11

Jones, Marjorie, 133–34, 178
Judaism, 74, 142

Kai-shek, Chiang, 60
Kaufman, Robert, 142
Kehoe, William, 55
Kelley, Florence, 39
Kelley, Robin, 140
Kleeck, Mary Van, 55–56
Klehr, Harvey, 42
Khrushchev, Nikita, 73, 116
King, Martin Luther, Jr., 136, 160
KPFK, 123–25, 127, 131. See also *Com-
  munist Commentary*
Kutulas, Judy, 96

Labor Defense League, 44. *See also*
  Industrial Workers of the World
  (IWW)
Labor's Non-Partisan League (LNPL),
  79, 95, 99, 101
League of Nations, 42
League of Women Voters (LWV), 33
Lenin, V. I., 6, 8, 39, 42, 102, 109, 197
Line of March, 180
Locke, William J., 55
Locomotive Engineers Journal, 58
Los Angeles Labor Council, 56
Los Angeles Police Department, 16,
  81, 96, 166–67. *See also* Red Squad
Lumumba, Patrice, 153

Magee, Ruchell, 172
Maoism, 165, 179
Marcuse, Herbert, 163
Margolis, Ben, 106–7
Marshall Plan, 105
Marston, Helen, 85
Marx, Karl, 8, 102, 109
Marxism, 39, 53, 77, 117, 142–43, 155,
  160, 163–64, 191

Red Scare (1940s and 1950s), 72–74, 109–13, 148, 194
Red Squad, 16, 81–82, 94. *See also* Los Angeles Police Department
Reed, John, 45
Reed College, 31
Reinhardt, Aurelia, 42, 53–55
Republican Party, 17, 22
Republican Women's Study Club, 56
Revolutionary Communist Party (RCP), 180
Richardson, Friend, 53–54
Richmond, Al, 23, 26, 62, 127
Roebson, Paul, 148
Roosevelt, Eleanor, 11
Roosevelt, Franklin, 100, 103
Rosenberg, Ethel, 110–11
Rosenberg, Julius, 110–11
Rosenblum, Bernard, 75
Rosenblum, Joseph, 74–75, 77
Rubens, Lisa, 23
Rubin, Danny, 186
Ruiz, Vicki, 90
Rumford Fair Housing Law, 122
Ryan, John A., 22

Sanchez, Alvaro, 84
Sanford, Edward T., 52
San Francisco Chronicle, 65, 69
San Francisco Examiner, 57, 69
San Francisco general strike, 62, 85–86
San Francisco International Radical Club, 48–49
San Francisco Preparedness Day bombings, 40, 46
Sanger, Margaret, 39
San Quentin Prison, 22, 51, 54, 168
Savio, Mario, 143
Schaffer, Robert, 10
Schenck v. United States, 52

Schneiderman, Rose, 40
Schneiderman, William, 66, 79
Scottsboro Boys case, 94
Second Great Migration, 134, 153
Shaw, Anna Howard, 31, 41
Sherman, Lou, 79–80
Shireik, Maudelle, 188
Sides, Josh, 144
Simons, May Wood, 37
Sinclair, Upton, 55, 86–87, 96, 99
Smith Act, 5, 109–10, 112, 118
Socialist Party, 1, 35–40, 42–43, 49, 74, 189
Socialist Woman, 37
social protest movements (1960s), 19
Soledad Brothers Defense Committee, 167–68
Soledad Prison, 167–68
Southern California American Civil Liberties Union, 95–96, 196
Southern Christian Leadership Conference (SCLC), 13, 137, 146, 170
Southern Conference for Human Welfare (SCHW), 140
Soviet Union: and American Communists, 10, 12–13, 17–18, 64–65, 69, 87–88, 98, 116–19, 133, 141, 147, 164, 173, 177; and international developments, 60–61, 66–67, 88, 100, 116–17, 126–27, 183–84, 193; leaders of, 6, 103–4, 117, 184
Spencer, Anna Garlin, 28, 41
Spinoza, Alex, 95
Spock, Benjamin, 168
Stalin, Joseph, 73, 76, 103, 117, 190
Stanford University, 56
Stegner, Wallace, 17
Strong, Anna Louise, 39, 147
Student Non-Violent Coordinating Committee (SNCC), 137, 141, 155

Young, Clement C., 53, 56–58
Young Communist League, 2, 71, 75,
   78–80, 89, 91, 100, 127
Younger, Maud, 30

Young Pioneers, 75

Zagarell, Michael, 161
Zetkin, Clara, 30

IN THE WOMEN IN THE WEST SERIES

CPSIA information can be obtained at www.ICGtesting.com
Printed in the USA
LVOW07*2253160715

446592LV00004B/14/P